UNSPEAKABLE TRUTHS AND HAPPY ENDINGS

Human Cruelty and the

Sidran

Unspeakable Truths is a passionate, thorough, and "for everyone" discussion of very divisive issues. It comes in the nick of time. There have been legitimate concerns about the role of mental health professionals who, in an effort to help traumatized clients, sometimes destroy families. Yet the value of reviewing past traumatic events in order to make peace with the past is obvious. Coffey's book is remarkable for its balanced view of the roles and limitations of telling, listening, psychotherapy, and psychotherapists in the healing process. This book heralds a new and more enlightened era of help for those who must speak unspeakable truths and be more assured of happy endings.

Charles Figley, Ph.D.
Professor of Family Therapy and Social Work, Florida State University

Unspeakable Truths is unique because it explores the genuine similarities between diverse types of traumatic experiences. This beautifully written book brings much needed intelligence to the discussion of trauma therapy.

Ellen Bass
Co-author, *The Courage to Heal*

Unspeakable Truths will undoubtedly prove helpful to many people. I applaud Ms. Coffey's wonderful ability to listen.

Jeffrey Masson, Ph.D.
Former director of the Freud Archives
Author, *The Assault on Truth: Freud's Suppression of the Seduction Theory*

This is not a book written from the perspective of the victim or the perpetrator, or even from the viewpoint of the therapist. Instead the reader enters the narrative of a professional writer and we follow her on a journey of discovery as the unpalatable reality of trauma hits home. Ms. Coffey has let herself get involved and through her vivid descriptions and interviews we get a sense of the price she has paid for that involvement. As she warns us, "trauma stories are inherently unbelievable" and yet the unfolding of her willingness to listen, to learn, to grapple with complexity, ambiguity and horror provides us with a model of responsible and responsive engagement as the silent bystander is transformed into an articulate, compassionate, and committed witness.

Sandra L. Bloom, M.D.
Author, *Creating Sanctuary: Toward the Evolution of Sane Societies*
Executive Director, The Sanctuary, Friends Hospital, Philadelphia, PA

This excellent and well-balanced book shows how sensitive listening to traumatic stories can make them more bearable for the tale-teller. The author's lucid writing and her intelligent sensitivity make *Unspeakable Truths* a most valuable tool for survivors, friends, family, and even therapists — for anyone who must come to grips with their reactions to traumatic events. *Unspeakable Truths* is an indispensable resource.

Danny Brom, Ph.D.
Director of Research of Amcha, The National Israeli Center for
Psychosocial Support of Survivors of the Holocaust

With *Unspeakable Truths* Coffey has achieved an extraordinary goal; she has made "unspeakable truths" of human cruelty eminently readable. This is an important contribution; knowledge and awareness of human cruelty encourages us to heal cruelty's reverberations and to prevent cruelty's repetition. Yet accounts of trauma are ordinarily too unpleasant and too threatening to be heard by even close friends of the victim, never mind the general citizen. Coffey's achievement rests on the high quality of her writing and perhaps most of all, on the frequent and well-timed inclusion of her own disclosures and self-analyses regarding how it was for the author to hear these very accounts when told by the victims. Read this book with its compassionate and open-minded accounts of human cruelty and you will find it stretches your heart and mind.

Jennifer Freyd, Ph.D.
Professor of Psychology, University of Oregon
Author, *Betrayal Trauma: The Logic of Forgetting Childhood Abuse*

For far too long, the needs of people with traumatic stress conditions have not been adequately addressed by the Nation's public mental health system. The timing of this book is fortuitous, given the current environment of rapid change offering us unprecedented opportunities to improve on the ways we serve vulnerable individuals. *Unspeakable Truths* is a timely publication that provides us with a chance to participate in a new dialogue. We trust that this book will lead to meaningful differences in the lives of traumatized individuals by significantly contributing to improvements in the quality of public mental health care that they receive.

Robert W. Glover, Ph.D.
Executive Director
National Association of State Mental Health Program Directors

This is a disturbing book, waking the reader out of tired assumptions. Neither a mental health professional nor a survivor, Coffey brings a fresh perspective to a topic too often ruled by predictable polemics. The accounts are harrowing, and Coffey has the courage to leave the reader without easy answers. This book "for survivors and their friends and family" is a valuable resource for those struggling to understand human cruelty and its consequences.

Kenneth S. Pope, Ph.D., ABPP
Co-author, *Recovered Memories of Abuse: Assessment, Therapy, Forensics*

Unspeakable Truths and Happy Endings

New Trauma Therapy

REBECCA COFFEY

The Sidran Press

Lutherville, Maryland

For more information, write to The Sidran Press, 2328 West Joppa Road, Suite 15, Lutherville, Maryland 21093; phone 410-825-8888; fax 410-337-0747; e-mail **sidran@access.digex.net**; or visit our website **http://www.sidran.org**.

Printed in the United States of America

Book design by Stephen Kraft; composition by Blue Heron

Library of Congress Cataloging-in-Publication Data

Coffey, Rebecca.
    Unspeakable truths and happy endings : human cruelty and the new
trauma therapy / by Rebecca Coffey.
        p.   cm.
    Includes bibliographical references and index.
    ISBN 1-886968-04-7 (hardcover : alk. paper).—ISBN
1-886968-05-5 (pbk. : alk. paper)
    1. Post-traumatic stress disorder.   2. Violence—Psychological
aspects.   3. Psychic trauma.   4. Victims—Mental health.
5. Recovered memory.   I. Title.
RC552.P67C64 1998
616.85'21--dc21   97-30737
                                                                          CIP

Contents

To my dear friend, Elaine. Thanks for the loan of your outrage.
I tried it on. It fit.

And to my equally dear friend, Vera Work, who died in 1994 of cancer
as she approached her 62nd birthday. Thank you for your help, Vera.
I miss you and I know many who do.

PREFACE

THIS IS A BOOK ABOUT HUMAN CRUELTY, CRUELTY'S VERY REAL consequences, and the equally real opportunities for emotional recovery, many of which are embodied in specialized trauma therapy.

There are many good books on the market about childhood abuse. Few exist, however, about the emotional aftershocks of war, street crime, domestic violence, Holocaust, rape, political terror, and other forms of human cruelty. This book is for survivors of all types of trauma and for their friends and supportive family members.

Because this book is for survivors and their friends and family, it is what the publishing industry would categorize as either a psychology or recovery book. Typically, such books are written by survivors or mental health professionals. Within the last few years, however, the credibility of survivors and of mental health professionals specializing in therapy for survivors has been questioned. A spate of articles and books has lampooned the rhetoric of victimhood and a few of the practices of trauma therapy. They have unjustly made all survivors sound like complainers and all trauma therapists sound like quacks.

Much of the uproar has been about recovered memory, a phenomenon that most authors have naively tied only to the stories of survivors of childhood sexual abuse. In fact, in my research for this book, I learned that the phenomenon crosses trauma boundaries. Certainly, people who encounter extreme human cruelty when they are adults are more likely to find their memories unshakable than ephemeral. Still, war veterans, Holocaust survivors, and retired police officers all told me about recovering long-lost, verified memories of horrible brutalities they suffered as adults.

The phenomenon of false recovered memory, too, crosses boundaries. This I learned from a man who had survived the Holocaust. I mentioned to this man that an abundance of psychiatric literature suggests that sometimes survivors at least temporarily forget much of what happened to them.

Quite without prompting from me, this man volunteered that sometimes, when survivors ultimately remember, they get their facts jumbled. He recounted for me a conversation he had once had with a fellow survivor. In that conversation, the fellow survivor described a newly recovered memory.

The memory was of a horrific episode of loss. It was also, moment by excruciating moment, a precise recounting of someone else's testimony in the movie *Shoah*.

For some unknown reason, this man's friend had completely confused cinema with memory.

Even for survivors whose memories have always been fixed, questions about the role of remembering and the credibility of memories can preoccupy. Such questions are central to many survivors' lives and to their ongoing encounters with trauma's aftershocks.

With truly compassionate help and in their own due time, survivors often resolve such questions. Survivors' progress toward recovery often seems impeded, however, by those very people to whom they turn for help.

In the course of my research for this book, again and again I heard from survivors that friends, family members, and even some therapists are generally unable to let them speak freely about what they remember and about the depths to which they are affected by their memories. Seeking to stifle the rage and fear that hearing traumatic memories evokes, listeners blame survivors for the strength, relentlessness, and even the content of their memories. They render survivors' personal truths completely unspeakable.

Indeed, the truths in memories of violence and degradation are unspeakably horrible. But this book sets out to speak them. It contains the detailed testimony of a score of trauma survivors. And it recounts those tales while prodding all its readers to tolerate both the memories' undeniable horror and their occasional uncertainty.

In doing so, this book takes its cue from the 19th century neurologist Jean-Martin Charcot. Sigmund Freud and others before (and since) Freud created elaborate theories to discredit the veracity of traumatic memories. Charcot dismissed such theories as follows: "La théorie c'est bon, mais ça n'empeche pas d'exister." Translated, this means, "Theory is fine, but it does not prevent facts from existing."

The central point this book makes derives from Charcot's truism. Theories about error in memories of human cruelty are fine. In fact, they are more than fine. For one thing, they illuminate much about the very real unreliability of memory. For another, they allow us all to rationalize 'til the cows come home, and thereby live happily and industriously despite clear and present danger. But while such theories are immediately serviceable to the listener, they do not prevent the facts about human cruelty from existing. We are all at unquantifiable risk. Friends and family members upon whom the sword of Damocles has fallen need the rest of us to shear ourselves of fears and prejudices enough to listen. For if we persistently hold the essence of their truths in deep suspicion, how are they to be assured that we still care about them? How are they to fashion anything resembling a long life with a happy ending?

In this book, I argue that, as thinking and caring inhabitants of a menacing world, we must all learn to hear unspeakable truths. At the same time that we risk accepting the truths about violence and degradation that survivors' memories hold, we must reasonably engage critical thinking when memories of violence and degradation stretch the limits of our credulity. We owe it to survivors to listen compassionately; we owe it to ourselves to listen prudently.

Listening both compassionately and prudently is what truly expert trauma therapists do.

It is what the friends and supportive family members of survivors must learn to do.

It is what survivors must learn to do for themselves. We must all take care to meet the extraordinary emotional demands that unspeakable truths place on us.

As I have said, this is a book for survivors and for their friends and family. It lives to help, and I hope this book does some good.

I hope it shows skeptics that they may have prematurely chosen sides in a debate about memory and personal responsibility much more intricate, far-reaching, and potentially damaging than they could have imagined.

I hope it teaches people to tolerate ambiguity.

I hope it leads survivors' friends and family towards a necessary and conscientiously examined trustworthiness.

I hope it ratifies survivors' subjective experience of human cruelty and infuses them with real bullheadedness about recovery and about their chances of being heard. I hope it guides survivors towards careful, ethical, and eminently sensible trauma therapy. And, indeed, I hope it accomplishes some of what critics of recovered memory therapy and the rhetoric of victimhood have set out to accomplish. I hope it steers survivors clear of the significant ethical failures of some incautious trauma therapists.

As I have pointed out, books like mine are usually written by either survivors or trauma therapists. But this book of unspeakable truths and happy endings probably could not have been written by either a survivor or a trauma therapist. If it had been, no one would take it seriously. The recent flurry of books and articles deriding self-identified survivors for the content of their memories has rendered survivors' and trauma therapists' opinions on matters of memory newly suspect.

I am neither a mental health professional nor a survivor. I am a writer who specializes in health and mental health topics. I am not a direct party to the now nearly rabid debates about matters of victimhood. I hope that my third-party status exempts me from the wholesale suspicion that has befallen the personal competence and motives of survivors and trauma therapists who have authored books. Indeed, I also hope I escape the aspersions that have been cast by some survivors and trauma therapists on the personal competence and motives of researchers in memory and hypnosis who have authored perfectly appropriate warnings about improvident therapy practices.

I hope that this book will help everyone calm down a bit. I hope that skeptics of the rhetoric of victimhood will give this book's survivor testimony a fair and dispassionate hearing. I hope survivors and their advocates will concede that considerable intelligence resides in skeptics' advisories about cathartic trauma cures.

Some of what I have put forth here is clearly incendiary; I am avidly pro-survivor while remaining enthusiastically pro-skeptic. My naive hope, of course, is that representatives of both survivor and skeptic factions will find limitless merit herein. I hope this knowing full well that, instead of pleasing everyone, I may simply have peeved them all.

Therefore, I have one further hope that merits expressing.

I hope that my critics will break what has become form in appraisals of recovery and psychology reading. I hope that they will confine any censure for this book to remarks about the merits of its arguments and not to assumptions about the character of its author.

* * *

Many people read copies of this book prepublication. A few found the testimony of one survivor very unsettling.

It is perhaps extraordinary for a writer to suggest to her readers that they need not carefully consider all of the material at hand. However, because of the difficulty some prepublication readers had with one survivor's testimony, I do want to offer a caution.

The testimony about which I am concerned is that of Madeline Goodman, a woman who was gang raped and nearly murdered. Her testimony appears at length throughout the book. According to my prepublication readers, the viscerally difficult part of her testimony is limited; it is only in the first half of Chapter Three.

Madeline Goodman lives. She is not a homicide statistic. And while her testimony as a whole shows that even people who have suffered the worst can eventually have recovery within their grasp, I do think that some of her testimony might be very painful to read, especially for friends and family members of homicide victims. I therefore advise such readers to simply skim or even to skip her testimony in the first half of

Chapter Three. (That testimony resolves with "Till the day she died my grandmother couldn't remember anything or she was heavy into denial. I couldn't talk to her about it. She got really upset.")

I do hope, however, that readers who bypass the truly frightening parts of Madeline's testimony will read the commentary interspersed with that testimony.

I don't believe that Madeline's testimony in the remainder of the book will prove terribly disturbing; her testimony there functions much more as evidence of her survival than as evidence of her near demise.

★ ★ ★

I have based my writing on three kinds of research: interviews with trauma survivors, interviews with clinicians and legal experts, and the writings of others. All three types of sources are cited in the "Notes" section of this book. I encourage readers to refer to the "Notes" section, for I have used that section not only to cite my sources but also to discuss some studies in greater detail and to refer readers to additional materials of interest. However, it is not necessary to read the "Notes" section to appreciate the message of this book.

I do want to begin this book by acknowledging my predecessors and their important contributions to my thinking. Judith Herman with *Trauma and Recovery: The Aftermath of Violence—from Domestic Abuse to Political Terror*, Lawrence L. Langer with *Holocaust Testimonies: The Ruins of Memory*, Jeffrey Jay with "Terrible Knowledge," and Jeffrey Moussaieff Masson with *The Assault on Truth: Freud's Suppression of the Seduction Theory* all courageously re-framed standard psychiatric literature and prejudices in ways that made sense to me. The impact on my understanding of human cruelty and its aftershocks made by Helen Epstein's *Children of the Holocaust*, Lenore E. Walker's *The Battered Woman Syndrome*, John P. Wilson, Zev Harel, and Boaz Kahana's *Human Adaptation to Extreme Stress: From the Holocaust to Viet Nam*, Diana Russell's *The Secret Trauma: Incest in the Lives of Girls and Women*, David Finkelhor, Richard J. Gelles, Gerald T. Hotaling, and Murray Straus's *The Dark Side of Families: Current Family Violence Research*, Bessel A. van der Kolk's *Psychological Trauma*, van der Kolk, Alexander C. McFarlane, and Lars Weisaeth's *Traumatic Stress: The Effects of Overwhelming Experience on Mind, Body, and Society*, Daniel L. Schacter's *Searching for Memory: The Brain, the Mind, and The Past*, Kenneth S. Pope and Laura S. Brown's *Recovered Memories of Abuse: Assessment, Therapy, Forensics*, and Jennifer J. Freyd's *Betrayal Trauma: The Logic of Forgetting Childhood Abuse* also cannot be understated. And I offer a deep and extended curtsey to Ellen Bass and Laura Davis. *The Courage to Heal*, a recovery book for adult survivors of childhood sexual abuse, may have occasionally overstated its case. I have no doubt, however, that with its boldness and wisdom it saved many a life.

* * *

A convention used throughout the trauma stories in this book requires explanation. For the most part, in order to protect survivors, myself, and this book's publisher from lawsuits alleging libel and invasion of privacy, I have changed survivors' names as well as identifying characteristics of their stories. However, in certain cases, trauma stories implicated only nameless masses of people or perpetrators who are long dead. In such instances I was able to give survivors the option of having their real names used. A star next to a survivor's name indicates that his or her real name has been used. The absence of a star indicates that, for legal reasons, a pseudonym has been assigned to the survivor and identifying characteristics of his or her story have been changed.

ACKNOWLEDGMENTS

I AM INDEBTED TO MANY PEOPLE FOR THEIR HELP. FIRST AND foremost, I owe a deep thanks to the trauma survivors who shared their stories with me. I hope that this book serves as both a voice and a platform for them.

Many experts in the field of psychological trauma gave freely of their time and information. They are Dr. Bessel van der Kolk, Professor of Psychiatry, Boston University; Dr. Matthew J. Friedman, Executive Director of the National Center for PTSD, U.S. Department of Veterans Affairs and Professor of Psychiatry and Pharmacology at Dartmouth University Medical School; Dr. Judith Lewis Herman, Associate Clinical Professor of Psychology at Harvard Medical School and Director of Training at Cambridge Hospital's Victims of Violence Program; Dr. James Jaranson, Director of Medical Services at the Center for Victims of Torture in Minneapolis, Minnesota; Dr. Yael Danieli, Director of the Group Project for Holocaust Survivors and their Children in New York City; Drs. Laurie Anne Pearlman, Karen Saakvitne, and Daniel Abrahamson, Research Director, Clinical Director, and Administrative Director (respectively) of the Traumatic Stress Institute in South Windsor, Connecticut; Drs. Mark Hall, Dena Rosenbloom, and Sandra Hartdagen, staff clinical psychologists at the Traumatic Stress Institute; Dr. Stuart Kleinman, Attending Psychiatrist, Forensic Psychiatric Clinic, Criminal and Supreme Courts of Manhattan in New York City and Assistant Professor of Clinical Psychiatry at Columbia University; Dr. Lucy Friedman, Executive Director of Victims Services Agency in New York City; Dr. Ellen Brickman, Associate Professor at the School of Social Services of Fordham University; Dr. Lois J. Veronen, a clinical psychologist at the Human Development Center of Winthrop College in Rock Hill, South Carolina; Dr. Christine Dunning, Professor in the Department of Governmental Affairs at the University of Wisconsin in Milwaukee; Dr. Denise Gelinas, a therapist in private practice in Northampton, Massachusetts; Dr. William Halikias, a psychologist in private practice in Brattleboro, Vermont; the late Vera Work, a therapist in private practice in Brattleboro; Dr. Martha B. Straus, a clinical and community psychologist with University Associates in Psychology in Keene, New Hampshire; Dr. Estelle Disch, Associate Professor in the Department of Sociology at University of Massachusetts in Boston and co-founder of the Boston Associates to Stop Therapy Abuse (BASTA!); and Dr. Lisa Oransoff, Clini-

Acknowledgments

cal Director of the George B. Wells Human Services Center in Southbridge, Massachusetts. In conversations with these experts I learned much about the nuances of trauma and recovery. For their help I am very grateful.

I also owe a special thanks to Linda Valerian, Volunteer Coordinator at the Center for Victims of Torture in Minneapolis; Deborah Spungen, Founder of Families of Murder Victims in Philadelphia; Susan Sweetser, co-founder of Survivors of Crime in Essex, Vermont; Bonnie Dwork and the Holocaust Writers Workshop in Forest Hills, New York; and Phyllis Woodside and the New Hampshire chapter of Parents of Murdered Children.

Thanks to Cathy Lauden and Laurie Bayer for their clerical help. And many thanks to the people who volunteered to comment on drafts of this manuscript. They are Bob Schwartz, Kate Dodge, Martha Straus, James MacDonald, Deborah Krasner, Jody Kamens, Annie Frelich, Danny Sobel, Vera Work, Sherry Frazier, Laura Fine, Leonard Foglia, and Cor Trowbridge. Their comments were often contradictory, but always enlightening. Their gifts of time, enthusiasm, and insight were indispensable; for those gifts, I remain very grateful.

The Helping Hand Strikes Again

1

AMERICANS SEEM AS TITILLATED as they are scared by the horror and tragedy played out in our headline news. We love dread so much that we have built much of our literature and entertainment industry around it. Books and movies tweak the feelings of vulnerability that stories of violence and coercion inspire and then reassure us with happy endings based on myths like the inevitable triumph of good over evil and the infinite resilience of the human spirit.

In fact, the dread to which we Americans are so attracted seems well-founded. The United States Department of Justice says that as many as 850,000 rapes, robberies, and assaults with firearms are committed each year in the United States. Eighty percent of Americans will be victimized by a serious crime at some point in their lives, or so the National Institute of Justice predicted in 1990. The Bureau of Justice Statistics says that criminals are increasingly likely to be armed and dangerous. Recent survey data gathered under the auspices of the National Institutes of Mental Health from 6,159 female students at thirty-two colleges indicated that 15% of college women have experienced rape since their fourteenth birthday.

Unfortunately, the idea that the human spirit, if truly innocent, invariably rallies seems not as well-founded as our communal dread. According to Dr. Dean G. Kilpatrick, Director of the National Crime Victims Research and Treatment Center of the Medical University of South Carolina, victims of crime are about ten times more likely than the general population to become depressed. One in every five women who has been raped attempts suicide. Over 40% of rape victims have suicidal thoughts.

Even a cursory look at these statistics is unsettling. We can shrug off fear by wisecracking that life will eventually kill us all. In some way, most of us probably have accepted the fact that we eventually will die. What we probably haven't accepted is that we may not get to die when dying would be easier than surviving. Crime, sexual assault, war, incest, and family violence will push many of us not to personal extinction, but only to its brink. Our selection as victims will be undeserved. The forces acting against us will be outside our control. We will not be saved by avenging heroes. While some will find their spirits resilient, many of us will be left degraded by the experience and ostracized by society. The reason for our social exile: We will be living proof that not all stories end happily. And the possibility of unhappy endings to true stories with innocent protagonists is an unspeakable truth too personally threatening for almost anyone to acknowledge.

For example:

* * *

At the beginning of World War II, roughly nine million Jews lived in Europe. Some escaped to the East or West or survived in slave labor camps, ghettos, forests, or by being hidden in the underground. But two out of three were murdered during the war. Most were gassed and then burnt, although many were unceremoniously shot and shoved into mass graves. No more than 75,000 seem to have survived the concentration, labor, and death camps.

In 1945, six years after Germany began its first offensive of World War II, the Nazis began fleeing their camps; it had become clear to them that the Allied liberation armies would soon roll in. When the liberators finally arrived at the camps, they were rarely greeted by cheers or applause, as most of the camp survivors were near death from hunger, thirst, and disease. Survivors lay, barely able to breathe or rise, among the people who had expired in the days since their captors' departure had left them without food or water. Most survivors had lost everyone in the world they loved. Most of those who were healthy enough to get about seemed devoid of feeling, completely passive, even roboticized.

International relief workers organized the chaos by feeding, clothing, and registering many, and by burying or hospitalizing many more. But efficient as the relief workers were in their huge logistical effort, no organized plan for survivors' psychological assistance was set forth by any nation or group of nations.

Dr. Paul Friedman, one of the first psychiatrists to have contact with survivors during the process of liberation, wryly admits: "We accepted the theory that the very fact of survival was evidence of physical and psychological superiority — without looking too closely at the implications of this statement." The blind assumption seemed to be that as these few, somehow superior Jews' bodies recovered their strength, their psyches would recover, too.

The assumption about physical and psychological superiority wasn't limited to relief workers. In that assumption the rest of the world, too, found comfort. It gave the world license to continue self-congratulatory victory celebrations and to rally around comfortable ideas like the triumph of good over evil and courage over cowardice. The assumption blinded celebrants to the fact that perpetuating heroic myths might compound the misery of the very people they had just fought to liberate.

The surviving Jews saw the cruelty of the hoax, but couldn't speak. They knew that many of the millions who had died were both courageous and noble. They knew, too, that not even the fearful and common had deserved their deaths. They knew that the Jews who survived the Holocaust were not infinitely resilient; they would carry the scars with them always. But when survivors tried to publicly and openly account for what happened to them and their loved ones and to talk about how it affected them emotionally, the world insisted on its right not to hear the truth. It was just too horrible to assimilate.

In an incisive analysis of the effects of victimization and social isolation on Holocaust survivors, Dr. Yael Danieli, Director of the Group Project for Holocaust Survivors and Their Children in New York City, writes: "Survivors' war accounts were too horrifying for most people to listen to or believe. . . . Survivors were . . . faced with the pervasively held myth that they had actively or passively participated in their own destiny by 'going like sheep to the slaughter' and with the suspicion that they had performed immoral acts in order to survive."

Having fought to liberate the Jews, the world began to exile them.

The pattern of revictimization for survivors of the Holocaust is strikingly similar to the pattern of revictimization for many survivors of human cruelty today. Because something extraordinarily calamitous has happened, a survivor feels a compelling need to process the trauma psychically while being supported by family and friends who care. But just when they are needed most, family and friends back off. "Survivors are isolated, which makes them feel even more vulnerable," says Dr. Lucy Friedman, Executive Director of the Victims Services Agency in New York City. This leaves the trauma survivor needing to speak socially unspeakable truths: The world is not safe. I have been reduced, destroyed.

In response, says Dr. Friedman, "We tell them to 'put it all behind them,' and that they are 'indulging themselves.' We resent the onslaught to our more comfortable world view."

As a culture, we don't like complainers. When trauma survivors insist on speaking their unspeakable truths, it can begin to seem to us that they are obsessing. They appear a bit crazy in their determination to tell, and we think perhaps they are exaggerating for effect. Finally, we begin believing that the trauma was somehow earned.

"Most of us believe that we, and by extension, those we love, are insulated from disaster," says Dr. Friedman. "Trauma destroys this belief. To integrate it, we have to either acknowledge that we, too, are powerless or that the victim, in some way, precipitated the trauma. And society encourages the thinking that the victim participated in the situation leading to his or her trauma. By believing that the trauma was somehow earned, friends can distance themselves from the survivor's situation and make them and their family seem less vulnerable."

Richard Bikales★ survived the Nazi Holocaust.

"I could only talk to other people that survived. Even now it's very hard. Even if they listen, they don't understand. The words aren't there that really describe what's inside me. How do you describe the feelings? How to describe the events? How do you describe the horror? I don't know."

Barbara Palermo's 28-year-old son was murdered.

"Unless you are personally involved in this type of death, people really don't want to hear it. So it kind of puts you in a position where—who do you speak to or who do you say nothing to? And it shouldn't be that way. I see old friends and they say, 'Hi, Barbara, how are you today?' And you always say, 'Oh, I'm fine, how are you?' You could be eating away inside on any given day, but you still say, 'Oh, I'm fine, how are you? How are the kids?'"

Dorian Davis is a retired police officer.

"I don't know how many people have died in my arms. Little kids. People don't know that. But I remember all this stuff. And it comes back to me. When I build around the house, I pick up a hammer and what will come to my head is 'hammer,' and I'll remember that this woman's husband hit her on the head, knocked her out the window, and she landed in the driveway, and it was wintry, and blood all over, and I was with her when she died. The other cops were upstairs. I was the only one, alone with this woman. Her face was like mush and she was bleeding. And all that comes back to me now. And at the time—I don't tell anybody—I held her hand.

"So it's impacting my life today. I really have to fight it. It's like sometimes I want to tell somebody, 'Gee, I saw a person die.' Or, 'Hey, life sucks, life's dangerous. You've got to be careful because you can really get fucked over big time.' But you can't just go up and tell somebody. I've tried, and it's inappropriate. I feel like an asshole."

Instead of taking her to a doctor or the police, Madeline Goodman's father and grandmother took her to a psychiatrist for hypnotism to forget being gang raped.

"All the way home as I sat in the back seat of the car, I said to myself, 'I will never forget. I will never forget.' My father and grandmother must have overheard me talking to myself because they kept interrupting me and making me respond to their unrelated questions. I went deep, deep within myself and told myself to 'always remember, always remember, I'll always remember.' When we got home, I sat on the couch in our living room. And I said to them, 'And you know what? They put a ball and chain on my ankle.' My father walked out of the room in response to my statement and headed for the bathroom. My grandmother spun around and spat out, 'Shut UP! I never want to hear another word about it!' and left the room."

Christine Dodge was sexually abused throughout her childhood by her father.

"My parents were very young when they had me and my two other sisters who were closer in age to me. They were able to have another child when I was 16. I felt that she was being sexually abused by my father so I confronted her about it. We went to a movie or something and I said, 'Deb, are these things happening to you, because they happened to me? And I am worried about you because of the way you have been behaving.' And she said, 'Yes.' And me and my best friend and my husband went directly to the police. I didn't really want to go to the police. I was like, 'Well, why don't we just confront the family about it?' and they said, 'Chris, you are crazy. It is not going to work that way, because the family is not going to take this very well. Go to the police.' It turned out that child abuse was founded in the case, but they did not have enough evidence to go on with any kind of prosecution or even a civil case with it, so my sister is still in the home and I do believe that she is still being sexually abused.
And I felt that Deb had thought I had kind of abandoned her after getting her into all this trouble by telling her story to the police and everything. See, I was not allowed to see her and set things straight. I have limited access to Deb now and I am not allowed to see her without a chaperon.

"My sisters are very angry that I went to the police. They have a lot of reasons. They tend to deny a lot and it happened on my grandfather's birthday and they thought that was terrible. They are angry at me for messing up the birthday. And they have a reality that they have invested in very strongly, you know, their denial about what happened to them in the home is very important to their survival. I have made it harder for them to survive."

Paolo Williams was working in a clothing store when a robber murdered his boss.

"Sometimes I am depressed, because at times I think about maybe if I had taken the scissors. There were scissors. See, this girl I know she said, 'Why didn't you grab the scissors?' Somebody else says, 'Why didn't you just try to fight the guy, too?' You see, people tell you things like this, it just makes you feel even more guilt. Then you say to yourself, 'Maybe I could have done this, maybe I could have done that.' But the truth? Maybe this, maybe that, but you don't have a chance to maybe do this or maybe do that, because when someone is holding a gun to you, you're frightened, because what is running through your head, it's the fear. It's fear right then and there. You think you're going to die. You don't think about, 'Well, let me try to do this or that.' No, you're just thinking, 'This is it,' you're not going to live no more, you're not going to see your family. That was what was running through my head when that guy had the gun pointed at me."

Patricia Berry's seven-year-old boy was murdered by the teenager across the street.

"I know that when I gave my victim impact statement to the court, it was very, very strong. It came from the bottom of my heart. I said to myself as I got up, 'Well, Jimmy up there in heaven, look down on me, because you're going to be proud of me after I'm done.' I told the court that what had happened had hurt to the core. It changed my life, it changed me as a person, and I had every right to have things go my way in court as much as I could get them to. And after I had spoken, I figured that was done and it was over with. But the defense attorney stood up and said that he wanted on the record that my statement was going to psychologically damage his client. It felt like I had blown up a balloon and somebody just went 'pop.' It was awful. I still feel like I wanted to take that—he was shorter than I was—and if I'd been closer to him I swear I would have taken him by the neck and shaken him, just like that. It was like, 'I had the chance, my one last chance, you little turkey!' And just with his one statement. Why did he have to say that? I had the right. But he wanted to make me feel guilty for hurting his client. He had to get that last word in."

Despite their years of professional training, psychotherapists are not immune to protecting their own precious beliefs about invulnerability at virtually any cost. When they do this within the therapeutic relationship, inevitably they rebrutalize trauma survivors. Dr. Yael Danieli's research into the psychological effects of trauma on Holocaust survivors illuminates the damage that a demand from society for silence can do to trauma survivors. This research also sheds some light on how mental health professionals communicate to their survivor clients a sense that bringing to therapy tales of abject terror imposes an unbearable burden on the therapist.

Dr. Danieli conducted open-ended interviews with psychotherapists working with Holocaust survivors and their children. She found that some therapists admitted to numbing themselves emotionally whenever Holocaust stories left them feeling overwhelmed. Others acknowledged not entirely believing their clients. Some said they had even accused their clients of exaggerating. Some therapists told of repeatedly forgetting the details of survivors' stories or of becoming impatient at hearing the same Holocaust story again and again. Some therapists said they lectured their Holocaust clients and admonished them for complaining. Others told of insisting that their clients "leave the Holocaust behind them" and talk only about the "here and now."

In her discussion of her study, Dr. Danieli points out that the participating therapists responded to the interview questions with "great eagerness and astonishing candor." It seems reasonable to infer from her observation that the therapists interviewed realized and respected the profound effect the Holocaust had on their clients' current emotional states. Apparently, however, regardless of how enlightened and compassionate their theoretical stances were concerning human cruelty and its emotional aftershocks, therapists routinely failed to incorporate such compassionate principles into their clinical practice. In psychological self defense, they interpreted the urgency of survivors' need to understand what happened as a lingering and unhealthy obsession, and not as a natural and entirely appropriate response to the trauma they had suffered.

Survivors have stories they need to tell. Unfortunately, these are the very stories that we who are their friends, family, and therapists seem to need not to hear. But if we refuse to listen to their tales, how are they to regain their lost sense of kinship with the rest of humanity? And if we do try to rally, if we could try to listen, how are we to help when the very act of listening undermines the psychological defenses we must maintain in order to live in our increasingly violent society?

Mary Margaret lost two sons when they were murdered in separate violent crimes.

"I have a problem crying in front of people, but after my first son died, I did. Not intentionally, it just happened. It was three months after my son was murdered, and the therapist said, 'Oh, you'll be okay. You're a young woman. Get on with your life.'

"'Well, how do I get on with my life? That's why I'm here! I don't know how!'

"He was just very insensitive, so I had to leave therapy. Because I probably would have gotten physical with him. I really would have. That's how angry he made me."

Amy O'Keefe grew up in an environment of pervasive physical and sexual abuse. In her forties she sought therapy.

"It was in the first year of therapy, and I left a session and I thought, 'When did I first really get depressed?' And I thought about if for a week. When it came closer to the therapy day I was getting more anxious and having more feeling and more feeling and more feeling. It was like my feeling was coming back to me for the first time in my life but it was overwhelming. So I went to the appointment about an hour and a half early and I cried quietly in the waiting room the entire time. When I got into the session I broke down and my therapist said, 'What's going on?' and I said, 'Well, I remembered the first time I got depressed.' And then I literally walked through in a 40-minute therapy period an episode of abuse that happened one day. I literally went back there in time. Although I knew I was sitting in my therapist's office and I knew he was there and I knew he was listening to me—I wasn't split off or whatever—I was back there in feeling. I'm crying, crying, uncontrollably crying. I couldn't stop.

"So when I was finished looking at that day, the feelings subsided and I came back to being in the room and looking at him and I couldn't take a reading on him. He wasn't really there like he had been there before. We talked about it and he described what he had just seen as an 'almost psychotic experience,' which made me retreat completely. Those are words that shut me down. I was fearful of being crazy and his words sounded like I almost was."

Monica Reed has been having violent outbursts since being sexually abused.

"My therapist's position is that I've got to really straighten out and start being responsible, stop having these kinds of violent attacks. I've got to stop it right now and I have to take control of things. And here I am saying, 'I don't have any control. I don't know how to be controlled. Will you please tell me how?'"

2

IN PREPARATION FOR WRITING this book, I interviewed survivors of human cruelty in the company of their therapists. All of the therapists were experts in the field of traumatic stress. All of the people I interviewed had thrived in therapy. I was encouraged by my research. It was apparent that no matter how violent the interpersonal trauma, no matter how complete the betrayal and resulting loss, people could, indeed, return to a state of emotional health.

To friends who asked how I could tolerate listening to trauma stories I replied that I was finding ways to cope. It had yet to occur to me that I was able to tolerate hearing these particular trauma stories primarily because they were told by people in whom recovery was so remarkably apparent. It had yet to occur to me that I had met only people selected by their therapists as evidence of at least partial recovery. It had therefore yet to occur to me that there might be therapy "failures," as well, and that the fact that these "thrivers" entered therapy at all might mean that while their experiences had injured them, they had not entirely broken them. The survivors had retained enough faith in human potential and decency to call a therapist, to give another human interaction a try. It had yet to occur to me that if life can kill you it can probably also damage you beyond repair.

On a snowy December day after my first few months of research I went to SelfHelp Community Services in the Queens borough of New York City to listen in on their Holocaust Writers Workshop. As I entered SelfHelp's building, I was terribly nervous. I had been nervous all morning, and I was beginning to understand why in full force.

In preparation for attending the Holocaust Writers Workshop I had read *Massive Psychic Trauma*, which I had been told was a remarkable book detailing the psychological devastation that the Holocaust wrought on its survivors. I had read the book through three times. I had absorbed nothing of it. Apparently I was so afraid of the material that I couldn't retain the information on the pages.

On the subway to Queens I tried to calm myself by imagining how the meeting would begin. The facilitator would probably introduce me and ask me to explain to everyone why I was there. I thought I would give some version of my standard spiel: "The book I am writing is about emotional recovery from catastrophic human cruelty like crime, sexual assault, war, the Holocaust, incest, political terror, and family violence. I am writing the book because, with disastrous results, survivors of human cruelty often turn to mental health professionals who know nothing about dealing with the special issues raised by trauma like yours. However, within the last few years, some psychotherapists have made real progress in identifying the unique aftershocks of such trauma and in devising ways to help survivors overcome them.

"My book will let trauma survivors know that others have suffered as they have. It will tell them that specialized care exists, and that although it won't erase what has happened to them, care from a specialist in psychological trauma can accelerate the process by which survivors begin to manage their pain."

I noticed that I had not imagined myself explicitly saying "recovery is possible," something which I normally said in my opening spiel. It was fairly clear to me why I hadn't.

I hadn't imagined it because I knew on some level it would be in unimaginably poor taste for me to say such a pap thing to people who had lived through the Holocaust and been liberated into a world that made no effort to help them heal psychically. I could not go in front of a group of Holocaust survivors and insinuate that there was a comfortable wellness that, if they hadn't yet discovered, they should be aspiring to. If I did and I was lucky they would be too polite to force me to see the truth of their "sickness." These were people whose trauma had not lasted a moment or a few hours. The majority would have survived years of intense degradation, terror, and helplessness. What was widely considered the most civilized region in the world at that time had come to a sudden consensus that these individual Jews and everyone they loved should be exterminated. The Holocaust survivors I was about to meet had seen human nature for what it is. It is genocidal. People who weren't actively murderous raised well-dressed, well-fed babies not far from the stench of burning ones and played with their children on train platforms as caravans of boxcars stuffed to the brink with terrified families rolled by to their deaths.

I realized that while "recovery is possible" is a seemingly plausible premise for a book, I had better stop and ask myself some very simple questions: Is recovery possible for everyone? What does recovery mean? If it implies a path from sickness to wellness what does the term imply about the victims of violence? That they are sick and that society and its members (including parents who rape their children, husbands who beat their wives, and all other perpetrators of cruelty, including mass murderers, secret police, Fascists, Nazis, petty criminals, and so on) are well? And couldn't I re-wound the Holocaust survivors who had kindly invited me to listen to their tales by blustering about with my own uninformed ideas about trauma and recovery?

Some of the survivors I was about to meet might have survived torture at the hands of doctors. Could I really suggest to them that mutilated psyches can be entrusted to medical-establishment psychiatrists? In Hitler's Europe, at the first sign of cracking under the emotional strain of life in the camps, a Jew was usually exterminated, no questions asked. Could I suggest at this workshop that openly acknowledging emotional strain can be entirely safe? Many Holocaust survivors had survived for years on the hope that one day their persecution would be over. They would tell the world what happened to them. The world would acknowledge their suffering. Change. War and degradation would be a thing of the past. It would be like a miracle. But when they finally made it out of the camps or out of hiding, they had discovered that their stories were too overwhelming to be believed. Too often, people like me treated them like complaining pariahs. The world didn't change as they had hoped. In fact, in a universal sense, their suffering had been truly for naught.

My reading of Dr. Danieli's work had taught me that, as the years went on, Holocaust survivors had only each other to whom to turn. And turn they did. Together they allowed themselves to remember human nature as they had seen it in all its horror. They helped each other accept the fact that the world has two kinds of "normals"—one for them and one for everybody else. Then, in life-affirming defiance of their brushes with individual and collective extinction, they started new families. Their babies would be their miracles, as would be their new lives, and they would make the best of both. They would have a victory, after all.

Yes, it seemed to me that I could preposterously offend the people I was about to meet by suggesting they turn their attention away from the miracles they had wrought and toward symptoms of life-long distress relating to the trauma of the Holocaust. By announcing that only relatively recent developments promise hope I would be implying that their youths had been wasted and that, for all the intervening years, Hitler had remained in some measure triumphant. I would be saying that their lives, their miraculous children, were not victories. I would be saying that they were sick and that they needed help. I would be spitting in their faces.

And, to be honest, I couldn't imagine ever truly recovering from an experience as horrible as the Holocaust. Why, then, would I even mention recovery to Holocaust survivors? Because I need to feel that their ordeals and losses somehow hadn't really had the impact I know they must have had? Would I be hoping survivors could just forget? If those things had happened to me I'm not sure I would want to forget them even for an instant. Why would I want to be put at risk by purposeful naiveté? And if barbarous things had happened to me, wouldn't I know that in some very significant way my current strength of character, my wisdom about the world and its people, would have been shaped by those experiences? Would forgetting those experiences also lead me to deny my strengths and my wisdom? "What is recovery, anyway?" I found myself wondering. "Is it forgetting? Denying? Suppressing?"

Needless to say, I felt like a bit of a blockhead by the time I entered the door marked "Holocaust Writers Workshop." Then a frail, elderly woman who introduced herself as Sarah Straus came up to me with her eyes shining as excitedly as if she had swallowed a light bulb. She asked if I was "the visiting writer." She showed me where to hang my coat and asked me to have some tea with her. Her look of expectation was wonderfully unremitting. She made me feel somehow as special as a Christmas tree, though the image was, of course, wrong for the setting. Gradually some of the other workshop members joined Sarah and me. They were all exceedingly polite, which helped a bit to put me at ease. But I remember hoping, as Sarah introduced me to everyone, that they would concentrate on my Biblical first name and not on my Irish surname, and therefore not suspect me of being like other Americans who had turned a deaf ear to their tales.

Nervous as I was about my integrity as a listener, I was there specifically to hear these survivors' stories, and that was a powerful enticement for these people, as it proved to be to all the survivors I interviewed in the course of writing this book. These Holocaust survivors had been meeting several times a month for fifteen years, reading aloud to each other the most minute details of their Holocaust experiences. They wrote for posterity, for their children, for catharsis, and for artistry. They wanted to be heard in the same way that any writer wants readers. They wanted to be believed in the same way that any survivor who bears witness wants to be believed.

We sat in a circle in a cozy room just a few feet away from an elevated subway track. The trains roared by right outside the window, and the sound of the trains as well as flushing pipes inside the building were so loud that they occasionally obscured the recording I made of the meeting.

There were five presenters that day. Sarah, whose mother was murdered by Hitler's army, told an especially loving tale of a day as a child when she tried to abide by her mother's lesson never to take anything larger than a pinhead. The story wasn't about death and destruction. It was simply an homage to a woman who was long gone and still missed. Sarah's husband, Albert, read about a young woman who risked her life over and over to give him and his brother refuge. Martin Grumwald's story was about escaping Hungary and travelling to America. Embedded in the story was a modest memorial to a woman whom he had romanced under apocalyptic conditions; although she survived the Holocaust, she killed herself in despair shortly afterward.

As I listened I began to believe that, in the hierarchy of suffering, these particular Holocaust survivors had not endured much. After all, their readings were primarily of escape, not capture or death. Maybe I was in the wrong place. Maybe I needed to find Holocaust survivors who had suffered more than the members of this group had. Then I realized the lie to that thinking. In order for a story to be about escape, something has to be escaped. And Nazi-occupied Europe and its death, labor, and concentration camps were the very real "somethings" for these people. For fifteen years now they had been recording and telling each other their histories of death and destruction, escape and freedom. Fright contraposed with consolation was probably for most of them an unshakable theme, for these were people who, after all, had somehow survived. The fact of their survival seemed to remain wondrous to them. It was clearly as important to them as the fact that they had almost succumbed.

I watched them give each other nods of approval and encouragement. As I watched, I realized that recovery has little to do with forgetting, denying, or suppressing. Rather, it involves the ability to insist on the recognition that one's degradation and despair truly happened, but that survival happened, as well. Recovery, I thought, has something to do with integrating into one's life the reprieve of survival along with the horror of trauma.

Then Richard Bikales★, a concentration camp survivor, read a piece:

"The Faith of a Survivor"

When we were fighting for simple, naked, raw survival, this in itself seemed to be the overwhelming purpose in life. But we did not just want to survive. We wanted to live to see the day when Hitler and his bloody empire would crumble. We believed with every fiber of our being that no matter how all-powerful and invincible our tormentors seemed, one day they would be broken, and we wanted desperately to see that day.

When Hitler was defeated, we had achieved this all-consuming goal. We had survived. We had stayed alive. We had held out to see reduced to utter helplessness the men in power who had set out to destroy us and who had hunted us as their prey. We had seen the last dying wish of millions come true. So no matter what happens in this life, we have acquired a basic conviction that in the end, good wins out over evil. Not a childish, naive division of the world into good guys and bad guys, but a fundamental belief that human goodness is the norm and that the vicious, the brutal, the unconscionable, is an aberration which in the long run cannot prevail. This faith has helped us feel that life and people are worthwhile after all. It has given us the strength to live with our memories.

I was shaken and moved. Here, sitting beside me, was a man who gathered enormous comfort from the conclusion that good triumphs over evil. I was troubled by my empathetic response not to what he had been through but to the lesson he had drawn from his experience. As a political stance I knew I didn't buy his conclusion. Wasn't the inevitable triumph of good over evil one of the very myths I had set out to debunk? Why, then, did I feel so touched? In such total agreement?

Richard introduced a second piece. "Last year my wife, Charlotte, and I decided we were going to go back to Poland. When we left in '45 we had sworn we were never going back to that cursed country because of what happened to us there. But as time went by we both had an urge to go back. So last year, after so many years, we went back. And we went to the place where my parents had been killed. This was a death camp called Belzac. Belzac was very special in this way: It was the first death camp, where they experimented with how to kill hundreds of thousands. In fact they killed over 600,000 Jews and 1,500 Poles who had helped Jews. So it was a horrible place. And the machinery wasn't functional. I read about it, I couldn't believe. It was one big horror story. And the night before we had to stay in a small town not far from Belzac, and I couldn't sleep. So I wrote to my parents a letter that night."

Then he read it:

To my parents, my beloved Vati and Mutti.

As we are making our way onto the field of horror, where you were so brutally tortured to death by fiends from hell, to be martyrs for your children and for a better future world, we have a deeper understanding of what you have done for me and Charlotte. Now that we have returned to Poland, and are stirring up our past, it has become clear to us that the thousands of miracles, and they were thousands, which led us through the Hitler firestorm, could not possibly have been coincidences. We understand how you made a terrible sacrifice of sending your son Norbert [my brother] to France to spare him from Poland, the tears and pain it caused you, and how you thus saved his life. And we also believe with every fiber in our being that you, in the last gruesome days, hours, and minutes, had prayed with all the strength you were capable of that Charlotte and I should be spared the cruel fate that had befallen you. Your prayers were so all-consumingly desperate that they were heard by somebody.

You brought us up to become decent human beings. You never said to us, not even in the slightest way, that we should become good Jews, only that we should grow up to be good people, and that we should become well educated, not just well schooled. But most of all, acquire wisdom and compassion.

I firmly believe that you willed upon us that in decisive moments, decent human beings would enter into our lives. So it happened that under the most incredibly difficult circumstances we found those decent people of compassion and wisdom whom you had sent to us. Decent Germans, even SS. decent Poles, decent Ukrainians, people, total strangers who made it possible for us to survive the crazed designs of the Nazis. You had taught us that only rabble indulges in the hatred of other groups of people. We have never forgotten your teachings and have always endeavored to do you honor. Charlotte and I have a powerful desire for a world without hatred. We have striven to plant this feeling in our children, your grandchildren. Even in Poland, at this dreadful place, do we recognize a gripping bond with you. Although the tears and sobs will overtake Charlotte and me, we also sense a profound peace, a consciousness that we are one with you. We want to bring this consciousness back to our new homeland in America, and we want to erect there a fitting memorial for you.

Your children, Richard and Charlotte.

That Richard knew something I didn't know was painfully clear. He had managed to reach an equanimity about his life and the world in general that I had not managed to reach about my relatively untroubled life or about the world.

To this day I remain humbled by Richard's world view. I have spent a good deal of thought trying to work out a fit between his conclusion—"that in the end, good triumphs over evil"—and my own belief that myths such as the inevitable triumph of good over evil inflict a second wound on survivors of human cruelty. I have finally resolved the differences to my satisfaction and, I believe, enlightenment. Richard was not talking about a myth. Something is only a myth to you if you've never seen it happen. But Richard had witnessed the triumph of good over evil on an epic scale. He was not espousing an unfounded or defensive assumption imposed on him. He was bearing witness to the public and private moments of heroism that had saved him. With great cause he had accommodated into his personal world view both evil and good. He knew first hand about degradation and triumph. He remembered exactly what had happened to him. And he had molded his memories into a powerful and realistic personal philosophy.

I was still resonating from what I heard from Richard when the last workshop writer, Walter Keats★, read what seemed to be a chapter toward the close of a chronicle of his Holocaust experiences. After escaping from Dachau, Walter had joined the British army, serving as an interpreter and ultimately helping in the courts at Nuremberg. The chapter he read told of an R&R leave during which he travelled toward Vienna.

> Soon our bus had crossed into Bavaria and drove through the picturesque landscape, climbing a mountain road to higher elevations. We halted briefly at the town of Berchtesgaden for a light snack at an inn that provided complimentary refreshments courtesy of the U.S. Army, and continued up into the mountains through lush forest greenery to the German dictator's retreat which was a lookout of many historical events in recent years.
>
> I was very keen on seeing this place, which had been in the news so much. We passed the SS barracks with its checkpoint, all now deserted, and pulled up at the once handsome building, now a bombed-out shell. There was a guide and I entered the place with beating heart. Here I was, a Jewish young man who would never have dreamed to come here, a place where history had been made, where world leaders had been humiliated, and dictators had planned world domination. I had taken part to vanquish these evil men, and there was a pride rising in me as I walked through these burned-out premises.
>
> I entered the large study with the huge picture window, now only a great jagged opening in the wall, permitting a breathtaking view of the surrounding mountains. The guide pointed out a building in the distant mountainside which had belonged to Field Marshall Göring, who recently had ended his own life. We went through the spacious living quarters and came upon the bathroom of Eva Braun, the dictator's mistress. The full-length plate glass mirror on the inside of the door was shattered, and I could not resist picking some fragments off the floor as souvenirs.

At this point, and without missing even a beat in his recitation, Walter gave a tiny, proud smile, whipped out of his breast pocket a card-sized fragment of the mirror and passed it to his neighbor in the circle. As the shard of glass passed from hand to hand, Walter read the paragraph's last sentences: "From an historical point of view, this excursion was very rewarding. It showed how the mighty had fallen."

What I saw as Walter finished reading was a wonderful snapshot of survival, of victory. Five decades later, the woman who had preened herself in front of her mirror for her genocidal lover was long dead and humiliated. A group of elderly people sat in an extremely noisy, wonderfully warm room a continent away on a winter's day. For fifteen years they had met. Together they had remembered every detail of horror. Somehow most seemed able to remember the minutiae of hope and love that had peppered their lives in the midst of it all. By mutual support they had changed the direction and timbre of their lives fundamentally. Now, with eyes wide in wonder, they passed the shard among them until the power of the moment passed. To paraphrase Richard Bikales, the last dying wish of millions had evidently come true.

* * *

The narrative core of this book is the detailed testimony of a handful of survivors of crime, sexual assault, incest, Holocaust, war, and family violence. Although some of these tales are inherently shocking, they are not included for their shock value. These are the stories of people who have suffered horribly but are at some point in the process of emotional recovery. The presence of their stories is a purposeful attempt to dispel the certainty of many trauma survivors that no one who has suffered as they have could ever again attempt to live a full life.

Throughout this book I have juxtaposed survivors' testimony with the reasoned commentary of experts in the field of psychological trauma. I have also noted my own observations about what I saw, heard, and felt when meeting with survivors. In doing so I do not intend to present myself as an expert on psychological trauma. Far from it.

I am a writer and a documentary videographer who specializes in psychological topics. Typically, I begin a project from the perspective of no or little knowledge about the topic that I am investigating. By reading professional literature and interviewing mental health experts as well as people working towards recovery, I gradually acquire information about discrete areas of mental health care. I use this information to create educational pieces that I hope help members of the general public understand otherwise perplexing mental health topics and work out satisfying, personal solutions.

The ability to approach psychological topics objectively is a skill I have worked hard to refine, for it is central to my trade. However, in researching and writing this book, I frequently found myself unable to shed personal biases. Time and again, as I listened to trauma stories I became aware of the full complement of prejudices I hold about human cruelty and its victims. I see now that these prejudices are rooted in beloved beliefs about my own invulnerability. I also see the lengths to which I will go to protect those beliefs. Try as I did to listen with an open heart and mind, at some point I emotionally backed out of virtually every encounter with a survivor. When trauma stories turned especially grisly, I usually sat with as attentive an expression as I could muster on my face and dissociated my thoughts and feelings from what I was hearing; sometimes, though, when a survivor's words broke through this relatively benign defense, I colored what I heard with a faint wash of blame and suspicion.

Because the professional literature had warned me that such reactions are common, I was usually able to catch myself in the act. Still, each time, my failure to remain emotionally engaged with the survivor and his or her tale appalled me. I felt uniquely unfit for the job of compassionate listening.

My more rational self now knows that such failings are virtually automatic defenses nearly impossible to defeat. But learning to accept and to overcome my failures has been difficult. I therefore include a chronology of my own reactions to trauma stories to help readers assess their own reactions and to make the following point: If and when you find yourself tuning out anguished voices, know that you are only human. Then try listening again.

The Struggle to Understand Trauma

3

To study psychological trauma means bearing witness to horrible events. When the events are natural disasters or 'acts of God,' those who bear witness sympathize readily with the victim. But when the traumatic events are of human design, those who bear witness are caught in the conflict between victim and perpetrator. It is morally impossible to remain neutral in this conflict. The bystander is forced to take sides.

It is very tempting to take the side of the perpetrator. All the perpetrator asks is that the bystander do nothing. He appeals to the universal desire to see, hear, and speak no evil. The victim, on the contrary, asks the bystander to share the burden of pain. The victim demands action. . . .

[From J. L. Herman, *Trauma and Recovery* (New York: Basic Books, 1992), p. 7.]

THE STRUGGLE TO UNDERSTAND TRAUMA is the struggle to empathize with the victim and not the perpetrator. It requires us to understand that the unusual and malevolent can intrude on the usual and innocent. It requires us to accept that no matter how foolishly or irresponsibly a victim has behaved, it was the aggressor who rendered the victim helpless and who bears sole responsibility for his actions. By extension, it requires us to accept the following unspeakable truth: If, for one person, foolishness does not account for helplessness, for ourselves, no amount of precaution can absolutely preclude it.

The struggle to understand trauma is the struggle to hear in trauma stories the truths that they hold about vulnerability and helplessness. This is a struggle for us all. People who have never been traumatized by violence or malevolence must abandon their sure footing on safe ground. Survivors must abandon their footing in self-blame and shame. Bad things do happen to good people.

★ ★ ★

MADELINE GOODMAN: "I was a toddler, about three years old. I was sitting on the couch downstairs and my father said, 'Look, Madeline, I have a new toy for you.' He had his penis out of his pants. He said his penis was a squirt gun and if I moved it up and down real fast it would squirt. He tricked me into masturbating him. Then my grandmother came down the stairs and he quickly put a pillow over himself so he wouldn't get caught. And I thought it was such a great game that I removed the pillow, and said, 'Look, Grandma!' She went berserk. She got very mad and I started to cry. I ran up the stairs. And while she ran up after me my father kept saying, 'She won't remember anything, she won't remember anything, she won't remember anything.' My grandmother grabbed me at the top of the stairs, held tight onto my shoulders, and shook me, saying, 'You better just forget it ever happened.' And I did, I did indeed. I forgot it happened. And I didn't get that memory back until November, thirty-five years later.

"When I was in high school my father used to sneak into my room while I was sleeping and molest me. I don't believe it was anything more than molestation through my pajamas.

"The first memory I had of the gang rape was this year. That would be twenty-three years later. I remembered it because I was alone working late and thinking to myself—I'd been in therapy for the incest with my father and saying to myself, 'How could I have gotten so messed up from this? I have memories of my father molesting me, but there's got to be more. I've been working with it and there's just got to be more to remember.' Instantly I received a flash in my mind of a newspaper headline. I see in big, bold print on the front page, 'Rapists at Large!' This image came to my mind as if a flash bulb had gone off in my head. I knew immediately that, yes, I was there! This did happen to me.

"I was alone in the elevator. I let the corner walls hold me. When I got to the ground floor I went straight to the library and I remembered how the guys who raped me had burnt the dog. I started getting a lot more memory fragments. And even today I get a clarity now when I think back. I can see more scenery. More greenery. The spring. The leaves were starting to bud. Sounds filter in I would rather not hear.

"It happened at a party. I was 17. I need you to know how I got into this party. I was in high school walking down the hallway and a little short pregnant girl, Theresa, came up to me and said, 'Madeline, there's a party coming up and you just gotta go. You gotta be there.' She named a bunch of guys. She rattled off about four or five names. None of them were familiar to me. But I told her, I said, 'I don't know any of these guys, but thanks for asking me to go, because I really want to go.' I loved going to parties, it was so much fun. And I felt special that I'd been invited.

"This girl picked me up at around 11 A.M. on a Saturday. My parents had left for a weekend of sailing. On our way to the party we smoked a joint. And the girl was acting so strange. She's not talking to me. I thought it was the joint, maybe she had a bad response to the joint we smoked. She parked her car on Flynn Creek Road. And I said, 'Where are all the other cars? Where are all the cars?' But she just kind of motioned with her head for me to get out. I got out of the car, slammed the door, and then she followed. 'Theresa, come on! Come on, let's go!' She was lagging behind. And I thought, 'Man, this broad can't even smoke marijuana!' We're walking into a big field and she's staying way behind me. And I keep hollering, 'Come on, Theresa! Let's go!'

"And all of a sudden there's a big fellow coming toward me. He's really big. And he's lumbering towards me. And I say to Theresa, 'Come on, what are you afraid of? Come on!' And the big fellow comes over to me and he puts his arm around me and as he does that, I'm still hollering for Theresa. And then a needle goes in my side."

* * *

I first met Madeline Goodman in the reception area of an outpatient clinic for victims of violence. We had both arrived early for a session in which she would tell me her story in the company of her therapist.

Madeline is forty. She is clearly intelligent, poised, and pretty.

Several times during our initial chat I noticed Madeline flinch when I gave specific answers to her questions about what I had learned through my research about the emotional aftershocks of violence. The flinches were not at all like wincing. They were more like quick looks inward. She always recovered with a broad smile that seemed designed to mask the fact that she had been momentarily "away" and hadn't paid attention to the last few words I had said.

During the session with her therapist, as she recounted her story, I noticed much larger flinches. At those times she seemed to mentally drift off. Gradually the drifting off became more pronounced. In fact, she seemed to occasionally enter completely into the past. In the transcript of our session, these periods are usually made subtly evident by her use of the present tense. During the session her presence in the past was more unmistakable. While telling her story, she would get up, wander about the room, and dramatically relive what she was saying.

What she was saying became particularly painful for her to recount. As the story picked up momentum, Madeline's demeanor seemed, to my untrained eye, a little bizarre. Her behavior, combined with the fact that she told every detail of what she remembered, threw me into a panic. What she had said so far wasn't all that scary. But I knew we were only at the prelude. What would happen when she got to the actual rapes? Would I have to hear every sensory detail? Would her behavior become more bizarre, perhaps violent? I realized I could no longer tolerate even the prospect of what she might say.

Excusing myself and leaving was impossible, for I knew that Madeline was going through the pain of telling as an act of trust and faith. She trusted me to be able to hear her. She had faith that if other women who had been raped could read her story in my book they would somehow be strengthened. I had to stay.

So I struck a deal with myself. For as long as my responses to her felt out of control, I would pretend that I was watching the particularly brilliant soliloquy of a playwright/actress. Once I was calmer, however, I would have to reengage my appreciation for the reality of her situation.

This worked. And from the emotional distance I had created for myself I was able for the first time to notice the syrupy self-contempt and irony with which her voice was frequently sugared. I noticed that when she spoke of her own inability to ward off danger, she used somewhat archaic forms of speech, which made her sound as though she were a child reading from an early readers' primer. As a dramatic technique (I told myself) this was brilliant; it highlighted her innocence, which threw the depravity of her father, and eventually the rapists, into relief. It also made me feel like I was watching a Stephen King movie: As she described her approach to the suspiciously remote field I could imagine hearing cinematic birds of innocence begin to sing and then a sting of spooky music warning me that something truly shocking was about to happen.

But mostly what I noticed was the continuing urgency of her voice. Each and every syllable was forced out of her mouth. Madeline the Playwright/Actress, I decided (in my last few seconds of self-imposed emotional distance), is the anti-e.e. cummings. If her monologue were a poem, it would be written in all caps.

Having calmed myself, I began to really listen, which was when I learned what the urgency was all about.

★ ★ ★

[Note to the reader: Some pre-publication readers found parts of Madeline Goodman's testimony to be very disturbing. Madeline was gang raped and nearly murdered. She survived the attack, and her testimony as a whole shows that even people who have suffered the worst can eventually have recovery within their grasp. However, some of Madeline's testimony in this particular chapter might prove particularly painful to read, especially for friends and family members of homicide victims. The author therefore advises any reader who wishes to skip this testimony to proceed to page 28 and resume reading after the "★★★" and at the start of the author's commentary, which begins with "For many of the twenty-three years between the gang rape. . . ."]

Madeline: "A needle goes in my side. I spin around real quick. I said, 'Wait a minute! Wait a minute! I think a bee stung me.' I didn't know it was a needle. Then I looked up and said, 'What is it? Did you do something? Did you stick me with something?' And he nodded 'Yes.' And he called me his little angelic being—because I was dressed in white, I guess, is why he said that. 'Well what did you give me?' I had to hold very still. He said that the needle had broken off. And I couldn't look. I couldn't look. I have always hated needles. He told me to hold very still so he could get the needle out of my side. And all I think he did was inject me with more of the drug. It did not hurt. He was very gentle putting it in the second time.

"I knew I only had seconds to get this big lumbering guy to like me because he said it was LSD and maybe something else, too. Who knows what it really was? All I knew at the time was that I was afraid of LSD. I had never done anything but marijuana. And I was afraid. I didn't want to have any kind of a bad trip so I knew I had to get him to like me, to watch over me. I began to get very weak, not being able to walk, very weak. I stumbled. He picked me up in his arms very easily. Just lifted me right up, cradled me in his arms, and walked into the party. I was very, uh, flaccid. He carried me in. I still had very good hearing. I wasn't seeing well or I had my eyes half shut from fear. Now a little short guy came over, bouncing over to him, saying, 'I don't believe you did it! You did it? I don't believe you did it! You did it? I don't believe you did it!' I guess he was talking about 'it' being me being injected with the drug.

"The big, lumbering guy brought me over to a box springs with no mattress. He laid me on top of the box springs and I was tied to the springs. I could still move around. [Pause.] I could still sit up. [Pause.] My wrists were tied. [Pause.] I could still turn. [Long pause while Madeline turns and 'sees' and 'hears' what she saw and heard then.] I could still turn. Yes. And I sat there a long time. I was listening to music. Someone had a radio on listening to the old songs of the sixties and I just listened to those songs. I would lay flat out on my back and look at the sky. I could raise my head and I could see the surrounding trees. And if I turned this way [Madeline turns in her chair to look left], off about 200 yards away—and it might have only been 50 yards—there was a station wagon. I can't quite make out what's going on over there at the station wagon. But there are a lot of people and there's a rocking motion.

[Pause. She seems to be 'watching' and trying to figure out what's going on in the car.] Rocking. Rocking. They yell at me, 'You quit looking over here or you're going to be next!' [Madeline begins to cry.] And they scare me. [Her crying soon stops.] But I was very curious. I couldn't make out what was going on over there. I was definitely [pause while she decides what she's feeling] scared. [She laughs.] After they yelled at me I wouldn't look for what seemed like an hour. Could have been only a few minutes. I would stare out at the field again. [Self-contemptuously.] But I had to go back and look at the people over at the station wagon. I kept looking back there. And they continued to yell at me.

"I finally figured out there was some kind of sex going on over there. There was Theresa, the pregnant girl, on her hands and knees on the back flap of the station wagon. I believe she was somebody's girl-friend. She had blonde hair. And she's rocking on her hands and knees. Rocking. Rocking. And there were probably four or five guys there all waiting their turn. And even she yelled at me, too, to quit looking.

"And I lay tied down on the top of that box springs with no mat-tress and I just look at the sky. And hours, what seem like hours, go by. And I have to go to the bathroom. And someone walks by and I tell him, 'I have to go to the bathroom.' And he unties me. I slide down. I'm trying to find a private place, but I'm so screwed up with the drugs. I don't know what direction is safe and I can smell dried leaves. [Madeline stops as though she's looking at dead leaves.] I see the dead leaves. I think I have a private place. Then going to the bathroom, urinating, my pants are down. Four or five guys come over and they start oral sex with me. And I am seeing these penises with little hats on their heads and the crack on the end of the penis looks like a smile to me and I also see eyes. And I'm cracking up. This is making me laugh so much. So I'm there, trying to get my pants up, trying to go to the bathroom, finish and get my pants up. A bunch of guys are coming over. They're masturbating and some are ejaculating on my face. I had bangs in those days and these wads of semen are just hanging there in my hair on my face. And I'm pointing and laughing at each individual penis because it has this bizarre little hat on, which I guess was a thumb, but to me with the drug I was injected with it looked like a little hat. And I just pointed and laughed at each one. And I mean, I am laughing hysterically! This bums the guys out so much, it just bums them out to where the guys who hadn't ejac-ulated yet lose their erections and get disgusted and they go, 'Aggh. This isn't any good,' and they turn and walk away and leave me alone.

"I get my pants up and I'm staggering around trying to figure out just what is going on. I can't make sense of anything. And I walk by a girl who's huddled down by the wheel hub of a car. She's crouched down, her hands to her face, and she's crying. And she's tied up. I walk by her. I see that she's tied and crying, and I'm alarmed. Why is she tied up? 'Will you help me? Can you untie me?' I say to her, 'If you're tied up, there must be some reason.' And then she looks at me, and she says, 'Oh, you're the girl who ....' She never finished that sentence. And to this day it drives me nuts. [Shouting.] Who *what*? Who *what*? I want to know. *What was she going to say?*

[More quietly.] "And I'm wandering around so much that they take me back over to the box springs. I believe I'm tied up again. One of the girls that was having sex with the guys walks over. By this time the drug has really kicked in. I cannot respond when she talks to me. She calls me Honey. 'You all right, Honey?' And I only respond by blinking because I can't talk. And I'm not all right. I can't talk. I can't get up. I'm not all right. And I'm laying flat on the box springs again and I am able to open my eyes. I can talk to her with my eyes but my voice is not working and she picks up my arm and it flops back down. And she hollers out, 'Hey, Mitchell! I think you gave your girlfriend too much.' And eventually he comes over and looks at me and I think I was injected with something else, but where I don't know. Perhaps the arm. I see the girl who brought me, Theresa. She's with two other women. She's bringing them into the party. I sit up and they're coming through the field. And I holler out to them, 'Hey! Go back! Go back! It's not safe here!' I hold my arms up. I show them I'm tied. 'Go back! Go back! It's not safe here.' I think I called out three times. Maybe this is a voice I only hear in my head perhaps. Perhaps it was a very tiny voice, and I think I'm yelling but because of the drug I'm not able to warn them. It's too late. Here comes that big, bumbling oaf again. He's got a gun."

* * *

For many of the twenty-three years between the gang rape and when the memories returned, Madeline was addicted to drugs and alcohol. During the years of her addictions she was, by her own description, sexually promiscuous. But for the last seven years, Madeline has been clean and sober, and has relied on God to pull her through some hard times.

When her memory of the gang rape finally returned, Madeline became suicidal. She heard in her head a constant chorus of criticism and loathing, all directed at her. First her father, then her grandmother, then her own voice could be heard telling her what a fool she'd been to let herself be entrapped and raped and what an ass she had been to let herself be dominated and molested by her father in the first place. At night,

Madeline lay down with a loaded shotgun beside her and kept all the lights on. She was easily spooked by unfamiliar sounds. Sleep was difficult to come by. As she lay awake she contemplated murderous revenge on everyone who had hurt her.

Madeline is not a violent person by nature. It is just that her newfound memory and all the fears and anger it evoked couldn't be shaken. She suffered waking flashbacks to the rape and, whenever she did sleep, nightmares about events that might or might not have been part of the actual rape, she couldn't tell.

Madeline's previous therapist had insisted that the reason her memory of the rape was so elusive was that it was not Madeline who had been raped. Considering her history of promiscuity and drug abuse, the therapist suggested, might she really be the girlfriend of one of the rapists, someone who had, in fact, arranged and abetted a rape? A perpetrator who, by some hallucinatory logic, had come to identify with her victim?

It's an interesting theory, and one that ascribes a whole shovelful of diagnoses to Madeline, all of them freighted with contempt. Sadistic. Deluded. Hysterical. Evil. But the specific problems Madeline had been suffering—anxiety, depression, suicidal thoughts, hypervigilance, sleep disturbances, concentration difficulties, self-loathing, nightmares, flashbacks, and problems with intimacy and addiction—are some of the common emotional aftershocks suffered by victims of violence.

Unfortunately, the fact that her previous therapist's and Madeline's interpretations of her story were widely disparate is not terribly unusual. Ideas of helplessness and vulnerability are difficult to accept even for psychotherapists; undoubtedly, therapists' self-protective denial has something to do with many diagnostic failures. But while the interpretations that some therapists give post-traumatic symptoms are deplorable, many others fail to diagnose the traumatic roots of clients' problems for an entirely guileless reason: The emotional aftershocks of trauma closely mimic the symptoms of a variety of psychiatric problems.

For example, one might easily call Madeline's insistence on sleeping with a loaded shotgun "paranoia" were one to disregard the fact that she was not fabricating a threat but merely responding with due vigilance to the knowledge that a large party of malevolent strangers might at any moment be licking their lips over her. The phenomenon that I witnessed, in which Madeline seemed to enter an altered state of consciousness while recounting her trauma, is one of several types of what the psychotherapeutic profession calls "dissociation," or a sometimes trance-like disturbance of memory, identity, or consciousness that is common to trauma survivors. With its extremities of emotion that are unrelated to the reality of the present, this type of dissociation can be intimidating to witness. To be honest, I wondered whether Madeline was psychotic when I watched her shout warnings of danger—"Hey! Go back! Go back! It's not safe here!"—to the wall of her therapist's office. In fact, dissociation only seems crazy when one fails to appreciate the fact that being pushed to the brink of personal extinction is not an experience that one easily shrugs off. For Madeline, the act of consciously remembering invited the abyss to intrude into her consciousness in full emotional force, again overwhelming and devastating her, again rendering her helpless to think clearly or calm herself.

Confusion regarding the interpretation of post-traumatic symptoms are not the only matters muddying diagnostic waters. Since the dawn of modern psychiatry, psychotherapists have noticed that traumatic memories are sometimes unavailable to a survivor's conscious memory. In therapy, survivors may complain simply of job, relationship, or sexual problems, or of anxiety, depression, or trouble sleeping. Psychotherapists investigating the vagaries of memory still do not know precisely how or why trauma survivors sometimes completely forget traumatic incidences. But despite current controversies within the psychotherapeutic profession about the possibility that certain therapeutic techniques may significantly distort memories as they are retrieved, there remains strong consensus among most therapists that traumatic memories can be forgotten.

Given that survivors do sometimes forget, it is perhaps easy to understand that a therapist might never suspect that the middle-class, successful businessman she hears complaining of nothing but a mystifying depression is an incest survivor. Similarly, a therapist might blunder by accepting as fact the assurances of a war refugee who, when asked about traumatic experiences, convincingly says, "I know the war was bad for other people. But I got out. Nothing very bad ever happened to me."

While the specific mechanisms of post-traumatic amnesia remain unclear, the phenomenon makes some intuitive sense. As Dr. Mark Hall, a psychotherapist at the Traumatic Stress Institute in South Windsor, Connecticut, explains, "It seems spectacular that someone would not remember family violence or something like wartime torture or a gang rape. It's easy to understand how someone else would think, 'What a fantastic and unusual situation you were in! And how horrendous! And instead of that being some pinnacle in your memory it is instead unavailable!' On the surface, that attitude makes entire sense. But that attitude also assumes that when someone is being tortured or raped she is openly taking it all in. I don't believe that's what happens. I believe that what happens is that victims psychologically defend themselves against an assault while it is happening. That is the beginning of shutting memory down."

Unfortunately, repressed traumatic memories don't seem to rest in peace. If they did, symptoms of post-traumatic stress wouldn't plague so many people for whom the traumatic memories remain unavailable. "One of the dilemmas of interpersonal trauma that has been repressed is that, while someone may not consciously remember the interpersonal trauma, they may be reenacting it constantly," says Dr. Karen Saakvitne, Clinical Director of the Traumatic Stress Institute. "They may be reliving it in the context of current relationships. Even when they are 'forgotten,' memories can still be present and pervasive. I've heard it said this way: People continue to tell their stories whether or not they are aware of it." Seen in this context, Madeline's history of promiscuity and drug addiction is not surprising.

Clinical observations of discrete populations such as war veterans, crime victims, incest survivors, and war refugees have amply shown that, regardless of whether trauma survivors have repressed their traumatic memories, there may be a span of years or even decades between the actual traumatic event and the onset of stress symptoms. The bulk of Madeline's post-traumatic symptoms appeared twenty-three years after the trauma, a delay that is by no means extraordinary. The years between trauma and onset of emotional difficulties confound many therapists, causing them to doubt the connection that a survivor may have explicitly drawn to an underlying trauma and to explore elsewhere in the survivor's psychological history for clues to the problem. It is understandable that many survivors who clearly remember their traumatic pasts find this dogged probing into the non-traumatic past insulting.

But these categories of diagnostic failure pose interesting dilemmas. Certainly they point to formulaic trauma-sensitive stances for therapists to take: When the client has symptoms reminiscent of post-traumatic stress, aggressively scrutinize the client's history for trauma; so as not to revictimize your client with skepticism, accept as fact whatever trauma stories you are told in the therapy session; and if a client assures you that the trouble is trauma and nothing else, do him or her the courtesy of investigating no further.

The dilemmas lie in the question of whether such formulaic stances constitute a groundwork for good therapy. It seems reasonable, for example, to assume that there is a fine line between aggressively urging a reluctant client to rummage for buried memories and imposing theories about victimization on a client who may have no history of trauma, but may simply be anxious and depressed. Just how doggedly should one look for trauma? It also seems reasonable to assume that memory can play tricks, especially when memories have been steeped over time in emotion and maturation. Could even a trauma-sensitive therapist therefore assume that, no matter how true a memory may feel, it may not be historically factual in its entirety? And with all due respect to the overwhelming nature of trauma's emotional aftershocks, it makes sense that a survivor's entire psychohistory would have played some role in his or her interpretation of and response to trauma. Does this not imply that a thorough investigation of non-traumatic aspects of a client's psychohistory would almost always be enlightening?

Certainly one answer common to these questions is simply that the art of psychological diagnosis involves diplomacy — probing gently for issues the client may not have already discovered and resolved, and doing so while forthrightly assuring the client that a deep-seated neurosis is not what one necessarily expects to find.

But this answer leaves unresolved the issue of how far the client's version of reality can be trusted, and to what extent conflicting desires and impulses might have led the client to twist reality. It is an issue that has preoccupied psychotherapists since Freud's time.

In the late 1800s, the psychiatric elite in Western Europe used a catchall term — "hysterical" — for many mystifying behaviors that reflected severe emotional upheaval. It was a rather belittling term usually reserved for women. At the time, it was fashionable to observe, classify, and catalog hysterical behaviors. One of the most prominent members of the psychiatric elite, Sigmund Freud, went so far as to try to discern the roots of these behaviors. Almost to a person, Freud's hysterical clients — women and, indeed, some men — told him astonishing stories of being raped and otherwise sexually assaulted as children. Far from having his judgment clouded by revulsion and rejecting his clients' claims out of hand, Freud believed them. In 1895, with colleague Josef Breuer, Freud published *Studies on Hysteria*, which introduced a theory of trauma-driven dissociation supported by clinical examples from Breuer's patient population. And at an 1896 meeting of the Society for Psychiatry and Neurology in Vienna, Freud boldly read a paper, "The Aetiology of Hysteria," in which he declared that the symptoms of hysteria were a direct result of childhood sexual trauma.

For the members of polite Viennese society in attendance that evening at the Society for Psychiatry and Neurology, the implications of Freud's statement were appalling: considering the prevalence of hysteria, incest and childhood sexual abuse must be rampant. Socially and politically, all hell broke loose for Freud. In the end, even he found the idea of high incidence of childhood sexual abuse too bizarre to be believed. (Surveys conducted beginning in the late 1970s and continuing into the 1990s, however, indicate that childhood sexual abuse is anything but rare. In 1995 Dr. David Finkelhor of the Family Research Laboratory at the University of New Hampshire analyzed the results of nineteen surveys from that period, surveys in which adults were asked about their experiences as children. As a result of that analysis Dr. Finkelhor estimated that at least twenty percent of women and between five and ten percent of men experience some type of sexual abuse as children.)

Under enormous pressure, Freud revised his position and ascribed his patients' hysteria to thwarted, infantile desires for sex with one parent and murder of another. Polite society and the psychiatric profession proved quite willing to believe that self-proclaimed victims are almost always frustrated perpetrators. The theory that would one day be called "Oedipal" was born and quickly applauded. Freud, and virtually all psychotherapists for much of the next century, saw tales of early sexual abuse as figments of hysterical adult imaginations and as evidence that the tale teller, who had projected his or her own sexual and homicidal drives onto another, was an unreliable attestant.

Seen through the lens of Freud's Oedipal theory, the assessment Madeline's first therapist made of her story of rape — that Madeline, who claimed to be an incest survivor, was not the victim but one of the rapists' abettors (perhaps continuing the pattern she established early in life of projecting her violent and sexual impulses onto another) — seems perfectly sensible, even profoundly so. One must assume, however, that if the therapist used the story of incest as grounds for distrusting the story of rape, she did not avail herself of modern epidemiological data. The data are astonishing.

In a 1986 study of the sexual assault histories of 930 women in San Francisco, sociologist Dr. Diana Russell, then a Professor at Mills College in Oakland, California, discovered that two thirds of those women who were sexually assaulted as children were victimized again as adults by rape or attempted rape. Dr. Russell found that only 35% of women with no childhood history of sexual abuse were victimized as adults by rape or attempted rape. Studies in 1989, 1990, and 1992 confirmed the phenomenon of revictimization first reported by Dr. Russell.

Of course, a skeptic might challenge Dr. Russell's findings with the following questions: Did the adult women who reported having been raped correctly remember their childhood experiences? Were their childhood memories not, instead, "hysterical" wishes? And were their reports of rape not, by extension, suspicious? The skeptic might cite as support for his or her misgivings the improbability that such a high proportion of any group of people might be raped as adults. Adult survivors of childhood sexual abuse hardly walk through life with cardboard signs on their backs saying, "Easy Mark." Surely—the skeptic might say—some twist of mind is at work here.

In fact, a twist of mind may be at work here, but it is probably a different twist than the one implied by Freud's Oedipal theory. Therapists working in various pockets of the trauma field have found that survivors of all types of trauma tend to repeat their survival experiences, sometimes literally and sometimes symbolically. For example, war veterans frequently become police officers, where once again their lives are on the line. Traumatized children usually reenact the trauma quite concretely in their play: A mommy comes into the dollhouse and beats up a baby; Santa Claus insists that a young child take off his pants.

Sometimes, in reenacting the original trauma, survivors put themselves at great risk. This is the case with crime victims who return again and again to the scene of the crime. It may also be true, though less obviously so, for incest survivors who enter dangerous marriages or stumble into perilous situations like the one in which Madeline found herself. What on earth was a 17-year old girl doing driving around stoned on marijuana, in the company of a girl she hardly knew, and going to an unchaperoned party in an isolated field held by a group of men who were strangers to her?

The complete answer to "blame the victim" questions such as these may lie in a look at why survivors reenact their traumatization. Trauma therapists have put forth several explanations: to give a happy ending to a story whose horror still plagues them; to prove to themselves that they now know how to handle such situations; to relive the moment of escape or reprieve, which is the moment when the survivor felt most aware of how precious life is; to assuage their trauma-induced biological addiction to the brain's defensive response to overwhelming fear and helplessness. The one that I think best explains Madeline's behavior, and that quiets any tendency of mine to blame her for her predicament, boils down to this: One of the things a child learns from being chronically abused is how to be abused. As Dr. Laurie Anne Pearlman, Research Director of the Traumatic Stress Institute, explains, "Where did a person like this ever learn what is dangerous, what is safe, who can be trusted, how to protect herself, how to say no? Certainly not in abusive families where there were no boundaries and where to say no was to risk—rejection is too mild a word. Disintegration of sorts. How can we expect that as a young adult this person can make judgments and say, 'This feels safe; this doesn't; I can trust you; I can't'?"

$$\star \ \star \ \star$$

[Note to readers: What follows is the last of the two pieces of Madeline's testimony that some prepublication readers found very disturbing. The author advises any reader who wishes not to read this piece of testimony to proceed directly to page 44, where author comentary resumes after the "★★★" with "When I started my research. . . ."]

Madeline: "Mitchell, the big guy, pulls out the gun and he motions with the gun. He points it at the two new girls. And he grabs one girl's purse. He pulls something out of it. It looks like a piece of jewelry or something. [Sounding a little confused, while she tries to 'see' what's been pulled out.] Maybe it's a wallet. I don't know.

"It becomes dark out. [Softly.] I know the girls are taken to the station wagon. I'm still tied to the top of the box springs. Something has happened to the music. The music's not playing any more. A bonfire is lit. People are always walking by. There are guys walking by my box springs and they go over to the station wagon it seems like every ten minutes or so. I can see their shadows walk by my box springs. I think I ask somebody's girlfriend for something to drink. And she brings me a Schaefer. [Madeline smiles.] Brings me a Schaefer beer. I always liked Schaefer. I think I can only drink a couple sips. She walked by again, that girl that gave me a beer. I call to her but she doesn't pay any attention. I tell her, 'I'm cold. I'm cold.' And she ignores me but I keep calling out to her. 'I'm cold.'

"She finally does come over with a big moving blanket. I'm so grateful to her. She says [Madeline shouts abrasively], 'You know, you're becoming a pain in the ass!' And I kind of just laughed it off. But she scared me. I think I had asked her previously for a cigarette, too.

"It's dark out now. I hear a voice whispering my name, saying, 'Madeline,' over and over. I can't figure out where it's coming from. But Theresa, the pregnant girl, is hiding right behind me. And she unties me! Theresa unties me! She quickly gives me directions on how to get out of there. She says, 'The road is just that way. You just got to walk toward the road.' I can't see her hand signals because it's so dark, and I'm just nodding and agreeing, 'Yeah, yeah.' I'm still heavily drugged.

"I stagger into the woods again. I'm scared and I'm crying. I can't figure out where I'm going. I don't know how to get away. I stumble over these lumps in the field made by a hedgehog or mole or something. Stumbling over lumps of grass. I hear voices whispering in the bushes. 'No. Not that way. Not that way. Turn around. You almost made it. Keep going.' And I turn around and I'm crying and all I want to do is get to where it's warm and there's light. And I head right for the bonfire.

"And there, there's everybody. They have captured it looks to me like a collie dog. And they're putting gasoline on the dog. They're [a puzzled look] . . . yeah, they're putting gasoline on the dog. They had used the gasoline I guess to start the bonfire and [more slowly as she 'watches' and realizes what is going on] they are saturating that dog really well. Apparently the [quizzical pause] father of one of the guys had showed him how to do this, because he knew exactly what to do. He said, 'Now, you've got to let it just soak in really well.' I approached the bonfire and they were very, very surprised.

"'How did you get free?'

"'I just did.'

"And then they started to razz Mitchell, the guy that tied me up. 'You didn't tie your girlfriend up very good.' He gets real mad 'cause he's being razzed by the gang. [Pause.] The station wagon is still, ah, still very busy.

"Mitchell came over with a ball and chain and he's holding my ankle. I tell him, 'Oh, that feels good. That feels real good.' He just had a gentle hold of my ankle. He put this, I guess it's a three-inch clasp, on my ankle. [Madeline looks down. Then, matter-of-factly, when she 'sees' what's going on:] It's a ball and chain. And Mitchell says, 'Well, that ought to hold you.' I laughed, 'I guess it will.' And I come dragging that ball and chain closer to the bonfire. One of the guys is crouched down and says, 'Don't you get too close. We have other plans for you. We don't want anything to happen to you. Don't you try anything.' And I look at the dog. The dog is sitting there panting, so happy to have so many hands on him and to get attention. One of the girlfriends was there and was petting and soothing the dog. They're saturating the dog.

[Madeline's voice is beginning to rise.] "I become alarmed and drag my ball and chain over to the station wagon. Not too close, because it's scary over there. Not too close. I holler out to the girl who gave me the moving blanket and a beer and a cigarette. 'Debby! Debby! Debby! I think they're going to do something to the dog!' She yells at me [Madeline yells harshly], 'Can't you see they're out of control?! Can't you see that?!'

"I back off and drag my ball and chain back over—but not too close to the bonfire, because it's not safe there. They take a stick from the bonfire and they light the dog in different places. I hear the guy say,

'Now don't let him go until I say so. He's got to smolder a while.' Don't let him go until I say so.' Then I see the smoke curling up off the dog's fur. [Long pause.] The dog's fur. The guy says, 'Ok, *now!*' The dog *runs* away at top speed [voice trembling now] heading for home. [Very long pause.] And *I* see a beautiful, orange and red rocket-like projectile, three feet above the ground, following the contour of the terrain, heading away. [Derisively.] And *I* said, 'Ooooh. It went soooo fast!' What I saw was beautiful sparks. I didn't rationalize that there was a dog underneath them. [Crying.] I feel so sorry. I've always liked dogs more than people. I couldn't combat the drug. I could not save him. No, I couldn't help the dog. I couldn't even process what was happening. As soon as I would get a coherent, rational thought, the drug would take over and the thought would leave my mind. That drug really had me. And when I said, 'Oooh. It went so fast,' it cracked those guys up. They were laughing at least a full three minutes. They thought that was the funniest thing anyone had ever said. And as they saw me staggering around with my ball and chain, a face would pop out of the night and they'd stick their face in front of my face and say, in perfect imitation, 'Ooooh. It went soooo fast.' And start laughing all over again.

"I can't take any more. I go back to the box springs, to my moving blanket. I take my ball and chain. And I think I'm safe there. I'm very quiet.

"Debby walks by again and she says, 'Which one of those guys do you like? Which one do you think is cute?' I point to one, and I think he's called Chucky. A little short guy he is, not too tall. Chucky. And he's funny. Debby says, 'She picked you, Chucky.' Chucky comes up and sits on the box springs with me. I'm sitting Indian style with the ball between my legs and resting my hands and chin on the ball and he's talking to me and he's asking me all about my boyfriend, Tommy, who I just broke up with. Tommy had just come back from Vietnam, and he didn't know where his head was and he wanted some space and we had broken up I think just a couple days before this happened. I tell Chucky all about Tommy and how we used to date. Chucky wants to know every detail, how we were petting, where we were petting, where did it take place. I enjoy watching Chucky's eyes sparkle. His teeth are perfect and white, he has dark hair and dark eyes. A powerful build, a very masculine man. He is extremely disarming in the way he is speaking to me. He notices the ball and chain attached to my ankle and wants to take it off. I tell him, 'Don't bother, I'm using it for a place to rest my arms.' He laughs and releases my ankle anyway. I share my moving blanket with him. He asks me more sexual questions about my boyfriend, Tommy. He wants to know how Tommy kisses me and where he kisses me. We kiss each other. I feel sexually aroused. Chucky asks me more questions about Tommy between kisses. He wants to know if I have ever had sex with Tommy. He's surprised when I tell him no. 'No? Why not?' 'Because I want to stay a virgin till I get married. It's a big deal to me.'

"Chucky continued to verbally and physically seduce me. I finally tell him how I'd like to have sex with him. All of a sudden, boop! He jumps down and he hollers out, 'She wants to have sex. And she just wants it with me!' He carries me over to the station wagon. There's another moving blanket down on the back flap of the station wagon door. There's one or two girls in the well of the station wagon where the spare tire usually is. Chucky and I are on the back flap of the station wagon and he unzips my pants and I held them and I tell him, 'Wait a minute! Not like that! You're supposed to kiss first and, and all kinds of stuff.' And that big Mitchell guy comes over again. And all the other guys come over again and they're—I'm not alone anymore. There's these girls in the station wagon. They weren't there before. And I wanted to have sex with just that one guy, Chucky.

"The guys offer Chucky the reward of going first. He sticks his penis into my rectum. I begin to panic and plead. Then someone else started having sex with me. I'm on my hands and knees [pause] just like the other girls were now.

[A long pause while she remembers.] "A new man is having sex with me while I am on my hands and knees. I sense he's tall. He reaches over and massages my clitoris. I do have a climax, and when I do I grab my clitoris. Mitchell, I guess he's the leader of the gang, he's upset. He doesn't want to see it done that way. He says, 'Give me your hand.' I give him my hand. And he twists my arm. Then he takes my other arm and he twists it so that the backs of my hands are touching together. Then he brought it back this way and taped my wrists behind my back with electrical tape. My ankles are taped also.

"'Why are you doing that?' I ask.

"'That's the way we do it around here.'

"I become scared now. It's not easy to breathe. I balance myself using my chin and knees. I start asking, I look around and I start asking, I ask, I ask, 'Where's Tommy?' I start calling for Tommy. 'Tommy, Tommy, Tommy, Tommy, Tommy, Tommy!' I just keep saying that over and over again. 'Tommy, Tommy, Tommy, Tommy, Tommy, Tommy!' These guys are still having sex with me. And they're . . . I hear someone say, 'Who's she calling for? What's she saying? Who's she calling for?' And I think I spit out, 'That's my boyfriend, and he's right out of the Marines and he's going to kill you. He's got a gun.' And it bugged them enough where they take lights and they shine lights into the surrounding woods because I keep looking in that direction. I know Tommy's coming. I know Tommy's going to save me. I know Tommy's coming. And I'm wondering why he hasn't come yet. But I know he'll save me.

"And then I remember I had just broken up with him. And *then* I started screaming. Because I couldn't think of anything else to do. I started screaming. Long, glorious, wonderful screams, screams that are — if you had to rate them, you'd have to give them a ten. They were the absolute best screams. I can scream so wonderfully. So that is what I do. These long, long screams. But this is really getting these guys mad. And one guy takes off his shoe and I think it was a loafer. [Madeline turns in her chair.] I may be able to see. I can see he's doing something. He takes off his sock and shoves it into my mouth.

"The girls in the well, it's their job to, uh, grease every guy that's next. It's their job to grease the guys' penises. One girl also greases my anus. When this guy puts his sock in my mouth — it's very hard to breathe with a sock in your mouth and your arms tied back like that. I'm at such an awkward angle anyway, supporting myself on my chin and knees. But it gives them free access. I turn my head ever so slightly. One girl, she helps me dislodge the sock from my mouth. I see she does it on the sly so the guys won't see her helping me. I push with my tongue. We get it out, and no sooner do we get it out then [a little derisively] I'm screaming again. I'm screaming again! And a guy says, 'What's she screaming about? I thought we already did this one.' And here comes the sock again.

"And so, there's [long pause] a long time this goes on. One guy got mad and shoved a gun barrel into my vagina because I was screaming so much. 'I'll give her something to scream about.' And one other fellow said to the other guy, 'You idiot, that could have gone off.' It might just as well have, because I still feel a bullet shattering me from my coccyx up to my neck when I think of it, even though there was no trigger pulled.

"And I, uh, I'm being mostly sodomized. Still screaming whenever I get a chance. In comes the sock again. But this time I'm going to clamp down on this guy's finger. I'm going to nail this jerk. I bite down on it with all my strength — which was probably nothing. I will not let go. I will not let go. I got a sock and his finger in my mouth and I'm not letting go. I hold onto that finger and I nail it. I got him good. And all he does is pinch my nostrils; now I cannot breathe.

"I release my hold on his finger.

"He says to the rest of the guys, 'See? It works every time.'

"I have this sock in my mouth. I'm having trouble breathing. The girl in the station wagon, she says to the members of the gang. She says, 'Look at her eyes! Look at her eyes! They're too big.' And the sock is still in my mouth. Twist. I twist my head. That's all the movement I had. 'Are they going to kill me?' I'm thinking to myself. 'Are they going to kill me?' I can't breathe. I can't breathe. So, uh, the girl and I get the sock out again. I dislodge it with my tongue. And they say, 'If you stop screaming, we won't put the sock in your mouth.' What I do is, when I hear a fog horn—it's a foggy night and the bay is not far away—when I hear a fog horn I match my screams to the horn. I try to scream as long as the horn is blowing. I try to scream longer than the horn. And they even catch on to that because they say, 'Ah, you couldn't do it that time, could you?' And I *am* running out of air. And still I try. So the sock comes back in.

"And I know now. I know they are going to kill me, and I accept it. Then there's one last guy. They're all watching. I have the sock in my mouth. I cannot breathe. I cannot see. I can't breathe. I cannot see. I can still hear. I'm losing my vision. A girl says, 'Look at her eyes. They're bulging out. Look at her eyes.' And one guy is sodomizing me and I defecate and I hear him say, 'Oh. Just when it was starting to feel good, too.' The girl in the well gives a good push with her feet and pushes me onto the ground. I am face down. One guy is standing over me and says, 'Well, you're no fun!' I hear another guy's voice say, 'Clean her up and— is she dead? Clean her up!' A reluctant man comes over and pulls the sock out of my mouth real slow. He didn't want to touch me. He cuts the tapes off my ankles and wrists and says, 'I'm sorry, little girl. I'm sorry. I didn't mean for you to die.' Then he goes away. I'm left there. I believe my pants are still down.

"When I come to, it's dawn. I see frost on the ground, and I'm still heavily drugged. I don't know where I am. I'm just lying in a field some-where and I have my eyes open and the birds are singing. It's a beautiful, clear day. It's cold. And I look at the frost and one drop of dew with brilliant colors inside is rolling down a blade of grass. I watch that with an incredible intensity, and I think, 'How beautiful! That is so beautiful!' And I—is someone calling my name? Is it Theresa? There's a pregnant girl coming towards me. She's coming closer to me. I'm trying to get my pants up. She's coming towards me. Who is it? Is it Theresa? I'm not sure who it is. I'm scared again. I'm trying to get my pants up and stand. She's walking towards me. It is Theresa.

"She helps me get my pants on and we get back to her car. She's telling me, 'Come on, I'm taking you to the cops! We've got to go to the cops!'

"'No, no, no. I can't go to the cops. I can't go to the cops. My parents will kill me. I can't go to the cops. I forgot everything and I *will* forget everything. It just never happened. I can forget this ever happened.'

"We get into the car. As we're going towards my house I tell her to stop at Nancy Dunsberg's house. She's a girl I went to high school with and I slept over at her house a couple of times and so we stopped there. She does let me off there. I go into Nancy's back door. The door is unlocked. I startle her sister. I ask her, 'Is it OK to go up and see Nancy?' And she nods yes and I climb the flight of stairs. Nancy, as soon as I'm in the door, bolts right up in bed and she looks at me and she says, 'Madeline, what happened to you?' She takes me to the bathroom, white porcelain sink, and she's washing my hands with wonderful, warm water. She's washing my hands, washing my hands with so much lather and warm water. I collapse to my knees and I sob into the sink. She keeps saying, 'I understand, I understand, I understand.'

"'Oh, Nancy, it was so horrible. So horrible.'

"'I understand, Madeline. I understand, Madeline. I understand.'

"I tell her, 'Nancy, I got my period. I don't know why I got it. It's too soon to get it. I got my period and I don't know why I got it.'

"She tells me, 'It'll stop. It'll stop.' She goes into the bedroom and I'm left on my knees sobbing into the sink. She went into her bedroom and brought me a Modess pad. Nancy laid a white, beautiful, full-length cotton gown on the bed for me to wear. My friend Nancy.

"I tell her, 'I can't put that on, I'll bleed all over it.'

"She says, 'You put it on.' And she helped me get my clothes off. And she helps me put on the gown. As she helps me get my clothes off I notice she's behind me and she hesitates and just looks. She just stops. She was helping me get my clothes off and she just stops. She stops because she was looking at the mess back there.

"She let me sleep in her bed. I woke up. I had no memory. No memory at all. The whole thing was gone. I do remember making a phone call from her house. My sister answered. I told her where I was.

"When I finally do get home I'm sitting on the couch and the next thing I know—I'm still drugged, sitting on the couch—my father's looming over me, a big ogre of a man, very strong: 'Were you or were you not at the Flynn Creek Road party? Were you or were you not?'

"'I don't know, Dad. I think I was babysitting.'

"'You weren't babysitting! Your grandmother says you were there!'

"'Well, if Grandma says I was there, I must have been there.' I really don't know what's going on.

"He grabs my arm, we fly out of the house, hop into the car, he's driving real fast. We go to some friend of his who happened to be a shrink. I'm taken into the office. He shoots me with a drug . . . [laughs] *another* drug, I believe sodium amytal, perhaps sodium pentothal, some kind of truth serum. I am given hypnosis. They ask me questions. I can only nod or I have to answer yes or no. They ask me questions, 'Were drugs involved?' I answer yes. They reawaken the whole memory.

"And then I'm told to forget this ever happened, not to associate with anyone that was at the party. Don't ever be afraid of these people that did this to me. You realize you will not have any legal options.

"As I'm leaving I feel really good. I see the brick building we're leaving. I'm walking on the pavement, the driveway to the office. I look at my father. I feel good towards him. And I say to him, 'Do you know, Dad? It's a funny thing. I know there were lots of guys, but you know I don't remember seeing a single one. I remember hearing them, that's all.'

"Boom! My father grabs my arm again, spins me around, we're back in the shrink's office. I'm sitting down on the couch again. And my father's extremely agitated. And the shrink sees it and says, 'Peter, do you want a shot to calm yourself down?' He gives my father a shot. And he says, 'This is just some sort of residual memory. Don't worry about it. You better go and get Patty'—that would be my grandmother—'and have her come. I can give her a treatment, too. And you can begin to put this behind you.'

"We do go zooming back to get my grandmother. She is in the kitchen as we walk in to get her. She says to my father, 'Is it as bad as we thought?' And he says, 'It's worse.' He says, 'You can go and get a shot.' My grandmother is pacing in the living room. 'Oh, I let her go. I let her go.' She's taking full responsibility for everything, which is garbage. I was sitting on the couch. I say, 'Grandma. Go get the shot!' never realizing I would have to go back to the shrink's office. I was forced to go back— this will be my third time. I did not want to go back there. I make a scene, I start crying, kicking, fighting, spitting. Whatever I can do. They do have me in there. My grandmother is sitting to my right. I had no idea I'd have to recount everything again. I had forgotten what happened and they made me remember and now they were going to make me remember it all again. I just turned to my grandmother and with as much hate as I could muster, 'Yeah, I wanted to be fucked! Yeah, I wanted to be there! Yeah! Yeah! Yeah!'

"And the shrink, says to me, 'Now, now, now, Madeline. That's not what you told us the first time.'

"All the way home as I sat in the back seat of the car, I said to myself, 'I will never forget. I will never forget.' My father and grandmother must have overheard me talking to myself because they kept interrupting me and making me respond to their unrelated questions. I went deep, deep within myself and told myself to 'always remember, always remember, I'll always remember.' When we got home, I sat on the couch in our living room. And I said to them, 'And you know what? They put a ball and chain on my ankle.' My father walked out of the room in response to my statement and headed for the bathroom. My grandmother spun around and spat out, 'Shut UP! I never want to hear another word about it?!' and left the room.

"I fall asleep on the couch. I wake up and I have no memory of anything at all. No memory at all. Whatever they gave me, I couldn't fight that drug, either.

"I was due to graduate in a couple of weeks. Rumors of the Flynn Creek Road party were spreading everywhere. As I approached my girl-friends, they would suddenly stop talking to each other. I heard them say, 'Shhhh! Shhhhh! Here she comes.' One of the rumors I heard was that one of the girls raped had committed suicide. I also heard a rumor directed at me: 'And one girl went crazy!' 'No, she didn't go crazy. She just can't remember, that's all!' Then I heard laughter.

"After graduation, my father caught me in the back basement room. There was a little bathroom there. I must have been just coming out of the shower. He was hiding behind the door. I opened the door. I'm coming out. I believe I had nothing on or just a towel. And my father grabs me. I'm naked. There's a lawn mower running outside. My father starts—he's using his fingers to begin with and then he goes and uses his penis and he sodomizes me and he keeps saying to me, 'Is this what they did to you? Is this what they did to you? Is this what they did to you? Go ahead and scream, nobody can hear you. Hear that lawn mower? Nobody can hear you. Go ahead and scream. Is this what they did to you? Is this what they did to you?'

"And of course I have no idea what he's talking about.

"And my father—I don't want you to get the idea that my father's [pause] a bum. He always provided well for us. He was a brilliant man. Had a very high I.Q. But he definitely was mentally ill. He was addicted to pornography and women. He knew each family member's weaknesses and would prey on them. My father did, indeed, rape me. My grandmother did hear my screams. She got him off me. I remember turning my head up because once again in trying to get away from him I had fallen down onto my hands and knees. I was so grateful to my grandmother for getting him off me. 'Thank you, Grandma. Thanks, Grandma.'

"Till the day she died my grandmother couldn't remember anything or she was heavy into denial. I couldn't talk to her about it. She got really upset."

* * *

When I started my research, listening to trauma stories, I quickly noticed that I easily grew impatient with what I called their "packaging." I like my information delivered to me in predigested paragraphs with tidy topic sentences. I like the stories' crises to be neatly inserted at the moments where they can pack the most punch. I stifle a groan when I hear about too many unremittingly bad things happening; what I prefer are tiny bursts of badness leading up to one grand climax and an orderly denouement. Basically, I now realize, I prefer fiction.

Personal narratives, and trauma stories especially, are rarely neatly packaged. Ask someone to "tell me as much or as little as you want about what happened and how it affected you," and the teller is almost always going to tell you too much or too little. She will be distracted by leftover emotion. She will dawdle on details that have significance only to her, or she will rush through the logic needed to convince you of the import of a moment. When she finally demands, "See? See what my Aunt Peggy did to me?" you may be only vaguely able to piece together the sequence of events just described and may truly have no idea what it was that Aunt Peggy was supposed to have done or failed to do.

Trauma stories, in short, are inherently unbelievable. We listeners bring to the listening a desperate hope that what we are about to hear didn't really happen. The tellers often remain too awash in the emotional aftershocks of trauma to tell a convincing tale. Perhaps this is one reason we as a society provide only a helping hand that strikes again. Perhaps this is one reason therapists frequently take refuge in convoluted theories that rely on the premise that the uncorroborated witness always lies. Perhaps this is one reason survivors often fail to believe and encourage even themselves, and instead become mired in self-blame and shame.

I have learned that understanding trauma does not require one to believe every aspect of a trauma story. Especially for long-forgotten memories newly retrieved, the historical truth about the trauma usually remains murky. Nor does understanding trauma require one to believe that victims never in any way contribute to their victimization. It is clear that many do, either by unnecessarily exposing themselves to danger or because they never learned to recognize danger once it had reared its ugly head.

What I believe is necessary to an understanding of trauma is to see that sometimes confusion about facts, complicity, and peril are part of trauma's emotional aftershocks. Having listened to scores of detailed trauma stories I have learned to tolerate ambiguity. More importantly, I have learned to keep an eye on what I choose to believe and deny, and to acknowledge to myself that a refusal to believe all or part of a story may have more to do with my unreliability than with the teller's.

The failures of individual people are reflected in the failures of groups of people. As a group, the psychotherapeutic profession has long disappointed trauma survivors. Freud suppressed his data about childhood sexual abuse. Historically, soldiers traumatized by the horrors of war have been diagnosed as morally deficient or constitutionally cowardly. Holocaust survivors were left to their own psychological devices. Wives terrorized by violent husbands have long been diagnosed as overemotional, masochistic, and passive-aggressive.

However, in the late 1960s and early 1970s, two political movements formed—antiwar Vietnam veterans and feminists organized on behalf of battered and raped women—that were to have a profound effect on the psychotherapeutic profession's official stance towards trauma and its emotional aftershocks. (This bit of history is beautifully traced in Judith Herman's *Trauma and Recovery*.) Both groups were born of outrage over lives dominated by violence. Both groups were made up of people disappointed by society's response to their plight. While antiwar veterans founded rap groups, people working with battered and raped women borrowed the feminist consciousness-raising group format and created issue-focused groups. These intimate support systems allowed members a forum in which to retell and relive their traumatic experiences. They also helped raise awareness about the effects of psychological trauma. By doing so, they formed bases for effective political action. Veterans and feminists alike were assisted in their political action by handfuls of sympathetic psychotherapists and sociologists who had compiled a wealth of data.

In the end, the antiwar veterans were the more effective of the two groups in lobbying for recognition of what many were suffering psychologically. Veterans' psychic wounds had been suffered in the service of their country, and in a losing war that was perceived by many as unjust and unnecessary. In a sense, perhaps, many people came to see them as having "God on their side." Regardless of the reasons, veterans rightly insisted on and got some recognition of their sacrifices.

But there was probably another, equally powerful, reason why the plight of Vietnam veterans caught the heart of the psychotherapeutic profession sooner than did the plight of battered and raped women. For the most part, the professionals supporting women's demands for recognition of the effects of violence on their lives were themselves women.

They did not hold politically influential jobs. The professionals support-ing veterans' demands for recognition, on the other hand, included well-connected male psychotherapists who could pull strings. Many of those who worked for the Veterans Administration also sat on boards and committees of the Washington-based American Psychiatric Association, which is the most influential of the professional associations serving the psychotherapeutic profession.

In 1979 the American Psychiatric Association finally acknowledged that emotional trauma can profoundly wound people who, prior to their traumatic experience, were psychologically healthy. They formalized that recognition by incorporating into the 1980 edition of their *Diagnostic and Statistical Manual* series a diagnosis called Post-Traumatic Stress Disorder or "PTSD." The diagnosis defined trauma as lying "generally outside the range of human experience . . . (i.e., outside the range of such common experiences as simple bereavement, chronic illness, business losses, and marital conflict)" and described trauma's emotional aftershocks. (This manual was revised in 1987 and again in 1994.) In defining trauma and in describing trauma's aftershocks, the American Psychiatric Association relied on reports and literature compiled not only by veterans and femi-nists, but by therapists working with Holocaust survivors, crime victims, police and rescue workers, incest and childhood sexual abuse survivors, victims of torture, and survivors of natural and man-made disasters. Post-traumatic stress disorder was a concept whose time had come.

There were some problems with the 1980 diagnosis. The descrip-tion of emotional aftershocks missed such common reactions as depres-sion. Furthermore, the terse language of the diagnosis failed to convey much depth of emotion. The aftershocks listed had more to do with what veterans were suffering than the problems with which other trauma survivors grappled. And to a certain extent, the PTSD diagnosis suffered from its enlightened stance. In its attempt to free trauma-related emo-tional problems from stigma, it conceptualized trauma as an external phenomenon. In fact, as studies by researchers such as Dr. Herman of Cambridge Hospital's Victims of Violence Program have shown, some-times trauma is so long-lived that it becomes internalized. In *Trauma and Recovery*, Dr. Herman argues that this is the case with children who grow up in relentlessly abusive families, for wives who live their entire married lives dominated by unpredictably violent husbands, for prisoners of cer-tain religious cults, and for prisoners of war who spend many years in psychological and physical degradation. Such people have integrated daily brushes with extinction into their concepts of the routine and nor-mal. For them, trauma is an indelible psychic imprint. Its aftershocks ex-

309.81 Post-traumatic Stress Disorder, Chronic or Delayed

"The essential feature is the development of characteristic symptoms following a psychologically traumatic event that is generally outside the range of human experience.

"The characteristic symptoms involve reexperiencing the traumatic event; numbing of responsiveness to, or reduced involvement with, the external world; and a variety of autonomic, dysphoric, or cognitive symptoms.

"The stressor producing this syndrome would evoke significant symptoms of distress in most people, and is generally outside the range of such common experiences as simple bereavement, chronic illness, business losses, or marital conflict. The trauma may be experienced alone (rape or assault) or in the company of groups of people (military combat). Stressors producing this disorder include natural disasters (floods, earthquakes), accidental man-made disasters (car accidents with serious physical injury, airplane crashes, large fires), or deliberate man-made disasters (bombing, torture, death camps). Some stressors frequently produce the disorder (e.g., torture) and others produce it only occasionally (e.g., car accidents). Frequently there is a concomitant physical component to the trauma which may even involve direct damage to the central nervous system (e.g., malnutrition, head trauma). The disorder is apparently more severe and longer lasting when the stressor is of human design. . . .

"The traumatic event can be reexperienced in a variety of ways. Commonly the individual has recurrent painful, intrusive recollections of the event or recurrent dreams or nightmares during which the event is reexperienced. In rare instances there are dissociativelike states, lasting from a few minutes to several hours or even days, during which components of the event are relived and the individual behaves as though experiencing the event at that moment. Such states have been reported in combat veterans. Diminished responsiveness to the external world, referred to as "psychic numbing" or "emotional anesthesia," usually begins soon after the traumatic event. A person may complain of feeling detached or estranged from other people, that he or she has lost the ability to become interested in previously enjoyed significant activities, or that the ability to feel emotions of any type, especially those associated with intimacy, tenderness, and sexuality, is markedly decreased.

"After experiencing the stressor, many develop symptoms of excessive autonomic arousal, such as hyperalertness, exaggerated startle response, and difficulty falling asleep. Recurrent nightmares during which the traumatic event is relived and which are sometimes accompanied by middle or terminal sleep disturbance may be present. Some complain of impaired memory or difficulty in concentrating or completing tasks. In the case of a life-threatening trauma shared with others, survivors often describe painful guilt feelings about surviving when many did not, or about the things they had to do in order to survive. Activities or situations that may arouse recollections of the traumatic event are often avoided. Symptoms characteristic of Post-traumatic Stress Disorder are often intensified when the individual is exposed to situations or activities that resemble or symbolize the original trauma (e.g., cold snowy weather or uniformed guards for death-camp survivors, hot, humid weather for veterans of the South Pacific)."

From *Diagnostic and Statistical Manual of Mental Disorder,* 3rd ed. (Washington, DC: American Psychiatric Association, 1980) pp. 236-237.

tend far beyond those listed in the American Psychiatric Association's 1980 *Diagnostic and Statistical Manual.*

But flawed as it was, the 1980 PTSD diagnosis, with its clear-cut description of cause and major symptoms, was invaluable. It made it possible for psychotherapists to talk to each other and their clients about trauma and gave them a vocabulary that was free of concepts such as neurosis and failure. Trauma had once been seen as a test of one's fortitude; only the weak succumbed. By incorporating the diagnosis of PTSD, the American Psychiatric Association specifically acknowledged that trauma can cause lasting emotional harm and that surviving trauma psychologically intact is not so much evidence of one's mettle as a measure of one's luck.

In the words of Dr. Jeffrey Jay, Director of the Center for Post-Traumatic Stress Studies in Washington, DC, the diagnosis of PTSD "tacitly recognizes that the world can drive a normal person crazy." And, indeed, the world seems to be driving a fair lot of us in that direction.

In 1996 Dr. Margaret Wright Berton, a psychologist working with children and adolescents in San Antonio, Texas and Dr. Sally D. Stabb, an Assistant Professor in the Department of Psychology and Philosophy at Texas Woman's University in Denton, reported finding that 29% of the ninety-seven high school juniors surveyed had clinical levels of PTSD.

In 1992 Drs. Klaus Duch and Brian J. Cox, then both of the University of Toronto, reported finding that nearly five decades after the close of World War II, 58% of Holocaust survivors interviewed suffer from PTSD.

Data compiled by the congressionally mandated Vietnam Veterans Study indicate that as of 1988 approximately 480,000 Vietnam veterans still suffered the emotional aftershocks of violence. As of 1993, 31% of Vietnam-era veterans had been treated by the Veterans Administration for psychiatric and neurologic diseases, a category that includes PTSD.

According to a 1990 national survey conducted by Dr. Dean G. Kilpatrick, Director of the National Crime Victims Research and Treatment Center of the Medical University of South Carolina in Charleston, twelve million American women have had PTSD at some time.

How could the incidence of PTSD be so high if, as the American Psychiatric Association clearly stated in 1980, trauma lies "outside the range of human experience . . . (i.e., outside the range of such common experiences as simple bereavement, chronic illness, business losses, and marital conflict)"? By placing trauma conceptually outside the range of the "common," the APA's *Diagnostic and Statistical Manual* invited readers to believe that PTSD is a rarity and, by extension, that the majority of the millions complaining of trauma-related emotional grievances are malingerers.

Unfortunately, PTSD is not out of the ordinary because trauma isn't. Natural and man-made disasters may indeed be rare; but in American society, violence — and, by extension, trauma — is not uncommon. It is conventional. In fact, trauma has become so conventional that the most recent (1994) edition of the APA's *Diagnostic and Statistical Manual* makes no attempt to relegate traumatic stressors to the realm of the unusual. Instead, the manual narrates an eerily nondescript laundry list of crazy-making, everyday events.

"Traumatic events that are experienced directly include, but are not limited to, military combat, violent personal assault (sexual assault, physical attack, robbery, mugging), being kidnapped, being taken hostage, terrorist attack, torture, incarceration as a prisoner of war or in a concentration camp, natural or manmade disasters, severe automobile accidents, or being diagnosed with a life-threatening illness. For children, sexually traumatic events may include developmentally inappropriate sexual experiences without threatened or actual violence or injury. Witnessed events include, but are not limited to, observing the serious injury or unnatural death of another person due to violent assault, accident, war, or disaster or unexpectedly witnessing a dead body or body parts. Events experienced by others that are learned about include, but are not limited to, violent personal assault, serious accident, or serious injury experienced by a family member of a close friend; learning about the sudden, unexpected death of a family member of a close friend; or learning that one's child has a life-threatening disease...."

The legalistic language defining traumatic stressors in the most recent *Diagnostic and Statistical Manual of Mental Disorders* gains the manual some precision. It certainly goes a long way towards explaining the prevalence of PTSD in the general population. However, what the new language gains for the PTSD definition in clarity it loses in poetic impact. Certain things aren't supposed to happen. The old PTSD definition said as much. The newest PTSD definition says almost the opposite.

The fact remains, however, that as of 1994, the American Psychiatric Association has formally acknowledged that traumatic stressors are so rife as to be almost unremarkable. Therefore, the question to be asked is probably not, "How can the incidence of PTSD be so high?" Rather, it is, "How can the incidence of PTSD be so low?"

For considering the prevalence of violence and other traumatic stressors, PTSD is surprisingly scarce. For example, the results of a 1979 survey conducted by Dr. Diana Russell of the sexual assault histories of women in San Francisco suggest that one in four, or 25%, has been or will be raped (with rape being defined as completed intercourse obtained by force or by threat of force or when the woman was drugged, unconscious, asleep, or otherwise totally helpless and therefore unable to consent). Considering more recent survey data — of 6,159 female students interviewed at thirty-two colleges, 15% had been raped since their fourteenth birthday — the prediction seems tame if anything. But according to the national survey conducted by Dr. Dean Kilpatrick, only twelve million American women have developed PTSD at some point in their lives. This is equivalent to roughly 9.4% of the American female population. Rape isn't the only traumatic stressor threatening women. Even so, clearly not every woman who has been traumatized develops PTSD.

In some circles, calling attention to the relatively low incidence of PTSD is a delicate matter. By remarking on the low incidence, one is, in effect, wondering aloud why some people succumb emotionally to trauma while others don't. The query smacks to some of a return to ideas such as fortitude and mettle being the natural defenses of the morally sound while rage, anxiety, depression, and lingering fear are the earmarks of the deficient.

Still, it is undeniable that trauma doesn't always lead to PTSD. Some trauma survivors escape relatively unscathed and some don't. What social scientists studying trauma have found is that individuals do differ in their resilience to trauma. Studies conducted with war veterans and with victims of terrorist attacks indicate that the difference between those who thrive and those who don't lies in several places, some of them rooted in the coping skills and self-esteem developed in early childhood. For example, people who are thoughtful and competent in their daily lives, who are sociable, and who believe that they are the masters of their own destiny are sometimes more resilient to trauma. Likewise, people who can exert intellectual and emotional self-control under pressure sometimes fare well.

These findings are undoubtedly gratifying to those who would believe that people of real moral fiber might handily out-wrestle trauma. Such credits might find their complacency disturbed by another set of findings, however. Studies of traumatized children and adults have shown that regardless of how resilient someone is, if the trauma is strong enough, anyone will succumb.

For example, in a 1983 study of the ongoing effects on twenty-five children of their 1979 kidnapping and live burial, Dr. Lenore Terr of the University of California in San Francisco had a remarkable opportunity to assess how individual children, each with a supposedly unique level of pre-trauma psychological functioning, reacted to the same fierce stressor. Dr. Terr found that four years post-trauma, all twenty-five victimized children showed symptoms of childhood PTSD. These data indicate that the brutality and overwhelming terror of the stressor had rendered the children's various levels of pre-trauma functioning irrelevant in helping them resist the effects of trauma.

Another example: A team of researchers from the Traumatic Stress Study Center of the University of Cincinnati College of Medicine interviewed two hundred Vietnam veterans, noting their level of education and age at the time of service; evaluating the leadership roles played and the quality of friendships enjoyed prior to service; retrospectively assessing the veterans' pre-service mental health; determining how stressful their combat experiences had been; and discussing with the veterans how they had been received post-war by their family and friends. The investigators determined that threat to one's life and exposure to grotesque death far outweigh the effect of self-concept, coping skills, and post-war experiences in determining the degree to which a combat veteran is psychically damaged by war stress. Similar conclusions have been reached by investigators studying resilience to trauma in prisoners of war.

In other words, studies with both traumatized children and adults indicate that while individual personality strengths can help people survive trauma emotionally intact, everyone has a breaking point. The fact that some women survive rape emotionally intact while others don't may be because some women have better coping skills upon which to draw. It may have more to do, however, with the simple fact that some rapes are worse than others.

The defining experience of psychological trauma is most commonly considered the experience of utter helplessness when heroic efforts of mythic proportion are direly needed. Dr. Ronnie Janoff-Bulman, a Professor of Psychology at the University of Massachusetts at Amherst, writes in her book, *Shattered Assumptions*, "Extreme negative events that induce trauma are unique in that they force victims to come face to face with their vulnerability, with their essential fragility." And, as Dr. Bessel A. van der Kolk, Professor of Psychiatry at Boston University, explains, "Trauma occurs when one loses the sense of having a safe place to retreat within or outside oneself to deal with frightening emotions or experiences. This results in a state of helplessness, a feeling that one's actions have no bearing on the outcome of one's life."

If helplessness does create psychological trauma, the worst rapes would seem to be those in which the threat was most awful and the victim felt most helpless. Plotting escape strategies, scheming revenge, thinking or doing anything—even a symbolic something—in one's defense, would seem likely to protect one from feelings of helplessness. According to Drs. Ann Burgess and Lynda Holmstrom, who over the course of a year interviewed all rape victims treated in the Boston City Hospital Emergency Department, such cognitive strategies are exactly how many women defend themselves emotionally during brutal rapes in which they are unable to protect themselves physically.

Madeline's attackers began their assault by pharmaceutically reducing her mind to drivel. Whatever cognitive resources she may have brought into the party were the first possessions of which she was stripped. She couldn't plot or scheme. She could construct no wall of thought to protect her from the onslaught of emotion. In her own words, "As soon as I would get a coherent, rational thought, the drug would take over and the thought would leave my mind." Having disabled her in every way they could, a gang of men raped her to the brink of death. Her imminent death was pretty much the only concept Madeline was able to grasp, and after having been terrified, degraded, and sexually violated for 18 hours it finally seemed the least of her worries. "And I know now. I know they are going to kill me, and I accept it." Her loss of control could not have been more complete.

Feelings of helplessness born during the trauma can be compounded after the fact. For example, as Dr. Ronnie Janoff-Bulman points out in *Shattered Assumptions*, a survivor may believe that fundamental flaws in herself left her open to victimization. Being helpless to change the essence of her character, she may feel helpless to protect herself from further trauma. It makes intuitive sense that even a survivor who initially holds herself blameless for her victimization may eventually internalize any harsh judgments of friends and family and begin to feel helpless. It also makes sense that if a survivor's friends and family blame her for her victimization and she resolutely does not blame herself, she may see them as embodying a second, massive threat of character assassination against which she is helpless to defend herself.

Ideas about the effects that others' judgments have on survivors' feelings of helplessness are important, for such ideas point to ways in which friends and family can actually help trauma survivors.

Ever since World War II, military psychiatrists have assumed that soldiers fighting in small combat groups characterized by mutual encouragement and support sometimes derive feelings of self-worth and safety that protect than them from trauma's aftershocks. And a study of rape survivors conducted in the Boston area by Drs. Burgess and Holmstrom found that those who enjoyed stable, loving relationships with men during the post-trauma period recovered more quickly than those who didn't. Stable relationships, it seems, can help trauma survivors rebuild their faith in themselves and in the world at large.

Unfortunately, however, trauma can corrode even the most stable of social contracts. Dr. Lucy Friedman, Executive Director of the Victims Services Agency in New York City, has learned from her work with people who have lost a family member to homicide that "friends, relatives, and neighbors, out of a need to deny their own vulnerability, avoid the survivors or, at the very least, avoid the subject of the murder. These survivors, rather than being embraced by family and friends, are isolated. Rather than feeling protected by the social institutions they assumed would shelter them, they are pushed out, making them even feel more vulnerable."

Dr. Ellen Brickman is an Associate Professor at the School of Social Services of Fordham University. During the years she spent as Director of Research at New York City's Victim Services Agency, Dr. Brickman learned that women who have been raped find themselves in similar circumstances. "Partners of rape victims are frequently angry at and blaming of the victim," explains Dr. Brickman. "The anger and blaming aren't necessarily motivated by malice or hostility. A lot of it comes from the partners' sense of helplessness at not being able to do anything."

"People do not want to acknowledge that life can be tragic," explains Dr. Ronnie Janoff-Bulman in *Shattered Assumptions*. "We spend our lives preserving positive illusions about ourselves and the world. These same illusions, which are shattered in victims by the experience of traumatic life events, are threatened in others by the acknowledgment of such victimization. In the presence of victims, as in the presence of all stigmatized groups, people feel uncomfortable, ill at ease. For some, this discomfort results in outright, even hostile, rejection of victims. For others it results in avoidance of the victim. In the case of large-scale, massive victimizations, it accounts for the community's desire to forget, to draw a veil of oblivion over the horrifying events."

Losing the support of friends and family is of course a devastating defeat, especially for people who have recently learned another, more horrendous lesson about helplessness and loss. Feelings of rage, distrust, self-doubt, and isolation generated by the initial trauma can be compounded. Then, as Dr. van der Kolk points out, "ashamed of their own vulnerability and often enraged about the lack of help from outside, many victims lose faith in the possibility of meaningful and mutually beneficial human relationships." Having lost faith in the trustworthiness of others, many trauma survivors swear off emotional attachments, sentencing themselves to lives of isolation dominated by the conscious or unconscious memory of trauma.

As the transcript of my session with Madeline shows, twenty-four hours after her rape, brutal in circumstance and for the fact that Madeline's inner defenses had been rendered impotent by drugs, Madeline's mind rallied to her defense. It completely suppressed the memory of the rape. Unfortunately, she returned home to a family who, alarmed by rumors, retrieved the memory for her only long enough to stomp on it and, in her father's case, to use it as erotic fodder for another rape. It is not hard to imagine how difficult it might have been under those circumstances for Madeline to rebuild her emotional resources, her faith in people, and a sense of control over her life and destiny.

Madeline's family's reactions to her rape may have been extraordinary for their ferocity. But if we are to believe the observations of Drs. Lucy Friedman, Ellen Brickman, Ronnie Janoff-Bulman, and Bessel van der Kolk, it is not extraordinary that immediately after the trauma Madeline was harshly treated by the very people one would most expect to help her. It is a profound and disturbing statement about our society that Madeline's experience with revictimization may be more typical than atypical.

Madeline's complete saga is particularly frightening to read, so much so that I suspect it is difficult for many readers to sustain their belief throughout the reading. My hunch is that most readers empathize with Madeline through much of the transcript, but that periodically—particularly during the post-gang rape episode in which Madeline is whisked off to the psychiatrist for hypnosis and later is raped by her own father—they shut off their compassionate responses.

Admittedly, my hunch is based on nothing more solid than an assumption that many readers would engage the psychological defense mechanisms explicated by Dr. Janoff-Bulman and others and would therefore be skeptical about helplessness in general. Trying to assess how such skepticism might taint readers' perceptions of Madeline's story, I gave Madeline's transcript a careful reading with my skeptical antennae raised high. Appraising its merits not as a first-person narrative but as a literary document, I realized that many readers would be left emotionally spent after the rapes; they would need a denouement. When they got the rape by the father instead, they might turn against Madeline. "This, surely, she is making up," they might say. "And if she has fabricated this, how much of the rest is real?"

Realizing that Madeline's story might push readers past the limits of their tolerance, I considered truncating it to make it more believable. But after hours of vacillating, I decided not to. Forcing first-person accounts of trauma to conform to the literary expectations of a general readership is the essence of revictimization. Listeners shouldn't do it. Neither should writers reporting the trauma stories they've been told.

Real life should not be held to the standards of popular literature. Sometimes a nice denouement simply doesn't happen. We must not assume that, just because victims in gothic horror novels rise post-climax like phoenixes from the ashes, real-life victims are never helpless for long. We must not extend our naive and defensive conviction that the virtuous ultimately triumph into an assumption that those who cannot triumph are of dubious virtue.

I ask any reader who did not believe Madeline by the end of her account to imagine how that lack of belief might have affected Madeline if the reader had been, for example, her therapist. Or her grandmother, who, according to Madeline, stumbled onto clear evidence that her son had enticed his three-year-old daughter into helping him ejaculate; who, according to Madeline, once caught her son forcibly sodomizing Madeline; but who, according to Madeline, never once conceded that her son was sexually inappropriate. Instead, she reminded Madeline that in her twenties and thirties Madeline had a drug problem. She suggested that the memories were hallucinatory delusions.

As her therapist or grandmother, could your harsh judgments make Madeline doubt her own ability to protect herself from further trauma? And if Madeline were willful enough to refuse your interpretation of her story, mightn't your continued derision seem to Madeline like an assault on her good name? On her sanity? Mightn't your complete lack of faith in her powerfully realized memories and strongly felt perceptions make Madeline feel just a bit crazy?

[Note to readers: By and large, prepublication readers did not find Madeline Goodman's testimony in the remainder of this book to be disturbing.]

4

BOB HOWE: "I WAS IN VIETNAM in '69 and '70. I was drafted. Go to war or go to jail. I figured I believed in the United States and when your country says you gotta go, you go. I went in as an infantryman. Because of my size—I'm not very big—I was a tunnel rat.

"There are mazes of tunnels over there. The Viet Cong had everything underground—hospitals, supply depots, ammo caches. I'd go find the tunnels and clear them. Tunnels had a lot of different booby traps in them. The enemy would dig out holes in the sides of caves, stick a grenade in there, pull the pin, tie a vine to it. When you crawl through and hit that vine the grenade drops. You got four to six seconds, which you can't do too much in. If we chased a man down there we threw a smoke grenade in and we'd tell him to surrender. If he didn't come out I'd put a gas mask on, a .45 in my right hand, stick a cigarette butt in my right ear in case I had to shoot down there. I'd stick my left finger in my left ear 'cause the concussion would blow your ear drums out down there. And I'd go down.

"I was also an RTO over there—radio telephone operator. I carried the radio. That's one of the main targets, the radio telephone operator or machine gunner. Anything with communications or one of your gunners. During my tour of duty I got my antenna shot off, I got four or five holes in my rucksack, two more holes through my radio from snipers and stuff. They always deflected off my radio or blew through my C-rations. Somehow it never hit me.

"A lot of things happened to me. My wife left me when I was over there. Lost a lot of friends. Picked them up and stuffed them in body bags, pieces of them. One night there were thirty-three of us on a hill. We got hit. Seven of us came off the hill in the morning.

"I didn't really care after a while about coming back so I started taking chances, doing a lot of foolish stuff, taking LRP [long-range patrol] missions. Take like four or five guys and you go out and do reconnaissance. You just sneak around out there.

"But I survived Vietnam. I didn't know if I was lucky or not. I think my big problem is that I came back from overseas. I'd done the best I could, what I thought was my job. It was a lot for a twenty-one-year-old-man to go in there and see the reality of it.

"My folks met me down at the airport when I came home from Nam. They had demonstrators down there and they were yelling and pointing. Security was trying to hold them back. They were waving signs saying 'Baby Killers' and all this stuff. I didn't understand what all that was about. It was like I was in war and then I was home, just like that. There was no shutdown period. Twenty-four hours later, boom! I was here. The world was different. Now the people around me didn't even seem to know that there were people dying out there, that there was a lot happening.

"Right after I got home I was on leave, up here in town, near the stone church. It was the first time I got involved with the protestors. I was going down the street. I just didn't understand it. I told them, 'All the signs and the yelling you're doing. You don't understand what you're talking about. You're going around full of crap.' And this guy says, 'How would you know?' And I says, 'I just came back from there.' It was the wrong thing to say. I was just kind of numb about the whole thing. And they pushed me out in the street, told me I wasn't worthy to walk down the sidewalks. People started spitting on me. I got really scared, angry. I didn't know what to do with it. A big part of me wanted to grab a club and start parting some hair. But I just went along. But things like that really stick with you.

"So then when I got out of the service in Fort Bragg I let my hair grow right away. I had my folks ship my motorcycle down to me. I didn't know what I was going to do with my life but I knew I was going to do some riding, try to get my head screwed back on straight. So that's what I did for eight and a half months.

"Mostly I just stayed away from people. At night I slept on the side of the road. In the woods I felt more comfortable. I just didn't trust anybody. I'd pull off the interstate, onto a back road where it was fairly clear. I'd go up through the brush and I'd turn around and come back so that if anybody followed my trail—I'd put sticks and branches down to cover me—they'd have to come right by my position and I'd know that they were there and I could get my stuff together. I always had it at night so I could just grab things. Everything was on the bike. I just took off. Pick up my sleeping bag, sit on that, hop on my bike and I'm gone. I just looked after me.

"There was a main group of us, we were going to have a reunion when I got back down in Myrtle Beach, South Carolina. I was the only one who showed up. A scrawny little guy on a Honda, you know?

"After I finished riding around I came back and started working, trying to pay off debts, look up my old wife. I just wanted to get back into life, put Vietnam behind me. I didn't talk about Vietnam. I had a lot of anger and stuff that I didn't know what to do with. You've always got jerks who're going to come up with dumb questions like, 'You're a vet, aren't you? Did you shoot anybody? What did that feel like? You ever see this and that?' I always felt like grabbing them and smashing their head against a wall or something like that. 'Wake up!' They just didn't know.

"I tried to just get back in, be part of the world, but I just had all this stuff I had to keep pushing down inside of me. The way there was to ease all that was I just worked. I slept three or three and a half hours at night maybe and other than that I worked.

"I just didn't understand people. It was like I was looking at people maybe for the first time in my life or something. Guys I worked with would swear about the place. 'Well, maybe it'll burn down! Jeez, I hate this.' And they were just going on, you know, bitching about everything. And I'd say, 'How long you been here?' 'Fifteen years.' 'Well if you hate it so much, how come you come back?' The next day it'd be the same thing. And I said to myself, 'My life ain't going to go like that.'

"People complain about the dumbest things. They don't know, life is so short. That's one thing Vietnam taught me. I come back with somebody sitting in a chair and he ain't got no legs on him. Somebody's got a patch around his head and he ain't got any eyes. And you pat him on the back and say, 'It's great to be going home, ain't it?'

"I thought I was dealing with everything OK until after I was back for ten, twelve years. I started slowing down a little bit. I had become diabetic so I couldn't work like I was. Just being a regular person and trying to sleep more. But things started catching up to me. I started to go asleep, wake up. I'd smell things. I could hear things. I could see things. It was just like I was there. Sit up in bed in cold sweats. It'd take me a few minutes to say, 'The war is over. I'm home. It's OK.' Then I'd get up and walk around the house. I'd need to go to sleep but I'd be scared to, afraid that I'd have dreams. I woke up one night underneath my bed. I was holding my bed up! [Bob laughs.] I thought I was in a tunnel and it had caved in on me. Kind of silly.

"I think one of my problems when I came back was the way we were treated. Made you feel like you were guilty, like you'd done something wrong. You want to yell out and tell them you hadn't done anything wrong. Just did what I thought I was supposed to do, you know?

"I made it through that. I tried getting help. I thought, 'God, you're a biker. Why don't you call the Vietnam Motorcycle Club, you know?' I called them up and, 'Yeah! Hey, Brother!' 'Yeah, what's happening?' So they go on telling me, 'Well, you got to get your vest with your colors on there that has your division patch and stuff.' I said, 'Wow! To be able to display my patch! That'd be kind of nice, you know?' Cause I *was* there. And there is security in numbers. With thirty other guys, you'd feel like you could maybe be proud of it or something. Maybe nobody'd mess with you.

"Everything was going fine. Then he says, 'Well, they like at least 650 cc's.' I says, 'Jeez, I'm puttering around on a little beater now. I got a little 350.' 'Oh, you got to have 650. That's one of the rules we have. At least that or bigger.' I says, 'What? Do you guys cruise all day at eighty-five or something? My bike won't burn up. You a bunch of leathernecks, a bunch of hard asses? What the hell's your club about?' 'Well, every club has rules, and this is the way it is. Wait until you get a bigger bike.' I said, 'You wait a minute.' I told him a few things. And I said, 'Look, you get anybody who calls you up. I don't care if they're riding a moped. I don't care if they don't even have a bike. I don't care if they don't have any legs, if he's crawling on his belly like a snake, you give him my number.' I says, 'I'll do anything I can for that man.' I says, 'You take your club and you stick that.' First, when I started off I was kind of excited about getting in with some other vets cause, hey, vets know vets, you know? Then it turned out I didn't have enough cc's between my legs, you know? My bike wasn't big enough. So it seemed like you were on your own. There was no help.

"I had been on my own through the whole thing—you got drafted and went in as a group with different guys from all over the place. You went through Basic Training together. Then you went out to California for Advanced Infantry Training for nine weeks. But after that you got your orders to go to Nam and you're on your own. You don't go over with anybody you've trained with or anything. They drop you over there. We came in, they started pulling the plane up, banked it hard to one side and said, 'Well, if you'd like to look down at the vacation capital of the world down there, see them little lights flashing? Well, that's our runway. They're getting incoming fire now so we're going to hang up here for a little bit.' I said, 'My God, this is going to be a long year.'

"So we landed, and all the way through you're by yourself. You get off and you're a new guy. We called them FNGs. Nobody wanted to be near you because you were going to get them killed. You don't know what you're doing but you've got to make it through the first couple of firefights on your own. And so you're like, 'Hey! Hey! What do you mean?! Come on, I got a whole year to go here!' After you survive that they kind of let you in a little bit. It was like you felt snubbed and pushed away. Before I left I seen myself turning, and I was like that. It was a survival thing. You're over there to survive.

"When you got ready to go, your tour was up, any way you can get there you've got to get back. I had three days I was supposed to be back in the United States already but I hadn't made it back to my freedom bird. All I know is the base with my bird's over that-a-way somewhere. So I hop on a mail bird. They say, 'Well, we're not going over there, but we're going over there. They got more birds than over here so maybe you can catch one out of there to your freedom bird.' I get over there and some other guy says, 'Well, we got a bunch of C-rations to deliver down that way. After that we're heading back up to this other place. I think you stand a good chance of getting a ride back in at this other place.' So I jumped in that bird. 'OK!' We went down to deliver some C-rations. They just hover above, kick them out both sides of the bird. Jeez, we started getting sniper fire. Boom! 'Man, I gotta go home! Get me out of here!'

"Everything you went through you were by yourself. And then I got here and for twenty years I've been by myself. Standing there watching parades go by and your kid goes, 'Dad, aren't you a veteran? How come you're not marching out there?' What the hell do you tell him? I'm scared to death? The people out here are going to wave, 'Don't Pay Your War Taxes' signs at me and 'Baby Killers' and spit on me and throw stones at me or something? I couldn't go through that.

"Now I've got a job as a school custodian, working nights. Been doing that for years, going in and doing my thing, leaving about the time any other people show up. Now all of a sudden I've got this promotion to acting head custodian, and my boss just has the rest of this week to break me in. A day job, with lots of clerical responsibilities, and I've got to manage people. I'm scared to death. I'm in the open now, in the daylight. I've got no cover and I'm open fire for snipers and people.

"It's spooky. I'm telling you, I'm scared. I start the job next week and then I've got until the end of June to decide to take the job permanently. It'll be more money. But I just feel like I can't think. There's so much new information coming in, about budgets and purchase orders and accounts. I try to concentrate and slap the little devils in me who're saying, 'Hey, you can't handle that.' But I *am* stepping out here in the light. It's like I'm being exposed.

"When I was an RTO, I kept saying, 'I don't belong here. I can't do this job!' But the guys remember me. They knew that when they needed a Medevac, I was the voice on the radio. When you're pinned down, I was the voice on the radio saying, 'Keep your pants on. I'm going to get you through this.' Well, today, I feel like I got help birds coming in and somebody else is screaming at me and somebody's hit, needs a Medevac. Get my other radio out, whip it up to the other channel, get a Medevac.

I see a bird who needs smoke. So I pop smoke out. I throw it out. 'We've got red smoke!' they say. 'Affirmative.' 'We've got two red smokes!' they say. Your enemy a lot of times will see what kind of smoke you're throwing out and he'll throw out the same, trying to confuse your bird. When you throw smoke out it does two things. It marks your location, plus the helicopter comes in and he can see your wind direction. They land into the wind if they can. So your bird starts heading over there, near the enemy's smoke! You start to pop a green smoke, but you've already said, 'Yeah, red smoke. Affirmative.' It's too late. The bird goes down there and the snipers start shooting at it and get through that fuel tank and there's a flash. You're going to be blown to the ground. You're going to look up and there's going to be pieces of fire going through the air.

"That same pressure that I had there is like today. I want the job. A part of me wants it. I want to be a regular person. I want to go home at night to my family. I want to walk around in the light. But I feel like I just walked out of my bunker and it's not quite safe yet.

"One day I was seeing a specialist for my diabetes. He started talking and he says, 'Are you a veteran? You're a Vietnam veteran?' I was like, 'I didn't think I had it wrote on me or anything, but why?' He said, 'You're a vet. I just knew it. What you need to do is join a support group.' He gave me a therapist's number.

"I called her up and I don't trust anybody. I asked her how old she was. I didn't want to talk to some young lady who read about Vietnam in some book or something, gonna hit me with a bunch of weird stuff. But no, this was somebody who was older and from that time and maybe could understand me better. I thought, 'Well, I'll go up there open-minded.'

"So I came up to the first meeting and I sat there. I didn't know these guys. I thought, 'What is a support group? Is it something where you sit around crying in your beer? Have a little pity party here? Poor me?'

"Everybody started introducing themselves. 'I'm Sammy, and I was a diver over there.' 'Dwight, and I was a medic.' I says, 'Yeah, I'm Bob. I was a tunnel rat and RTO.'

"We went around and started talking and sharing things. I really felt like, 'I know what he's talking about. This guy's not bullshitting. He knows.' [Bob smiles]. And so I thought, 'I think maybe I'll come back to another meeting.'

"By the time we got through I really felt glad that I did it and I was better for it. Just a chance to let things out. You could talk about things but know that you weren't alone.

"Then, last year, our town had a bicentennial parade. I marched in it. I did. They had a thing in the paper asking Vietnam vets to march. I got thinking about it and at first I says, 'Why? Why now after all this time?' The longer I thought about it, though, I said, 'Why not?' About two days before the march I said, 'Damn it. I'm going to march. I don't know what the hell is out there but I'm going to do it.' I started calling up the guys from the support group and trying to get some support. Well, one of the guys from the group, I talked him into it. He's going to go with me.

"All my stuff, all my medals—they're all in a box out in the shed. I got my bush hat out of that shed. That's what I wore over in Vietnam. Got my little calendar marking off my days in Vietnam. I got that out of the shed and put it on my hat. Biggest thing I was proud of was my CIB—combat infantry badge. I got that out of the shed, stuck that on my hat. Got my tunnel rat pin out. And I had a port division patch, my division I served with in Nam, I stuck that on the side of my hat. My wife says, 'You ain't wearing that gaudy thing!' I said, 'Damn it. This bush hat was good enough over there. It's damn well good enough for any parade they got here.' That was the attitude I had.

"I went there, to the parade. Other guys said, 'Hey! I wish I had my bush hat! Man, I like the hat!' I said, 'Thanks.' I said, 'This hat is what I wore in Nam. I finally got to wear it again.' A couple of guys had tiger fatigues on, they were all decked out. This other guy had a shirt on. He says, 'I was in the navy, a medic. This is my scrub shirt. I hope it's good enough for the parade.' I said, 'I think it looks damn good.' Another guy was a helicopter pilot. He couldn't walk. He was in a wheelchair. One guy was trying to push him up to the top of the hill, where we were starting, after pushing him about a mile down to get him a soda. That guy was burnt out. He said, 'I don't know. I've got to get somebody else to push Fred.' I said to Fred, 'I'd be damn proud to push you in your wheelchair.' I said, 'Don't let my size fool you. I may be a sawed off little runt,' I says, 'but I got you and your chair set OK.'

"Then I said, 'I don't know how you guys feel about this, but I'm a little bit nervous. A little spooked about this thing. I don't know how we're going to be received down there, if there are going to be people throwing things at us or spitting on us again.' I was surprised. There were a lot of guys that felt the same damn way and had the same fears.

"The parade was getting ready to start, and I was getting ready to start pushing Fred and somebody said, 'Wait a minute. We want to meet over here before we start.' There was this young man, nice fatigues, Desert Storm. He climbed up on a stump on the side there. He says, 'I write some poems, and I wrote a poem for you.' He says, 'I wasn't old enough when Vietnam was going on. I was just a young man and stuff. But I went to Desert Storm.' See, the reception we Nam vets got was so crappy when we came back that we wouldn't let any other veterans fighting any other war, conflict, or whatever you want to call it come back to that kind of stuff. This kid said when they came back from Desert Storm the most people they seen in the reception they got were the Vietnam vets. Vietnam vets had been there to make damn sure that these guys got welcomed home. The way we saw it, they'd done their job, you know?

"War is not nice. There's nothing good about war. But support the troops. They're just doing their job. We've always been fighting wars. There's people fighting wars right now, today. Dying today someplace we can't even pronounce. It'd be nice if there wasn't any war but I don't ever see that. But this kid wrote a poem and when he got through he came down to shake all our hands. And it touched my heart. I went up and shook his hand. 'Young man,' I told him, 'you touched my heart with your poem. That was really nice.' It just seemed like everything had been happening lately.

"So we headed out for the parade. I said, 'Boys. I don't know if people are going to get down in front of us or try to stop us. I don't know what to expect.' Well, none of us did. We were real nervous, you know? And I says to the guy I'm pushing. 'I may just run your wheelchair right over them. What do you think of that?' And he says, 'Go ahead! I'll hang on!' We had the American flag out one side of us and a POW flag out the other. Everybody carried a flag. They carried POW flags, MIA flags, or just pieces of bamboo symbolizing the people that are still over there and what they went through. I have a friend who was over there in '59 and was POW for eighteen months. They kept him in a hole. Tortured him. He's got no real scalp left. So yeah, everybody carried something.

"So we went down through there and people stood up when we came by. Applauded us. We had World War I and World War II veterans saluting us. The other guys I was marching with ran over and shook their hands. If I didn't have to push the wheelchair I'd have run over and shook their hands, too. It really felt like a welcome home. When we got over the crest of the first hill I could see for miles. I said, 'Damn it! Look at all them people down there!' Just waving and smiling.

"When we were marching along we were going, 'Hup, two,' you know, fall in step. I said, 'Let's let 'em know we're here!' Somebody yelled out, 'Amen!' [Bob laughs.] And then, 'Somebody call a cadence!' Well, we had this sergeant marching with us, I don't recall his name, a black man. And what a voice! A real thunder voice. And he started calling out cadence. He started singing out, and we sang all the way. Once you went through 'em a couple of times you got them.

> Got a letter in the mail.
> Go to war or go to jail.
>
> Took a boy, made him a man.
> Put a weapon in his hand.
>
> Took a boy, made him a man.
> Sent him off to Vietnam.
>
> Mama, mama, don't you cry.
> Airborne troopers never die.
>
> Don't believe a spoken lie.
> There are MIAs that are still alive.

"We sang that, shouted it out all the way down through there. We got people afterwards saying, 'Wow! I saw you in the parade!' and stuff. My mom came up to me after. Crying. She gave me a great, big hug. I just lost my dad. Cancer. I'd been thinking about him. She said, 'He'd have been real proud of you out there. He always was.' My dad wasn't a big one for words. But I believed her. And afterwards I did feel proud.

"My goal is to some day take out the medals and everything I got hidden in the shed again and put them on and take a walk down the street like any other veteran. We're just veterans. Our country told us to do something and we did it. Not that it was right or wrong. The medals say that you survived, you made it through there. That's all."

* * *

Researchers working with survivors of community traumata have noticed a curious phenomenon. Just as friends and family distance themselves from the concept of helplessness by blaming individual survivors for their trauma, communities that together have suffered some catastrophe either collectively select a scapegoat or begin to turn against one another. "A case in point," says Dr. Bessel van der Kolk, "is the attempts to 'explain' the problems of Vietnam veterans: they had no business being in Vietnam in the first place; they lost the war; they were 'babykillers'; or they all had preexisting character disorders." The conflict in Vietnam, catastrophic in terms of its death toll and questionable wisdom, tore at our country's morale. It was an intolerable national trauma with easily

Dr. Jeffrey Jay, Director, Center for Post-Traumatic Stress Studies and Treatment in Washington, DC:

"In 1978, some colleagues and I developed what now seems an almost naive plan of action to create meaning from trauma by taking the veterans in our program on the road, so to speak. We went with them to mental health meetings, businesses, churches, public halls, wherever we could get together a group willing to listen to their stories. At a time when there were no movies or docudramas or TV series about Vietnam veterans, when they were, in fact, overwhelmingly regarded as killers, dupes, social dropouts, failures and embarrassments, it required courage to go before an audience and talk about things most Americans wanted to forget. But for the vets, silence and forgetfulness were dishonorable and indecent.

"At one such meeting, an anguished young man I had been treating spoke of his job as a helicopter gunner. He told of endless, boring days punctuated by the indescribable power and terror of landing in a war zone with his machine gun blazing. The worst times, he said, were the seconds after his crew had picked up the wounded, when the helicopter lifted vertically from the ground and hovered, suspended in midair, until it could begin straight flight. During those seconds of transitional flight, the men were sitting ducks, the most exposed they could be, and the gunner described shaking uncontrollably and defecating in his pants in primitive, animal fear.

"Once, in the helicopter, he saw a captured Vietcong pull out a knife. In a moment of terror and rage, he pushed the man and his family out of the helicopter door from several hundred feet. 'What do you do after something like that?' he asked the audience. 'You land, and have a cigarette, which never tasted so good, maybe a beer . . . So when I go home, it's hard to just get a job selling shoes and pay the Sears bill. What do I say to my mom? Who on earth wants to hear this anyway?'

"After he spoke, there was the uneasy silence that is usual after such revelations. Finally, an older man rose, stood staring at the vet for about thirty seconds, and then said, 'I want you to know that I was in the Pacific in World War II. I landed on Corregidor. What happened to us was much worse than what happened to you, but I have never talked about it, I have never complained, and I never will.' He then picked up his coat and walked out of the room. The audience was aghast. Why hadn't the World War II veteran sympathized with his Vietnam counterpart?

"But the young vet was not surprised. He reddened in embarrassment and said softly that he understood what the older soldier was telling him, because other men who had been through past wars, including his own father, had given him the same message. 'What do you know about honor and courage and dignity? Why are you whining and complaining so shamefully—you are not the first to have sacrificed; you do what you have to do; can't you keep quiet about it?'

"To an older generation of soldiers, the young veteran had violated a fundamental code of privacy that rigidly forbade the public revelation of terrible truths. In return for the solace and comfort of belonging to the community, the World War II soldier had kept his silence, which had become a personal mark of sacrificial honor. But the younger man rebelled, and like a renegade priest of an arcane religion, demanded the right to tell the truth and to belong, to break the social taboo that isolated him in one way if he was silent, in another if he was not. 'A year ago, I couldn't do this,' he said, his voice growing stronger. But now I am ready to talk with anybody about what happened. Anybody who wants to listen. I am not going to go off to a bar anymore and drink it off.'"

From "Terrible Knowledge," *Networker,* November/December 1991, pp. 18-29.

identifiable scapegoats: the combatants, so young and naive that they were without influence in their communities when they left them to fight, and so traumatized by war that they were even more socially powerless upon their return. Millions fought; most had been drafted against their will. They were far from the perpetrators in this national catastrophe. In fact, they and their families were America's only real Vietnam war victims.

Studies with veterans have shown that one of the attributes that can protect someone from the psychological aftershocks of trauma is emotional (and chronological) maturity. The more psychologically developed someone is, the more developed are his or her emotional resources and coping behaviors. For this reason, a mature adult may be more psychologically resilient to trauma than a teenager. I wonder how old you must be to resist the aftershocks of stuffing friend after friend into body bags, of seeing buddies blown to bits before your eyes, of perpetrating blind, homicidal revenge, and of never having the luxury of tears because dropping one's guard means risking death. I don't know the answer. But, with the Department of Veterans Affairs estimating the number of Vietnam veterans still suffering symptoms of PTSD at 480,000, I suspect that 18–21 years old is not old enough. It is late adolescence, an age at which the opinions of others still matter dearly. Therefore, I suspect, neither is it old enough to easily withstand being publicly spat on by your contemporaries.

In *Trauma and Recovery* Dr. Herman points out that, "Returning soldiers have always been exquisitely sensitive to the degree of support they encounter at home. Returning soldiers look for tangible evidence of public recognition. . . . Hence the insistence on medals, monuments, parades, holidays, and public ceremonies of memorial. . . . Beyond recognition, soldiers seek the meaning of their encounter with killing and death in the moral stance of the civilian community. They need to know whether their actions are viewed as heroic or dishonorable, brave or cowardly, necessary and purposeful or meaningless." Soldiers from many conflicts have shared the public's ambivalence about war and realized how distorted the truth of war must be in order to glorify it. But our country has always accommodated their need for reintegration with sentimental displays of pride and gratitude. The young men and women who returned from Vietnam were the first Americans to be denied this kindness.

As with Madeline, I had emotional and visceral reactions to Bob and to his story. In his natural speaking style, Bob talks at a very rapid, matter-of-fact clip. When he gets anxious or angry, as he frequently did during our meeting, Bob's speech becomes infused with emotion, which makes him talk almost faster than my ears can hear.

During those portions of our meeting I became exhausted by the effort needed to make sense of what Bob was so excitedly saying. I found myself giving up and silently declaring those parts of the interview suspiciously incoherent. It was only later, when I had the luxury of stopping and restarting the audio tape, that the coherence of his story became quite clear. Remembering my impatience with Bob's anxiety and outrage led me to wonder again about revictimization.

Up to that point, my research had led me to believe that revictimization was rooted in the listener's unwillingness to confront the possibility that anyone could be innocently pushed to the brink of personal extinction. I had also begun to see how what I called the "packaging" of trauma stories, coupled with the listener's reluctance to hear, can make trauma stories seem unbelievable.

But Bob's story had not been as horrible as many I had heard. I could listen and believe. It was *solely* the packaging to which I objected. My petty resentment, not doubt, was the problem. Apparently, regardless of how worthy of empathy I believe a trauma survivor to be, when I find the fury, resentment, anxiety, and other aftershocks of trauma difficult to accommodate I am capable of blaming the survivor simply for hurting.

Dr. Jeffrey Jay of Washington, DC's Center for Post Traumatic Studies and Treatment has described with eloquence the reaction in which I caught myself red-handed. Trauma victims feel "isolated, terrified and exquisitely vulnerable, in need of protection, reassurance and safety. The traumatized victim is not inclined to make a quiet request for understanding, but feels driven to a howling, self-centered outrage that exactly corresponds in ferocity to the pain and terror of the trauma itself. At first, others are sympathetic and understanding, reassuring the victim with hopeful promises that life will soon be what it was before. But then, friends and family and even professionals become alarmed by all this excessive emotion about something that is, after all, over and done with. Alarm becomes impatience and then irritation with the selfish cries of someone who seems intent upon holding onto, even exaggerating, victimization, making irrational demands and refusing to heal."

5

SANDRA DONIKE IS AN ARCHITECT who was sexually abused by her grandfather throughout early childhood, beginning at about the age of two. During our meetings, Sandra never exhibited what I might have considered excessive emotion. Her social presentation was, instead, impeccable. I believe that by sheer force of her affability Sandra could make her story believed by virtually anyone. As a listener, I did not feel particularly invited to share her emotional distress, probably because distress was difficult to discern. But even if she were clearly still grieving over what had happened to her, I might not have minded empathizing and realizing that Sandra's misfortunes could have befallen me. Who wouldn't positively welcome an opportunity to emerge from childhood as strong and self-confident as she?

Sandra Donike: "Basically, my grandfather sexually abused me, and I'm not sure of the length of time, all those memories are not back yet. They come back in pieces. But I think probably for about four years from other things that went on in the family and from the timing of his death. I would say when it stopped I was probably somewhere around six or seven.

"There were a lot of things going on in my family at home. My father was an alcoholic. He wasn't a 'drunkard' alcoholic. Mostly he would drink too much beer or whatever and go lie down. I didn't know what was happening. But now, looking back, I'm sure he passed out. So he wasn't really there for all of us. And my mother and my sister formed an alliance and I was always sort of outside of it. And I felt that I needed to protect my mother. I couldn't tell anybody, especially her. This was her father. 'How would she feel? What would she do? It's terrible. I can't tell her that!' Besides, how could I tell her what I was feeling? Feelings weren't allowed in my family. If you were sad you were feeling sorry for yourself. If you were happy you must be doing something bad and you'd better stop it.

"My grandfather was such a remarkable figure. He was physically a very big man. He was powerful looking, anyway. He paid very special attention to me. I was his favorite grandchild, or so I thought. I obviously did not realize what was going on until — well, I knew I was uncomfortable. But I also felt that it was my duty and that it was required to get the attention I needed.

"I started to remember about the incest about six months after I started therapy. I had learned to deal with—actually, dealing with my father's alcoholism was easier than I thought. I can remember the first time I said, 'My father was an alcoholic.' And then I remember saying to myself, 'There's something else here. There's something else here and I don't know what it is.'

"One night a lot of memories came out in a rush. I wrote everything that I could remember. And it was almost like—well, the child in me spoke, I didn't. The child's words were what came out on paper. The child, I call her Lolly, was actually talking and I was writing. Because *I* couldn't verbalize it.

"I had had an argument with my husband, Vinny. I had never told him the little bits of what I was remembering about my grandfather in therapy. And in the middle of the argument it was like, 'You don't really understand what's going on here! You don't know what happened to me!' I was very angry. And everything came out on paper. Because the child within me actually wrote it for me, it felt like, 'Hey, I didn't say that. I didn't write that. The child did.'

"I think the child wrote the memories for my husband because I was so angry and my defenses were down. I was feeling pushed by Vinny, abused—not sexually, but that abused feeling came back and it was like, 'Oh yeah? Well handle this!' That's really what it was. 'Take this and see what you can do with it!' I unleashed my anger and my memories full force. And what I'd written had surprised even me.

"I was stunned that it came out because I didn't know those memories were there. When the memories actually came out on paper, it was like I had no control over their release. It was not conscious writing. It was like vomit. It was just coming out. Regurgitation of emotions.

"After I read it I was shocked and scared and upset. But there was a sense of relief. I remember feeling like [Sandra deeply inhales and exhales] it's out. And I'm still alive. My grandfather has not come back to get me. I told my husband and after a struggle he still loves me. We're still OK. And so I guess it's going to be OK. I'm not ready to go tell the world but I made one major step.

"Right after the memories started coming out I went through a kind of emergency stage. I remember a couple of times really thinking that I had gone over the edge. Thinking, 'Why did I do this? Why did I ever get into this? I was OK before! Things were not great. But at least I could survive, I could function. Now I can't! I can't!' There was one point there, and I don't even remember where in therapy, where things were coming so fast. I remember sitting on the porch surrounded by trees. It was a balmy, windy night. I really think I lost it. I was hysterical.

Karen Saakvitne, Ph.D., Clinical Director, The Traumatic Stress Institute in South Windsor, CT:

"'The child within' is a very useful metaphor for the part of oneself that is vulnerable and needy and wants holding and caretaking. Often that vulnerable and needy part represents the part of the self that has been abused. Because abuse is degrading, people often feel deeply ashamed about it, and negate and reject the abused aspects of themselves. One way they can eventually start to reconnect with those aspects is by distancing themselves from their own need a bit, seeing the abused self as a child within. In that 'not me' experience they can ask themselves, 'What can I do for that child over there?' A survivor may make the connection that she was a child when abused and may allow herself to care for the child part of herself in a way she can't allow herself to care for herself.

"The metaphor of the child within is a powerful therapeutic tool. But people's individual experience of that term varies widely. Some people, when they are talking about a child part of them, will use a different voice. For some people, the child within is experienced as a separate personality. But for most, 'the child within' is simply a vivid metaphor."

Sandra's therapist:

"It's not uncommon, especially with trauma survivors, that sometimes the memories or the feelings are sequestered over in a special 'place' inside the mind. And sometimes that place is so repeatedly used that it develops a 'personality' of its own. What Sandra is talking about when she says 'the child within' is this child part inside of her—Sandra calls her 'Lolly'—who has been a gatekeeper for the memories of incest. Lolly developed into a very distinct entity in Sandra that Sandra was not aware of until the issue of incest came up in therapy.

"Coming to grips with this little girl has been a challenging, interesting, and scary part of our work together. And I know for Sandra that the discovery of the boy named Charlie was another jolt.

"It's important to realize that people like Sandra are not necessarily 'crazy,' although often they believe they're crazy because they don't have any sense of why what is happening is happening. Obviously Sandra is not crazy. She has a lot of resources, a lot of skills, and forming Lolly and Charlie inside her has been her adaptation to her childhood trauma.

"There are a lot of abuse victims who have Sandra's unique kind of dissociation as a very important and primary defense. They have a real sense of people—separate, discernible parts of themselves—living inside them. For people who actually have MPD—Multiple Personality Disorder—the personalities are usually not all conscious of each other. That's how the dissociation serves the survivor—it creates a useful amnesia.

"For some survivors, like Sandra, that amnesia happens only occasionally, and for the most part they have a lot of co-consciousness among their personalities. Because she has tremendous co-consciousness, I would diagnose Sandra as having Dissociative Disorder Not Otherwise Specified, rather than as having MPD.

My husband had to come out to calm me down. I know there was one point where Vinny had to call my therapist. And that was a major thing to call, and to cry out for help, especially to my therapist because Vinny held him responsible for the emotional crisis I was in. There were several emergencies like that as the memories flooded back. I was in crisis off and on for about a year.

"My life was made up of daymares. These were conscious things going on where I would just get hysterical. I really felt like I was going crazy. I felt like I had crossed that little edge and they would just carry me and put me away and lock the door. I did have a lot of dreams, but I wouldn't call them nightmares, of going somewhere, trying to go somewhere and getting off the track.

"One night on the way home from therapy, just as I was finally beginning to believe that I wasn't crazy, the child within me—Lolly—said to me, 'There's somebody else in here. And he's dangerous.' And I thought, 'Oh my God.' I wasn't at all comfortable with the idea of having other personalities inside myself. And it was over the next little while that I realized the 'someone' was a little boy, because Lolly had distinctly said 'he.' And the reason that she felt he was dangerous was that he was on the opposite side. He wanted us to shuck our responsibilities and not worry about consequences. He isn't interested in duty.

"I call the boy Charlie. I have a sense that Charlie may have been created in part by Lolly. Although she is frightened by him, at the same time she is envious of his freedom. At first Lolly controlled Charlie. She kept him locked behind the door that holds back the memories. And while she feared what would happen if she didn't control him, she also envied him.

"I'm not sure if Charlie is some kind of 'living' metaphor for my grandfather—only safe if he could be locked away—or Lolly's view of males. The thought has occurred to me that maybe Charlie is also a metaphor for the incest memories, which, if they weren't locked away might come gushing out, and that would put Lolly, and I guess me, in danger. I also think that part of my problem is that I saw men in two roles—either the totally controlling, overpowering male that my grandfather was or my very weak, alcoholic and passive father, whom my mother could dominate. Either men were in total control or they were locked behind the door being dominated by a female of some kind.

"I told Charlie that in order for him to come out from behind the door and share in our lives he would have to accept controls and rules of behavior. He seemed quite willing to accept this and at some point was able to make judgment calls himself. Lolly had a very difficult time accepting that he would be let out without any extreme danger to her, that he could be trusted or that I was strong enough to control him and to protect her.

"I hope that even long after therapy is complete, pieces of Charlie and Lolly will always be with me. I know that sounds funny, but I hope they are. Lolly is a very strong little girl, and Charlie is fun. I think that you need Lolly's responsibility and sense of direction and loyalty. There has to be that sense of duty. But there also has to be, on the other side, Charlie's ability to let loose and run wild through the field and say — within reason, again — 'Let's just do it.' Even now Charlie and Lolly are starting to disappear. They're not as clear cut. Soon they'll be a memory. I'm beginning to equate my feelings about Charlie and Lolly to my feelings about people I haven't seen since grammar school. They are part of me because I remember them, and whatever happens to them, they'll be here with me because I remember them fondly. Charlie and Lolly really did keep me from going crazy. And so even as they merge and become very indistinct with the 'me,' yes, they'll always be part of me. I feel like they were good friends."

* * *

For survivors, their friends, family, and their therapists, the struggle to understand trauma is ongoing. The propensity to lay blame is nearly overwhelming, for it relieves the blamer of any responsibility to feel anguish or to alleviate that anguish by taking action. Survivors are shamed not only for their circumstantial helplessness but for the fact that in their suffering they have deviated from the socially seemly. At first I experienced Bob's outrage as suspiciously incoherent. Perhaps it was because Sandra's description of her own dissociative habits was so socially impeccable that I was not tempted to call her crazy but resourceful. Perhaps it was her therapist's kind and reasoned interpretation of her dissociative style that had allowed her to survive emotionally intact the discovery of two distinct personalities "living" inside herself and to tell me about Lolly and Charlie with such grace.

More than a decade has passed since incorporation of post-traumatic stress disorder into the American Psychiatric Association's *Diagnostic and Statistical Manual* series. Still, many psychotherapists continue to regard some of trauma's more confusing emotional aftershocks with contempt. Within the past few years, however, trauma specialists have made some strides in helping others of their profession shed that contempt and focus instead on the personal resourcefulness of survivors that those aftershocks make evident.

An example of this redefinition of symptoms as adaptive strategies can be found in the attitude of Dr. Laurie Anne Pearlman, Research Director of South Windsor, Connecticut's Traumatic Stress Institute. "In the same way that the environment shapes natural things — like goldfish grow to a size appropriate for their fish bowl and trees grow to the east when the wind blows to the east — people's personalities are shaped by their environment. Socially difficult behaviors arise in response to environmental stressors and realities in people's lives. I really believe that people do the best they can given what they have to work with. If people grow up in families in which they are deprived of the ability to get their needs met in mature and healthy ways, where they are not taught how to feel like they are whole people, where they are not taught how to make self-protective judgments, where they are not given the opportunity to learn to manage strong feelings, they have to just deal with that stuff the best way they can. Blaming them for their social and interpersonal failures is sort of like saying, 'Why doesn't a person on a desert island with no tools build a shopping mall?' Well, how would he do that? Wouldn't he just find something that he could break and pretend it's a shovel and do what he could with what he had? That's metaphorically what I believe many trauma survivors do when they try to build personal and social lives. And then, when we arrive from civilization, we say, 'Hey, where are the shopping malls?' forgetting that there are no resources with which to build those malls. We blame the person who has eked out an existence. Whatever he has accomplished should instead be admired given the paucity of any kind of resources."

Identifying PTSD as a valid diagnostic category was the first step in the psychotherapeutic profession's growing understanding of trauma and its aftershocks. The evolving awareness of how symptoms function as adaptive strategies has been a second step. This second step has paved the way for a third. By reexamining common stigma-laden assumptions about psychiatric symptoms, clinicians have begun to identify some of the aftershocks of trauma common to survivors of prolonged or systematic trauma and overlooked by the American Psychiatric Association's PTSD diagnosis.

For example, the American Psychiatric Association's 1980, 1987, and 1994 editions of its *Diagnostic and Statistical Manual of Mental Disorders* series list marked mood shifts, impulsive, occasionally violent antisocial behavior, and a deep emptiness or boredom as symptoms of borderline personality disorder, or "BPD." Historically, BPD has been ascribed to a constitutional aggressive drive, or, in plainer language, to being born mean. There are no data to prove a connection between contemptuous diagnoses such as BPD and failed therapy. But it seems reasonable to assume that such prejudices as a belief in constitutional meanness would contaminate any therapeutic relationship with hopelessness, leaving the therapist with the sole option of throwing up his hands at what nature has wrought.

And, in fact, a 1984 study of the results achieved by eleven therapists highly experienced in treating BPD found that only 10% of clients terminated therapy with what their therapists deemed successful outcomes. None of the clients achieved what their therapists considered a state of optimal psychological health.

Six years after that study was published, Drs. Judith Lewis Herman, J. Christopher Perry, and Bessel van der Kolk published convincing evidence that as many as 81% of people diagnosed as having BPD have childhood histories of profound physical, sexual, or emotional abuse. As a result of their discovery, many therapists working with people diagnosed as BPD have begun to shed some contempt-laden assumptions. They now entertain the possibility that people once seen as constitutionally mean are simply behaving defensively in what has been for them an unremittingly cruel world. Likewise, many therapists now acknowledge that a person's seemingly temperamental emptiness and boredom may be rooted in isolation born of shame and distrust; marked mood shifts and impulsive, even violent antisocial behavior may arise from a pervasive sense of vulnerability.

As the 1984 study of therapy outcomes indicates, BPD clients are difficult — nearly impossible, it seems — to help towards a state of optimal psychological health. The 1990 findings of Drs. Herman, Perry, and van der Kolk, however, may point to therapeutic opportunities for work with BPD clients. For example, explaining to a survivor of prolonged and severe child abuse that his unpredictable behavior may be a learned and highly adaptive response to a malevolently unpredictable world might profoundly affect the client's self image and ideas about his future. The client might be shown that unremitting external trauma has by and large disappeared from his life and that meanness as a response is therefore no longer necessary. Conceivably, such explanations could strengthen the client's commitment to therapy and to unlearning mean and self-defeating behaviors.

Doubtless, therapy for people who have accepted trauma into their concepts of routine and normal will always be a long, hard road. In fact, the recovery data for BPD are sufficiently bleak that it seems likely that trauma has distorted the personalities of many people so severely as to render them beyond help. Regardless, infusing both parties to any therapy contract with appreciation for the trauma survivor's abilities for self-protection seems a better groundwork for therapy than contempt and abhorrence.

There is a growing concern in the psychotherapeutic profession about the value judgments inherent in many psychiatric diagnoses such as BPD. This concern, combined with a general acknowledgment that the official PTSD diagnosis continues to describe inadequately the range and tenacity of aftershocks suffered by survivors of prolonged, systematic trauma, has led researchers to propose a new diagnostic category called at various times, "Victimization Disorder"; "Victimization Sequelae Disorder," and "Complex Post-Traumatic Stress Disorder"; it is now most commonly referred to as "Disorder of Extreme Stress Not Otherwise Specified (DESNOS)."

Judith Herman wrote the concept paper formulating the new category. In *Trauma and Recovery*, she points out that common to survivors of ongoing child abuse and to survivors of trauma such as the Holocaust, domestic violence, war, certain religious cults, brothels, and many prisons is the experience of being held captive by a coercive institution. In most such institutions, especially in malevolent families, the means of control is only partly force. Psychological domination also rules. Through a combination of threats and enticements the perpetrator strips the victim of autonomy. Many perpetrators are also adept at blinding their victims to the facts of the perpetrator's malevolence and the victim's domination. For example, it is not unusual for a woman to show up bleeding, bruised, and crying at a shelter for battered women, asking for temporary haven, but insisting all the while that her situation is somehow unique and that she is not actually a "battered woman."

According to Dr. Herman and to other researchers interested in obtaining for DESNOS status as a bona fide psychiatric diagnosis, the emotional ramifications of long-term psychological domination include those listed in the current PTSD diagnosis but also embody other, more profound psychic injuries such as extreme emotional dependence and destruction of the survivor's sense of self. Ironically, the emotional dependence is often focused on the perpetrator, who has long been the sole possible provider of occasional relief from the very terror he or she perpetrates.

These emotional ramifications are currently rather neatly described in the American Psychiatric Association's *Diagnostic and Statistical Manual* as behavioral styles characteristic of people suffering from Borderline Personality Disorder. But as Dr. Herman points out, while the language of the BPD diagnosis may adequately describe a recognizable constellation of behaviors, the term "personality disorder" implies a constitutional fault and as such may be misleading for clinicians seeking to understand the complexities of a person's emotional problems. "The clinical picture of a person who has been reduced to elemental concerns of survival is still frequently mistaken for a portrait of the victim's underlying character. Concepts of personality organization developed under ordinary circumstances are applied to victims, without any understanding of the corrosion of personality that occurs under condition of prolonged terror."

DESNOS is still so young a formulation that few hard data have been published to demonstrate that it holds a benefit for therapy. Its utility as a diagnosis is therefore unsubstantiated. True, the American Psychiatric Association's *Diagnostic and Statistical Manuals* have always been thick with unsubstantiated diagnoses. But in preparing the manual's 1994 edition, evaluation committee members for the first time took the laudable step of insisting on a wealth of data to support the inclusion of new diagnoses. (For practical reasons they could not hold already included diagnoses such as BPD to the same standards. To do so would have required billions of dollars of mental health research.)

Sadly, for lack of the time in which to accumulate the necessary supporting data, proponents of DESNOS as a diagnostic category failed to carry the day. But despite DESNOS's current purgatory as an outlaw diagnosis, its existence as a testable formulation seems a well-founded step. Its formulators number themselves as members of a larger movement in psychiatry recognizing, first, the ways in which trauma lies at the root of many mystifying and socially troubling behaviors and, second, the ways in which those behaviors may be adaptive strategies in a world seen as elementally corrupt. For people perceived to be constitutionally flawed, such a movement opens the door for hope and the idea of real, fundamental change.

Raising the issue of personality disorders and of antisocial, violent behavior necessarily raises the uncomfortable issue of evil and the question of whether evil is inborn. No data exist to prove that it is. Plenty exist to indicate that evil frequently breeds evil. Some traumatized Vietnam veterans murdered innocent civilians. Police brutality isn't every cop's problem, but it is a reality for many who have been psychically scarred by daily violence. The vast majority of adult survivors of child abuse can become loving parents; a disproportionate number, however, abuse their own children or allow their spouses to do so.

Regardless of the importance of realizing that antisocial behavior is often rooted in prolonged trauma, it would probably be foolish to base social policy on an assumption that all perpetrators are former victims. It would be even more foolish, it seems, to condone violence perpetrated by anyone. No matter how innocent a perpetrator once was, no matter how anguished a perpetrator may currently be, rape, torture, and murder are unconscionable acts.

An acknowledgment of the traumatic roots of evil, however, does point to possible problems with our penal system, which emphasizes punishment and isolation over treatment and reintegration. The brutalities of prison life seem more likely to create additional perpetrators than penitents. In theory, we don't want our prisons regurgitating onto city streets hundreds of thousands of freshly traumatized ex-cons primed for violence. Yet that seems to be exactly what they do.

Our society as a whole faces pressing questions of whether and how to rehabilitate violent criminals. We individual members of society face equally urgent questions about how to help the millions of nonviolent victims of violence. Can we overcome our own fears and prejudices enough to talk and listen? Can we remember that a survivor who hesitates to speak may not actually prefer to remain silent? Can we hear the moral complexities of what the survivor has suffered? Can we act fairly and compassionately? Can we risk imagining it all happening to us? And if we insist on expecting victims to ascend like phoenixes from the ashes, can we at least provide them a stable base from which to rise?

★ ★ ★

Madeline Goodman: "My father has recently died, which I'm very happy about. God took him out with cancer, which is a really good thing because I wanted to shoot him. I had a shotgun, I had bullets. It really worked out well because God gave him just the right amount of pain and everything and I didn't have to do anything. All I had to do was wait. And my father went to his grave denying any of this.

"With the gang that raped me — and there were twenty-seven that were arrested for raping the *other* girls, the ones who remembered and testified — I sometimes have thoughts of getting in a safe place, which I think would probably be a tree for me. Each time one of those guys walked by I'd shoot him. But I really would like to shoot them in the heart because that's where I feel it the most. It would definitely be vengeance. But I won't work on that either. I know I won't do that but I do have thoughts of that. Because I have so much anger in me.

"I always look for validation, you know — perhaps one of the other women that were raped that time, if one of them ever wanted to talk to me, I would like to talk to her. I look for them all the time. I am trying to unseal the court records so I can learn who they are. I found Theresa but she denies everything. She's not in too good shape, herself. But when I asked her whether what I remembered about her was true, she said, no, it wasn't her I was remembering. But we talked for a while and when I got around to saying, 'Twice, well, the person I thought was you tried to save me,' she started nodding her head in agreement. So maybe it was her I was remembering and she's just scared about coming forward.

"Oh, I forgot to tell you that in school—I had to go back to school after all this. Everybody was talking about me. I would pass by people, and they would say, 'That's her, that's her,' a lot of whispering. Me never making the connection, never having a memory. And then Theresa came up to me and wanted me to take a ride with her. And she was so earnest, so desperately pleading for me to take a ride with her after school. I said, 'OK.' We went to the field off of Flynn Creek Road. And we were looking for something specific, but she wouldn't tell me what. We went to the stream, and she went downstream and I went upstream and I saw something in the water. I could see movement caught on a fallen, half-submerged tree branch stuck in the water. I watched the movement of the water as it was trickling by. There was something black caught on the tree, waving with the water. I called to Theresa, 'Theresa! Come here!' And she came running up. 'What's that? Is it a body? What is that in the water?' It was the remains of the dog. I do remember the guys dumping it into the stream, because I heard a splash. It had been totally burnt except for the tail, and that's what I saw moving against the limb as the stream went by.

"About twelve years ago, a girlfriend of mine, Emily, had a party at her house. I was in the living room when she called me into her kitchen. 'Hey, Madeline! Will you come here a minute? There is someone who would like to meet you.' I enter the kitchen, the room is packed with people. They are watching my face intently. 'Madeline, this is Chucky Donovan. Chucky Donovan, this is Madeline Goodman.' I extend my hand. 'So very nice to meet you, Chucky.' We shake hands and exchange how do you do's. I turn and leave the room, happy to get back to my drink. My friend says to everyone in the kitchen, 'Well, I didn't see any recognition there, did any of you? But you, Chucky, you look guilty as hell! Now fess up, Chucky, fess up. That was the deal.' My friend Emily has told someone to keep me busy in the living room and not to allow me back into the kitchen. Later on I notice it has become very quiet in the kitchen for about an hour. Emily is calling to me again. 'Madeline, Chucky is leaving and he wants to say goodbye to you.' I return to the kitchen, extend my hand to him again and say, 'Very nice to have met you, Chucky. Take good care of yourself. Goodbye.' I go back to my drink in the living room. Eventually, Emily comes over to me and says, while looking directly into my eyes, 'Madeline, I know you don't know what I am talking about, but I am very, very, very sorry.' She has tears in her eyes. I return to my drinking. I don't question her.

"So here I am, forty years old. I've lived most of my adult life in confusion, chaos, escape in cocaine, alcohol and isolation, unable to sustain a long-term relationship, sexually dysfunctional, and will probably be in therapy for many years to sort this out.

"I know I have the right to walk the earth in peace. I know I am a person of worth because God created me in his image. I know I have the right to feel a full range of emotions, to sleep peacefully, to enjoy other people. I know I have the right to a healthy relationship with a man. I know I have these rights, I just can't seem to apply them to my life.

"But you know what's really bugging me now? Legally, I have no rights. I do not have the right to bring charges against the guys who raped me because the rape occurred twenty-three years ago and I could not remember anything related to it until it was sixteen years too late. My state does not have a law increasing the statute of limitations for people like me. It is time to change the law. I will try to change the law. Even though I may never be able to legally help myself, maybe I can help other people like me. Helping them, maybe, will give me the catalyst to become a person I can love.

"I found a quote by Jennierose Lavender in *The Courage to Heal* that I want to read to you. I changed it just a bit. It says what I feel.

> People have said to me, 'Why are you dragging this up now?' Why? WHY? Because it has controlled every facet of my life. It has damaged me in every possible way. It has destroyed everything in my life that has been of value. It has prevented me from living a comfortable emotional life. It's prevented me from being able to love clearly. I haven't been able to succeed in the world. If this didn't happen to me I could be anything today. I know that everything I don't deal with now is one more burden I have to carry for the rest of my life. I don't care if it happened 500 years ago! It's influenced me all that time, and it does matter. It matters very much.

"What I have told you tonight is the truth. It is a part of my life. I would like to end what I've said by saying my name.

"It is Madeline Joyce Goodman."

The Struggle to Overcome Trauma

6

THE IDEA OF THERAPY UNNERVES many survivors, and for good reason. The theoretical orientation of many therapists is that of pathologist: Psychic troubles are a sickness born of fantasy and self-deception. But the subjective experience of most survivors is that of quarry: Psychic troubles are rooted in the harsh reality of having been sighted, stalked, assaulted, duped. Survivors correctly sense that treatment with a therapist insensitive to the psychological aftershocks of trauma could teach self-loathing when self-respect is what must be learned. Therapy could erode whatever righteous clarity a survivor has salvaged about personal integrity. A therapist inexpert at treating trauma might simply dispense one psychological surprise after another to a survivor desperate for predictability. When an infusion of hope is needed, therapy could become a prolonged exploration of personal incompetence. When learning to establish and defend a faculty of authority about oneself is paramount, therapy might invite survivors to once again doubt their ability to judge what is good or right for themselves. Therapy might seduce them into once again ceding control over their hearts and minds to people who secretly hold them in contempt.

Acts of extraordinary malevolence push survivors to the brink of personal extinction. Acts of ordinary faintheartedness, indifference, ignorance, and blame fail to retrieve them. With foes and friends producing peril at every turn, deciding whom to trust can seem a choice without true options, and finding a therapist a daunting task, indeed. What, at a minimum, should a survivor expect from a therapist? What, at a minimum, should a therapist do to meet those expectations? What is recovery from psychological trauma? And how does one know when one has achieved it? These are questions of enormous practical interest to survivors and therapists.

In spite of the various psychological bombshells traditional psychotherapists have long dropped on trauma survivors, expert post-traumatic therapy draws heavily on a surprising source: traditional psychotherapy. The format is traditional. Post-traumatic therapy usually happens in private sessions once or twice a week between a single therapist and a single client. The goals of therapy are traditional. The trauma survivor moves toward self-knowledge, self-control, and self-help. The method of post-traumatic therapy is also traditional. By and large, talking relieves distress, as does the deepening relationship between therapist and client. All this is not to say that nontraditional techniques have no place in post-traumatic therapy. Stress management, cognitive therapy, behavior modification, hypnosis, meditation, expressive therapies like journal writing and art work, group therapy, and drug therapy frequently supplement talk therapy. But they rarely supplant it. As Dr. Bessel van der Kolk of Boston University explains, most trauma survivors benefit from one-on-one, psychodynamic therapy. It "allows disclosure of the trauma, the safe expression of related feelings, and the reestablishment of a trusting relationship with at least one person."

A steady rain of questions are being raised about the validity of traditional psychoanalysis. Learning that the Oedipal theory, one of the very foundations of classic psychoanalysis, rests on assumptions that are both treacherous and personally insulting convinces some survivors that a simple formula exists for selecting expert help: Choose any self-described trauma therapist over any self-described traditionalist. But a formulaic approach presents survivors with its own problems. For while much of traditional psychoanalytic theory may rest on faulty assumptions, the traditional psychoanalytic format, methods, and goals have met the test of time. Furthermore, many self-described traditionalists have informed themselves about trauma and its aftershocks. In fact, increasing recognition of the profound and lasting aftershocks of trauma seems to be the direction in which the entire psychotherapeutic profession is slowly moving.

What this means for survivors seeking expert help is that one cannot evaluate a therapist solely on the basis of the few words describing his or her theoretical persuasion. Therapists do rest much of their practice on the basis of their professional training. But perhaps as much as anything else, they rest their practice on their integrity and personal talents—on their perceptions, feelings, insights, intuition, and the degree to which they can hear unspeakable truths. "Pay more attention to the therapist's intellectual and emotional equipment than theoretical system," Dr. van der Kolk advises survivors. "Pay attention to whether the therapist really wants to hear the troubles you have to tell. Ask yourself, 'Do I feel validated? Is the therapist really listening to my story?'"

If validation is one important selection criterion, Dr. Judith Herman, Director of Training at the Victims of Violence Program at Cambridge Hospital in Cambridge, Massachusetts, makes clear a second criterion, and one that seems of equal importance: An effective trauma therapist empowers the survivor rather than imposes a cure. In *Trauma and Recovery*, Dr. Herman writes that post-traumatic therapy "is based upon the empowerment of the survivor and the creation of new connections. . . . [The survivor] must be the author and arbiter of her own recovery. Others may offer advice, support, assistance, affection, and care, but not cure. Many benevolent and well-intentioned attempts to assist the survivor founder because this fundamental principle of empowerment is not observed. No intervention that takes power away from the survivor can possibly foster her recovery, no matter how much it appears to be in her immediate best interest. In the words of an incest survivor, 'Good therapists were those who really validated my experience and helped me to control my behavior rather than trying to control me.'"

The dual formulation of validation and empowerment seems to be fundamental to post-traumatic therapy. At least it is what I observed in action when, in the course of researching this book, I sat in on therapy sessions for survivors. Granted, my presence in the sessions undoubtedly distorted them. Sometimes highly dissociative clients were able to banish from consciousness the fact of my presence and proceed with the session as though it were any other. But I would be kidding myself to think that on more than a few occasions I observed real therapy. However, while I probably didn't see much substantive self-discovery, I was able to observe therapeutic technique. And what I didn't learn about any particular survivor I did learn about the manners, so to speak, of post-traumatic therapy.

Time and again, survivors asked questions — about flashbacks, about perpetrators, about the tricks of memory, about how their own psychohistories may have made them vulnerable and may have colored their adaptations to life. I was relieved to see that, without fail, survivors' questions were welcomed as a contribution to the therapeutic process, not a distraction from it. Questions were always met with reasoned and clearly helpful answers.

The sessions I observed were undoubtedly more emotionally neutral than typical therapy sessions. In fact, they seemed as filled with prevention and education as emotion. Especially in cases of ongoing domestic violence and sexual abuse, therapists were concerned with survivors' physical safety. "Is he still hitting you?"; "Have you found a safe place to live?"; "Does your mother understand that she is not to come by without calling first and that she cannot see you alone?" Therapists taught survivors relaxation exercises. They taught cognitive techniques for coping with intrusive fears and images.

Post-session, most therapists confirmed my hunch about how my presence flattened the emotional content of the session. But they were careful to emphasize to me the significance of what I had been able to observe. Practical concerns of physical safety take immediate precedence. Once physical safety is guaranteed, education about the emotional aftershocks of trauma gives survivors some bit of mastery over their lives and symptoms. Physical safety and a measure of emotional predictability constitute the foundation upon which therapy can build.

Out of session, I talked with survivors about their therapy. I asked them how and why therapy works. I heard plenty of assurances that the talking in therapy helps; that the therapists' talking does so partly by giving survivors an objective body of knowledge about trauma's aftershocks; that survivors' own talking helps by clarifying for them their strengths and weaknesses and the methods they have used to manage post-trauma life. I heard that even the conversational pauses of therapy help. Standing back from experience, having a few moments to feel or reflect instead of react, is one way in which survivors gain control over emotions and thoughts. I heard that gaining control is paramount for people who have been robbed of it. And I heard that it is a necessary precursor to forging or continuing happy relationships.

I heard assurances that talking to a therapist is different from talking to a friend or writing in a journal; therapists can help survivors interpret their reactions to trauma and can make seemingly impenetrable behaviors and fears intelligible. I heard that friends and family interpret when they listen, but that sometimes their ability to listen is obstructed by private, unexplored fears. I heard that even when friends and family can truly listen, the interpretations they offer are restricted, fashioned as they are from a limited pool of lore. I learned that an effective therapist ratifies the survivor's subjective experience of trauma while calmly decoding trauma's aftershocks with seasoned sympathy and wisdom.

I learned from survivors that they felt cared for by their therapists. Many said that their therapists' steady presence in their lives taught them hope.

In short, I learned that the quality of the relationship between survivor and therapist can determine whether or not trauma is a lifelong dead end.

"What, at a minimum, should a survivor expect from a therapist?" I asked these survivors. These are some of the answers I heard: Constancy. Experience. Respect. Information. And, perhaps most importantly, an enormous capacity for empathy.

* * *

Brad Lambdus is a Vietnam veteran.

Brad Lambdus: "Twenty years after I came home, my life had no meaning to it at all. I was just existing. I didn't feel a part of anything. I just felt tired of fighting all the feelings I had inside of me, not understanding how to deal with all these things. I was tired of being high all the time, knowing that I could be something better but not knowing how to be better. Not having anybody out there see me for anything else other than just a dope addict or drug addict.

"When I first started therapy I was looking for answers. 'Jeez, how long I'm gonna be messed up like this? God, I can't handle this no more.' And I still get like that. It's not as bad as it was, I don't believe, when I first started. You got to be willing to open up, just gotta talk. Sometimes you don't feel like talking about something, sometimes you do. Sometimes I say, 'I don't want to talk about Vietnam.' So we'll talk about something else, you know. I guess a little bit chips off here and there once in a while and things do get a little better. My therapist picks at me sometimes and gets me to thinking about things that I really don't feel like talking about. Sometimes I leave here more upset than I was when I walked in and sometimes I walk out of here feeling a lot better than I did. It's all part of the process of getting better.

"I probably never will be totally recovered from that thing over there, you know. It will always be there but I will be able to live with it and deal with it a little better, hopefully."

Mary Margaret is an incest survivor. She lives in a high crime neighborhood.

Mary Margaret: "I had three children. I lost one son, he was murdered, in '87, and my older son that was twenty-two was shot on the second of last month, and he died on the 14th.

"I'm the type of person, I hate pity. But I needed to talk to somebody after my first son died. That, or really go crazy. So I went to therapy, and the more I came and talked, the more comfortable I got. I even was starting to laugh sometimes, which is very strange for me. Before therapy when I would laugh I would say to myself, 'What are you laughing for?' I always used to be very hard on myself for laughing or feeling anything fun or nice.

"Then my second son was killed. I was going to stop coming to therapy. I felt that it wouldn't do any good. But I've been back three times since it happened. It has helped. When it happened to my first son, I was just lost and really didn't know what to do with myself. And I feel that way again but not as intensely. I come in here. It helps. Because I've said some things here that no one else knows about."

Karen Hakey's son, Bernie, was shot in the head by a friend angry about an imagined slight.

Karen Hakey: "Because our son's murderer is a sociopath and because he has been proven to hold a grudge, I had a morbid fear of having him come to do me in. Bernie had been missing for a while. And it was only because I doggedly pursued Bernie's whereabouts that a murder investigation was launched.

"The murderer got off easy. And when Bernie's murderer was about to be released from jail, I found myself in stark terror of having him come to get revenge. I would waken at night in cold sweats and many are the times that I awakened crying out from my nightmares. I got some very good counseling and have brought those fears under control."

Because her mother was in and out of mental institutions, Lynne McCue spent her childhood in foster homes, some of which she describes as terribly cruel. Then, when Lynn was eighteen years old, her mother killed herself.

Lynn McCue: "I had grown up knowing that she would commit suicide, but I always thought she would do it by pills, because that was her previous method. Anyhow, I got a phone call from my grandfather saying my mother had killed herself. And my first question was, 'Was it pills?' And my grandfather said, no, it wasn't pills. She'd stabbed herself, three times. So she was desperate, she wanted to die.

My Grandma said, 'Would you like us to come get you?' and I said, 'Yes, please.' So she and my grandfather drove up north to get me. Then my grandmother and I were basically both mourning at the same time because this was her only child. I was upstairs doing my grieving and she was downstairs doing her grieving and somehow it just felt like one of us had to get it together. So I decided to contact a therapist.

"We did a lot of grief work. I remember the one thing that my therapist really tried to get me to do was to cry. I hate crying. I'm really bad at it. And that seems to be just the result of not being able to cry when I was growing up. But I do remember the grieving was a slow time in coming because you didn't talk to anybody about suicide. You still don't. It's a dirty word in our society. And so I didn't tell many people about it. My therapist and my family knew but that was it. The only times I would let anything out was when I had too much to drink at a party or something, and then that was bad. Not good at all.

"But then I had a dream. I dreamt I was going into this long hallway in a basement. It was like an office building. There were all these desks set up with telephones. I was walking past the desks and this phone rang so I picked it up and said, 'Hello, can I help you?' and it was my mother. And I was desperate. I said, 'Mommy, where are you? Tell me where you are!' She said, 'I can't tell you where I am right now but I'm OK.' And I said, 'But you died! You killed yourself! How can you be OK? It's awful being here. Why did you leave me? I miss you!' She reassured me in a very calming voice and said everything was OK and she was sorry but she had to do what she had to do. And I woke up.

"I didn't know what to think. I was a little freaked out. Was my mother trying to reach me? What does this all mean? When I proposed this to my therapist she sort of looked at me and didn't say much.

"And then she said, 'Lynn, do you think it's possible for your mother to try to contact you?' I didn't know. And she said, 'Think about it for a minute. Don't you think it was more like you were trying to reach out to your mother and resolve this whole issue?' And it just blew me away. Of course that's what it was. It had to be. And that really sort of helped me swallow the whole thing. And once that conversation was finished, in my dreams at least I felt like, 'OK, it's all right. She's at peace now. She's not in misery and it's time for me to get on with my life and that's what she would want.' And so I did. I continued with my school work, I continued working. And I continued therapy.

Maureen Terry was stabbed repeatedly inside her throat by a stranger who then stood over her, hoping to watch her die.

Maureen Terry: "Knowing that someone who didn't know me had wanted to kill me was strange. I could understand if someone who knew me had tried to kill me out of anger or something. But because someone who didn't know me had that much rage that he let out on me I saw the potential for everybody else in the world to do that. Intellectually I knew it probably wouldn't happen again, but emotionally I was having a hard time walking down the street.

"It was very hard for me to even leave the house. The first time that I was able to really get around I figured I would just go to the post office, which is only a couple of blocks from the house. I walked out the front door and I got about five feet and I turned around and I walked back. I couldn't. Everything that was out there just seemed like something that would hurt me. I had horrible nightmares and I wasn't sleeping at night, and any time I heard a noise I would jump.

"And then everybody said to me, 'You should get therapy, you should get therapy.' And it was in the back of my mind to do that, but at that point I couldn't talk, so I wasn't really doing anything about it. As soon as I was able to talk, I called Victim Services Agency, and ended up coming to the Crime Victims Center.

"Therapy turned out to be a lot of work. A lot of it in the beginning, for me, was just being able to verbalize what I was feeling. It was really hard talking about what happened to me and feeling those feelings again and thinking about it. And then learning how to relax and control my body. That helped me not be so fearful. We'd start at the top of my head and I'd tense my muscles and feel what that felt like and then relax that. And then I'd do that throughout my body, tensing all the different muscles and then relaxing them. Now I'm able to do it quickly so that it feels like a wave going through my body. I can relax right away. But learning how was a hard thing, because my body was so tense.

"Towards the beginning of therapy I was having a lot of nightmares that would stay with me all day long. We picked them apart in therapy and talked about the different things in them and why I might have dreamt what I dreamt. And things became so much clearer. It was really good for me to talk about the dreams because I started realizing what I was feeling and what was really going on. Fairly soon the nightmares stopped, and that was a relief in itself, being able to sleep through the night.

"After the stabbing I wound up allowing myself to be victimized in situations that I don't think I would have had I not been stabbed. For example, I allowed some people in my dance troupe to get away with things against me when I should have said, 'Stop, there's no reason for this,' or whatever. But I was just letting these things go on. And it was very disturbing to me.

"So another thing we did in therapy was we correlated my feelings about things that happened after the stabbing with feelings about things that happened to me in my past. You see, I had been physically abused when I was a kid, so I didn't grow up knowing how to say, 'No' to people and take care of my own needs. And it was real hard to deal with some of the unresolved feelings. But they kept coming up. Every time we dealt with something about the stabbing it would revert back to when I was abused when I was a kid or to my first marriage, which was to an abusive guy. None of those memories or feelings are really pleasant. It was exhausting and hard for me. It's still hard for me.

"But I know that in trying to avoid things I went through as a kid, I made the past something bigger than it was. By not dealing with it I was letting it still hurt me. Now I see that the people who hurt me when I was a kid can't hurt me anymore, you know what I mean? So it's not like there's still some sort of threat or something that I still have to be fearful about. My mom doesn't hurt me anymore. I actually have a good relationship with her now. My grandmother is dead. I'm no longer in my first marriage. These people can't hurt me. But by holding onto a lot of the feelings that I had about all this that happened to me when I was younger, I was allowing it to still hurt me. Now I deal with it bit by bit. There is still a lot of pain there, but talking about it and feeling the feelings has really helped me. And it's helped me deal with the whole stabbing incident. I feel better, it's taken the weight off me."

Paolo Williams: "A guy came in and was going to buy some coats and stuff, pulled a gun out to me, I was at the register. My boss, who was my friend, attacked him. The perpetrator's gun went off, I went down lying on the floor terrified. That's the end of the story. My friend was killed. My friend was killed. He was a very good friend.

"I was referred to this therapy center by the district DA. I have been coming for the last ten months. It has helped. You see when you go through what I have been through, it is terrible. It is terrible because you don't know where to seek help. You don't know who is who. What you're seeing is your friend on the floor. Your mind is not working. It's terrible. You cannot think straight.

"At first I got depressed. It got to the point that I wanted to kill myself. I wanted to kill myself because of what I was living through. It's like being victimized over and over again and it doesn't stop. I would rather be dead than be a victim.

"But I've been doing much better, thank God. For a while I took medication for my depression. I don't have to take it anymore. Now I'm not depressed. I'm angry. Therapy has helped me a lot. Coming to therapy helps you feel that there is support, that there are other people out there that have gone through what you've gone through. In therapy I learned ways of going about—if you don't have a good education, how to get a good education. How to join organizations. It's like opening up doors for much better ways and knowledge in your life so that you can go up against these dirt bags. It's like my therapist says, you've got to learn how to use your anger constructively to help other people, and not in a violent way. We've got to fight back and try to get these dirt bags off the street.

"I call them dirt bags because of the way I feel from inside. I'm pretty sure there's hundreds and thousands of other people that feel the same way. But people don't get involved. People don't scream or something like that. People have to get involved. This is the thing. People must get involved. You cannot just stand there and see something happen to somebody and not do nothing about it. No.

"I saw a purse get snatched on a subway platform. And I got involved. I felt great. I felt super. I felt so good. People just got to get involved, that's it. It doesn't mean you have to chase the guy and fight with the guy. You don't do that neither, cause you don't know if these guys got a weapon on them. You could get killed. You scream. I scream. When I heard the scream in the purse snatching I screamed. 'Hey!' And that distracted him and then I started going towards him and he fled. I was very happy that the lady was all right. She was all shaken up, but she was OK, and I was happy. Very happy.

"What I'm doing with my anger is I talk to a lot of people every day. Nice people. I try to make them alert about what's going on. A lot of times, people feel, 'No, it's not going to happen to me.' No. It could happen to you. It could happen to you. Don't say, 'No.'

"Sometimes people think I'm trying to like save the world. I wish I could save the world. But I try to make as many people as possible aware. I tell people who were victimized, 'Go. Seek therapy. I know how you feel, man. I know you got a lot of anger in you, you were violated. Go. It'll help you.' And scream. And scream."

Dorian Davis is forty-three years old, an ex-cop who won every street battle he entered. Even though many people might consider Dorian unusually lucky (he won, after all) he is on permanent disability for job-related post-traumatic stress disorder.

In casual conversation Dorian's post-traumatic stress is completely invisible. He is charming and funny. He refers to himself jokingly as Gentle Ben. He seems like Gentle Ben to me. He is exceedingly peace-loving. He explains that he is that way by nature and that police work only intensified his pacifism.

I am a little surprised, then, when he shows me that in nooks and crannies in and around his house loaded guns are hidden. Dorian lives in the woods in a house no bigger than most kitchens. It would be an easy house to defend. Having seen so much death, Dorian explains, life seems ephemeral, a treasure easily snatched away. Dorian is always ready to fight for his life.

Dorian Davis: "When I first went to therapy, I saw a therapist who just sat there and listened. I wasn't going to say anything because I knew the therapist was taking notes. Writing it down. I wasn't going to say anything that Freud could use against me. So I really didn't get very far.

"A while back I started seeing a therapist who works with survivors. She really participates in the sessions, and that helps. Because I can't get anywhere if I'm being defensive and afraid. I need participation.

"One thing therapy with this woman is giving me is a feeling that I'm not so bad off. She said, 'What you've been feeling is normal considering what you've been through. Other people I've seen have the same feelings, the same ideas.' So I don't feel like I'm in my own little world here.

"I trusted her fairly quickly, knowing that she dealt with trauma. So far we've done a lot of talking, but actually at first she had me drawing some pictures and things like that. She said it would help me think a little bit differently. Normally I'm skeptical of techniques like that but I wasn't this time because I know myself. I know I can sit and talk about trauma, and I have, for hours, and still get nowhere. But to have her say, 'Draw me a picture,' got me out of the talking level that kept me stuck in my head, seeing things the same old way.

"She asked me how I protect myself. I drew a circle. I have something I protect, my inner self, and I drew that in the middle of a circle. And the circle was all barbed wire, and the box inside is just solid steel, you can't get to it. Those are my feelings in the box, how I feel about what I've seen, what I've dealt with. Nobody gets to it, not even me. I can't even get to it. And she noticed that the barbed wire wasn't wound real tight. 'Is there anybody that gets in there, or anything that comes out?' she asked. And that started me feeling differently, like something does come out, you know, love for my children. So it was like the box isn't as impenetrable as I thought it was, and drawing it brought that out. If I had just sat and talked, I would have said, 'The box is steel. Nothing comes in, nothing comes out.' But seeing it on the paper and drawing it I learned I wasn't as boxed in as I thought I was. I don't know if it makes sense, but it worked.

"At our first meeting I asked her, 'How long till I feel better?' She said it never goes away, but you learn how to manage it. And just by saying that, it's like, 'Okay, I'll be able to manage my life!' But that's what you actually need to know, is that it never goes away, because you're wanting and you're thinking that you can think and hide it away. And when that doesn't work, it's like, 'Oh, shit, what am I going to do? It's never going to go away, this is going to plague me for the rest of my life. It's going to destroy me.'

"This is the background on what happened to me, minus the blood and guts:

"My buddy, Reilly, and I were called to take care of a 'domestic'— a family fight. A woman was being assaulted. That's all we knew. We were downstairs outside the place, and I got a strange feeling. I can't explain the feeling, but it was like something I never felt before. It was like electricity in the air. We don't know where in this building the domestic is, and this is a two-family building. So we're downstairs, outside, Reilly and I. We start looking around. We can hear somebody moaning but we can't figure out where it's coming from. So there's a very small door and one of those yellow bug lights, and very narrow stairs going up and we can hear the moaning coming from there. So Reilly goes up first and the door at the top is a little bit ajar, and we can still hear moaning. So Reilly pushes the door a couple of inches and all of a sudden the door comes back and hits him right in the head. Someone had pushed the door back. Knocks his hat off. We look at each other. We didn't say anything, it was nonverbal: 'Let's go.' We had our batons in our hand and we didn't know what to expect. No guns out. Didn't know what to expect.

"So we go in and there was just a little night light, so I couldn't see what was happening. And it was just a total ambush. All I know is that somebody was on top of us. First I just thought he was hitting us, because he was swinging. And I was swinging back with my baton trying to protect myself. And all of a sudden I felt this sharp pain in my chest when he stabbed me. As I fell back against the wall I could see him with

Reilly fighting. And he got Reilly from behind in the back. He's poised over Reilly ready to stab him again and I fired and shot him in the chest.

"And he's wearing a white T-shirt with a little alligator. And he looked at me, and I looked at him, and we just looked at each other for a second or two. I watched the blood and things just stopped. And then he collapsed.

"And Reilly's on the floor. I knew I wasn't—well, I didn't know what was going on with me, but I didn't care. It wasn't like I couldn't move. I went over to Reilly. I got his shirt off, and as I was over there, this big woman stood up. She had been behind the stove, and we hadn't seen her. And she walked out and she fell over. We didn't know it, but he had stabbed her twice in the chest.

"And Reilly's breathing, well, like he's going to stop breathing. I hear other cops coming up the stairs, and the guy that I shot moans. I said to the other cops, 'Handcuff that fucker!'

"So I helped Reilly down and another cop drove us to the hospital. But I didn't tell anybody I'd been stabbed. We put Reilly in the front seat, I got in the back seat. And I'm like, 'Keep going Reilly. It's OK. We'll make it.'

"We get to the hospital, we take Reilly in, and then I say, 'I've been stabbed, too, right here.' I remember sitting in the hospital emergency room, sweating. Beads of sweat are just coming off my armpits. And there were some other cops and I'm asking, 'What's going on? How's the guy I shot? How's Reilly?' I can hear Reilly moaning. But they are just staring at me. It's kind of like, 'What's going on here? Everybody's just kind of looking at me.' I want to know what happened to the guy I shot. And I'm starting to think this guy's dead. But nobody's telling me.

"So after I'm released they drop me off at home and I show up at the door. And I'm just like happy to be alive. 'I'm alive! I'm OK! I made it!' I give my wife a big hug. And I just wanted to make love, and just be alive. It's like, 'Whoa, fuck, I just almost got killed! But I survived!' But she was like, 'You just killed a guy?' And I could see this look on her face. And she looked like I'd done something wrong. And I'm not faulting her at all. But that's the way that went.

"So after three weeks I go back to work. I'm back out on the same beat, and nobody's saying anything. The police department isn't telling me about an investigation or coroner's report, whether it was a justifiable shooting. There's nothing coming to me to let me know that I did OK. So I'm lost. I don't know if I did OK, I don't know if I didn't do OK. 'Tell me *something*!'

"So six months down the line nobody's telling me anything. I say to myself, 'I don't know what to do anymore. Nobody's talking to me. I can't even talk to my wife about this.' So I went to the mental health clinic and talked to a counselor. He tried, but he just didn't know what was happening with me. But at least I got to say what happened. Ten sessions, an hour each. I put in a worker's comp claim to pay for the counseling, and the city came back with a refusal, saying that who am I to refer myself to a counselor. And my reaction is, 'Well, it's happening to me, I think I know what's going on here, you know, and I need some help!' Well, they refused to pay for that hundred dollars. And I really felt abandoned, angry, like, 'I almost got killed, my buddy almost got killed, and I killed this guy. Doesn't that mean anything? What is this all about?'

"If I quote statistics, it's because it's helped me. Only 2% of cops ever kill anybody. And 80% of those who do kill somebody end up not in police work after five years. I didn't know all this at the time. But what I went through was an unusual event.

"So I'm alone. And the system doesn't really know how to deal with me because shootings are so rare. So the city rejects me.

"So I got angry and I took them to task on it. I hired a lawyer to get the city to compensate me for the work-related counseling. I didn't know it at the time, but he was in cahoots with the city, trying to get me to settle the case and just let it go. They were going to give more than the hundred dollars if I would put it on the record that my problems weren't work related. Eventually I fired that lawyer and I got another one. He said, 'OK, this is very controversial. I want you to know something, that the whole state's looking at this case, and cities are looking at it from a monetary point of view. They don't want this to be job-related, and they're going to fight you on this.' I was like, 'Well, I'm a crusader. I'm going to insist because it really *is* work related.'

"But eventually I got emotionally tired of the fight and I begin saying to myself, 'Just go back to work and do the job and survive.' And so that's what I did. I got real hard-core. On the street my attitude was, 'You will not kill me. I will kill you before you get me, if that's what the police department wants me to do.' No emotions. I got good at it, good at being hard. Dink 'em and screw everybody. No support from the system.

"So the way I see it now is that I'm alone and people are trying to kill me. But most cops aren't experiencing this, OK? They haven't had somebody try to kill them. They haven't shot and killed somebody. People who haven't been through it have a hard time understanding a person who has. From the guys on the force I'm just getting the message that I'm a troublemaker.

"In the meantime I almost got killed by another cop, and I turned him in. And you don't do that. Cops cover for cops, they don't turn them in. So I'm getting further from any support from the police department. But this guy was brutal. We called him Mad Dog. Like he'd handcuff a guy and then beat him with his gun. And he kept doing stuff like that, but the system covered for him.

"It started like this: I got a call of a gang with a gun going into an alley. There's a new guy working with me that night, I'm breaking him in. So we see the guy with a shotgun and we follow him and his gang into this alley — a real alley, with brick walls on both sides. There's six of them. This new guy and I, we jump out, we get everybody up against the wall. We call for backup, and Mad Dog is one of the backup guys, OK? There's no sign of the shotgun now. In other words, they're submitting. I have my new guy doing cover while I'm frisking the gang. And I'm up frisking them, and I hear this Mad Dog cop next to me screaming and hollering like he always does, and all of a sudden I hear a shot go off inches above my head. It hits the brick wall. Stuff falls in my face. And I look around, and I'm like, 'What the fuck?' And Mad Dog's laughing. And I looked at the new guy, and I said, 'You didn't fire that shot, did you?' And he said, 'No.' So I just said, 'Fuck this.' I called for the supervisor, he took over, I went to headquarters. I told the lieutenant, I said, 'That's it. I'm reporting this guy.'

"To make a long story short, there were four other cops there, they didn't see anything. The one guy I thought was my friend, too, he didn't see anything. He slipped and fell. So I'm the only one who's seeing this complaint through. We go through the police board, which is like a trial, and I'm sitting in there facing this guy and I'm telling the police board that he's been out of control, and I also requested to be able to wear my sidearm in there because I don't know what this maniac is going to do. He's a real wacko. But because I've seen a counselor ten times I'm considered the one who's wacko.

"So after this police board hearing this Mad Dog comes up to me and he says, 'You fucking rat. I'm going to take care of you.' And — my poor wife — I sat up that night with a shotgun waiting for him to come to my house, because he said he was going to get me. My wife was like, 'Jesus!' And I don't blame her, I wouldn't have been able to understand that either. But I knew the threat was real.

"So he gets two weeks of suspension, and then he starts threatening me in the police department. And I had a couple of confrontations with him. One time he came in to where I was working, he was slapping his nightstick in his hand, and he said, 'I'm going to take care of you, you little rat.' And there were other guys in there. I'm sitting there, I'm stunned. Wrote up a report to the chief, telling him what happened, that I felt that I was threatened and can they do something about this. In the meantime, everybody else was on this guy's side. They don't want to see him get in trouble.

"So the department doesn't do anything about the incident, nothing at all. So I told the sergeant, 'If he threatens me, I want you to know, I'll kill him. If I have to, I'll kill him.' And they were like, 'What's the matter with you?' And I said, 'I know this man is violent, he's irrational. I've seen him beat the shit out of handcuffed people, and he's not going to hurt me.' And one of the guys said, 'This kind of sounds like a setup. Davis might just try to shoot him.' And because this clown is still around, 'backing me up,' I don't know if I'm going to get shot in the back, OK? Where am I safe? How can I survive all alone?

"And I'm into survival big time. Right about then, they're starting up a SWAT team. And that's just what I want. Because I think I'm in combat. And no matter what the rest of the P.D. thinks, the lieutenant on my shift knows that I'm a good guy to have with you when the shit hits the fan. So I'm on the SWAT team, and I'm the point man. First man through the door. I've got to be the most alert. I'm out there. I *am* the most alert. I am Mr. Ready!

"In the meantime, my regular duty is walking a beat, midnight shift. I get a call of a burglary of a house. I meet up with a cruiser driver and go to the burglary. The woman says the man was standing at the foot of the bed and he's got a rifle, and he was playing with her feet. Then he ran out of the house. So while we're standing at that house, there's another call of a burglary not too far away, walking distance, running distance. So we go down to that one. And somebody broke out a window, there's blood all over. The lady there says, 'Somebody's trying to break down my door.' And we're saying, 'We got a real nut here.' And while we're standing there, we hear several houses down a big smash, glass is breaking. 'OK, this is the guy,' we think. We get the call while we're standing right there. Sure enough, he's breaking in down the road. There's only two of us. We were sort of short on manpower at the time. So we do our tactics, me at one corner of the house, him at the other corner, good police procedure. This house is up on a hill. I'm standing back where it's dark though, real dark. And all hell breaks out in the house. Screaming, hollering—you know that kind of screaming when the shit's really hitting the fan?

"So I went running towards the front of the house, and as I came around the corner, there's a man coming down the stairs with a rifle in his hands, screaming, face bloody, a madman. I yell 'Freeze!' but he turned, pointed that rifle right at me, and so I shot him. I dove for cover, called on the radio, and while I'm doing this, there comes a lady running out of the front of the house, and this lady is screaming, 'You son of a bitch! You son of a bitch!' And I'm going, 'What's going on here?' And she's yelling, 'You shot my husband!' Well, the husband and criminal had fought over the rifle and then the criminal had run down the hill. So I shot the homeowner, OK?

"So my mind is like, 'Here I go again. I don't believe this shit.' Calling for the ambulance, the radio's not working, all these things that happen to us out there. Anyway, the medics come, and this guy's hollering and screaming. And this woman's saying, 'You shot my husband. You shot him, you son of a bitch.' And he's bleeding, and I'm saying, 'Oh my God, please don't let *this* guy die. I don't need this.' So he's screaming, and I'm sweating, waiting for the medics. And it took them a long time to get there. I'm standing there by myself. Then the medics come, taking his blood pressure, taking their time. I'm saying, 'Just get the guy to the hospital!' It's chaotic.

"So the criminal, he's down the hill with a couple of cops on top of him by now. So here comes our sergeant. I remember I gave my handgun to the sergeant, said, 'Here, I know the routine.'

"Our police department, maybe they've changed the procedures, but at the time, we didn't have a lot. When we get to the police station, the prisoner is being very belligerent. The lieutenant has *me* book the prisoner. Prisoner won't give me his fingerprint. So the lieutenant stands *outside* the booking room and says, 'Davis, take his fingerprint.' And that was all he had to say. It was like, 'You made me shoot this fucking guy. And now it's payback time.' I grabbed the prisoner by the neck. I took his noseprint after I beat the shit out of him. You know? They shouldn't have done that. Why the hell did they even let me in there?

"So after I finish choking the guy, I go out to the main desk and I hear the phone calls being made. 'Yup, Davis got another one, except this time he got the wrong guy.' That's stuck in my mind ever since. No I didn't get the wrong guy, I shot the right guy. I wasn't deer hunting. I shot this human being who was pointing a rifle at me. Thank God he didn't die.

"So now I'm really hard-core. Two shootings. No support from the system, and I'm not talking to anybody. Nobody's picking up any signs of anything, because the kind of thing I'm going through is just not recognized.

"Pretty soon word comes down that we got to get Davis off the street. Nothing is said directly to me, it's all through the grapevine. They put me in Youth Bureau. But I don't like Youth, they're just little criminals. 'Get me out of here! I don't want to talk to these kids when they call me an asshole. I don't need to have kids bombarding me with that now. I'm losing faith in the world here. Now I'm going to have kids giving me a hard time?' I want to be back on the street where I feel safe, where people are trying to kill me — that's where I know how to survive these days. So I say, 'I want to go back on the street. I want to be back in my uniform. It's where I need to be.' 'Well, we'll put you in Traffic. You can wear your uniform there, but you won't have to do much.'

"This is what I start thinking: 'Hey, they're trying something here.'

"So I go in Traffic, and I spend a year and a half in there, and in the meantime I'm still on SWAT, you know? Still doing it. And then I pass the test for sergeant, and so you have to promote me. I get to be SWAT team leader. And that feels good. Now I can really go for it, and I get to be in charge of third shift. New guys, all of them new guys. I get real dedicated to keeping these people alive, because *I* know people are trying to kill them. And the only way you're going to stay alive out there is by being tactically prepared, and that's what I taught them. And I was hard on them. I said, 'I will *not* let you people die. You *will* live, because I will teach you the right way to survive.'

"So this is all going on, and then another incident happens. This was my breaking point. I was working the desk that night, filling in for the lieutenant. And this man drove into the police department and said that he was with another woman and that his old girlfriend had spotted him fifty miles away and she'd started harassing him. He wanted us to find her and talk to her. Lo and behold, she pulls in behind him. And she comes in and she's off the wall, screaming and hollering. But it's OK, this is just another domestic. And we don't want to arrest her. 'All this guy wants to do is go home with his girlfriend and wants you to leave him alone. So why don't you let him go?' So I said to the guy that was working the desk with me, 'Come out here, we'll make sure that he gets off OK and she leaves.'

"So we had her get in her car and we told her, 'Take off.' It was a one-way street she had to drive on. She drove down the street, so we figure she's gone. I'm standing by the driver's door talking to the guy. And all of a sudden she turns around. She comes up the one-way street the wrong way, and she's heading right for the guy's car. I jumped up on the back of the car just before she hit. I smashed into the back window. A second or so later I jumped on the hood of her car, onto the ground, and the window was open a few inches. I reached in, shattered the window, and grabbed her by the throat. I was going to choke her. And right then, something inside me just said, 'That's it.' I didn't hurt her. But the other cop yelled, 'I was going to shoot her! I was getting ready to fire!'

"For me, it was like, 'I can't do this anymore. I cannot do this anymore. I can't do it.' I went through all the procedures, booked her, did everything right, everything OK.

"And I go to the hospital. My knees are hurt. I'm out of work for three weeks. I come back to work and I decide that I'm going to ask to be taken off the street. I've done nothing wrong in my career. I've got all my medals. I got the highest medal possible for the shooting incident with Reilly. I've never been disciplined. I've always been a good officer. I go in to the department and I say, 'I don't want to work the street anymore, I can't.' 'What do you mean, you can't?' 'I don't know what I need, except I know I can't work the street.'

"So they don't know what to do with this. The captain says, 'Well, I'll have to tell the chief.' And the chief called me in and, pulling an authority thing on me said, 'I don't know why you have a problem. I can't take you off the street. What is your problem?' And I looked at him, and I said, 'You've never done what I've done.' I got really pissed off, and he got scared, because he was an intimidating kind of guy but he wasn't able to intimidate me. I looked him right in the eye and I said, 'You've never done what I've done. Don't tell me.'

"After that he tried to make me look like a nut. They put me in what they call the police library, which was where they had the police board meetings. As we all know, police aren't great for going to the library, are they? And that hurt me so bad because I would go in there, and there's nobody in there, nothing to do. I'm alone. I'm the most decorated officer on the force and in charge of the SWAT team and they're treating me like I'm a nut. 'Because I went to you and asked you for help, you're punishing me?'

"Then they started with, 'If you can't work the street, we don't want you.' And they started to try to build a case to let me go.

"First they sent me to a psychologist. He gave me a letter backing me up and suggesting that they take me off the street but keep me in real police work. I've got all kinds of training. The force had spent thousands of dollars on me. I was a firearms instructor, SWAT team leader, I was an instructor in the police baton, in self-defense. I've got all kinds of qualifications, and they spent a lot of money getting me there.

"But as a result of the psychologist's letter they take me out of the library and just put me in another do-nothing job. And I'm confused as hell now. See, the chief didn't want to give me anything but a do-nothing job because if he put me in any assignment with real responsibility he would have to take one of his lapdogs out and put him on the street. And he wanted his lapdogs running everything in the force. And it was pretty clear I wasn't going to be a lapdog.

"The chief became my supervisor, and he gave me the lowest evaluation I ever had. He was trying to fortify his case against me. He called me into his office with the police commissioner there, and said to the police commissioner, 'The way I see it, according to this psychologist's report, Officer Davis shouldn't be carrying a handgun.' He said that. And to take a policeman's handgun, that's like dishonor. The commissioner didn't let him take my gun, but those were things that were happening on a daily basis. I can remember the chief seeing me in the hallway, and I'd always say, 'Morning, Chief.' And he'd say, 'How are you?' And I'd say, 'I'm fine.' And he'd say 'I don't know about that.' You know, shit like that.

"The chairman of the police board happened to know me because he had given me my medic training. And I could tell he liked me as a cop because I was professional and I really enjoyed the job and I liked helping people. But he had to go along with the chief. But he did come in and talk to me. He told me he knew I was getting fucked, but he couldn't do anything about it.

"Then I got a letter saying that if I couldn't do police work, there would be no place for me. Though the letter didn't explicitly say it, police work was being defined in the narrow sense of street work. They told me that they weren't going to go by the psychologist's recommendation and that they needed a psychiatrist's report to see if I could do 'police work.' At the time I'm getting divorced, and my world is falling into shit.

"They booked me an appointment with a psychiatrist. When I walked into this psychiatrist's office he looked at me and kind of growled, 'So what are you doing here?' And I'm thinking, 'Whoa, this is an understanding individual!' The police department had told me to take a couple of newspaper articles about the shootings and stuff, so I gave them to him. He reads them over. He never asks me anything. It was a bag job.

"So his written report backs up the original psychologist's report by saying that whatever is happening to me is work-related, but it backs up the police department in saying I can't be a cop at all. No suggestion that I do legitimate, non-street police work. I just shouldn't be a cop. So I'm defenseless. I'm going to lose my career, no doubt about it.

"Towards the end there I hired an attorney again. My lawyer negotiated an agreement with the city. It wasn't a lot of money, but I was proud of the agreement. They acknowledged that my problems were work-related. I got full retirement and disability. I got $55,000, which seemed like a lot then but obviously isn't because I've lost my career and I know I need psychiatric help but I can't afford it because, with no career, I've still got to raise two kids and somehow try to send them to college.

"Being disabled, being retired when I wasn't yet forty, it puts me in a place where I'm having a hard time now because people say, 'Where have you been?' What do you do?' I can't say, 'Hey, I have PTSD.' They expect somebody with PTSD to be out there hunting people down, killing people. So I'm ashamed. I feel defective when I see people of my generation having a good career and mine's been totally washed away.

"And when 'retired' really started to sink in, all of those feelings, all those dead people, all those dead babies, all those awful things that I saw, that I put in my mental knapsack, started to come back. And it was like, 'What is this about?!' When I saw the guy dead with his head blown up, it didn't bother me. I went out and had a cup of coffee after that. Well, now that I'm retired all this shit is coming back. I don't know how many people have died in my arms. Little kids. People don't know that. But I remember all this stuff. And it comes back to me. When I build around the house, I pick up a hammer and what will come to my head is 'hammer,' and I'll remember that this woman's husband hit her on the head, knocked her out the window, and she landed in the driveway, and it was wintry, and blood all over, and I was with her when she died. The other cops were upstairs. I was the only one, alone with this woman. Her face was like mush and she was bleeding. And all that comes back to me now. And at the time—I don't tell anybody—I held her hand.

"So it's impacting my life today. I really have to fight it. It's like sometimes I want to tell somebody, 'Gee, I saw a person die.' Or, 'Hey, life sucks, life's dangerous. You've got to be careful because you can really get fucked over big time.' But you can't just go up and tell somebody. I've tried, and it's inappropriate. If I do it, and I've tried, I just feel like an asshole.

"I don't go to cities because I'm fearful, I know what can happen. And it's not going to happen to me. I don't want to make it sound like I'm armed and dangerous, but I don't really feel safe unless I have a weapon within my reach.

"Mostly, by staying up here in the woods, I'm keeping myself out of situations where I'd feel the need to be armed. But I can't pretend that the world's safe, because I know that it hasn't been safe for me. That's why I run into trouble with socializing with people. I have trouble with relationships. The world hasn't been safe for me and I can't pretend that it is but I can't act out how threatened I really feel.

"So at our first meeting when my therapist said, "It will never go away but you learn to manage it," for me it was like, 'Okay, that's okay. It's never going to go away, but I *can* manage it.' Because I've managed a lot in my life, and if this is manageable, that's good news.

"Another thing that I've liked so far about going to this therapist is that she acknowledges what I've been through and how it has changed me both for better and for worse. So I'm not looking for other people to acknowledge it now. Because I can't expect the guy or lady down the street to acknowledge it, because it's something people don't want to know, or in relationships it's hard. Nobody's been where I've been, and yet I wanted them to know it and say, 'I understand that.' And it doesn't happen. So I'm letting go of that, and that's good, because then it's like, 'Okay, it happened,' but I don't have to carry it around with me, looking for acknowledgment from the whole world.

"A lot of themes we talk about in therapy keep coming back to how I dealt with things as a cop and how I continue to deal with things. It even goes back to my childhood. I grew up in a Marine Corps family, was brought up to be tough. 'Kill is what you're going to do.' That's how I was brought up. The drill instructor father who beat you and that kind of stuff. So now I look back on that. And I can see that by having some trauma in my childhood, it gave me empathy for the people I dealt with, which allowed me to understand them and be a much better cop. Police work involves relating to victims, seeing their viewpoint and having some sympathy for them.

"But having a sixth sense about victims also got me into a lot of trouble. Other cops used to say, 'Why is Davis always getting into shit?' See, I could see problems where other cops couldn't. And I can remember incidences — this is one very particular one. I was sitting in a patrol car with another cop. A woman had a guy on each side of her and they were walking down the street. This was midnight. And I looked at them and I said to the other cop, 'Something's wrong there.' And he said, 'What do you mean, something's wrong? It's just a girl and two guys.' I said, 'Something's not right there. Let's check it out.' We did. And those guys were kidnapping her. They had already sexually abused her and they were walking her — well, we just happened to be parked back in a parking lot, so when they walked by they were exposed. We saved her ass.

"So I think I had a gift for seeing. But that meant I was always in a lot of shit. A lot of guys couldn't understand it.

"I also know now that my childhood stuff with my father beating me and all was difficult for me later in one other way. When I sat in the police chief's office and he said, 'I don't know what your problem is. You shouldn't have a problem,' it was like being a kid in trouble and having adults turning their back on you. You ask your father for help. What does he do? He beats you up and tells you you're fucked.

"All this stuff in my Marine Corps family about being stoic and not turning to anybody for help kind of set me off to be isolated from the rest of the world. So for all my life I've been isolated and haven't had a way to learn what's normal for other people. I got set up at a very early age to not be talking to other people about what's happening.

"So here I am living all protected in the woods, and now I'm learning in therapy that maybe it's not good to be too isolated. And all this stuff I'm learning about the dangers of isolation help me make sense out of why I am finding my current experience with therapy more useful than the one where the therapist just sat and listened. My current therapist interacts with me. It's been like a partnership. She challenges me, poses questions to me. 'What do you think that might be related to?' she says. And if she says, 'Maybe it might be this,' I can say, 'No, it's not that. Maybe it's this.' It's an exchange, and we're both part of it.

"One thing I'm thinking of doing eventually is join a support group. Because learning from my therapist that other people have reacted to trauma the way I did has been so helpful. And I think there'd be a lot of comfort hearing it from another trauma survivor. Like hearing someone say, 'I've felt that,' or, 'I do that.' It'd be like, 'Whoa, gee, I'm not whacked out!' I just don't know what group. I don't really fit in with rape victims, or child abuse victims, or Vietnam war veterans. But even if I don't fit in I think that I would just like to go and listen, because I think that the reactions to trauma are probably very similar, no matter what the trauma.

"And I do want to make myself understood that, while I have anger about the way things went for me with the police department, I don't really blame the system because I don't think the system really knew. They fucked me but I can't take it real personal. And I don't know how to say it, but I wouldn't be who I am today if all this hadn't happened, and I'm glad I am who I am today. So it's like, I'm glad it all happened, because it's made me wiser. Sadder but wiser. I mean, if nothing ever happened, I might just be ho-humming through life like a lot of people do, and you can see them—they've kind of got a glazed-over look. That's one thing I don't have. I couldn't come up with a glazed-over look if I tried."

7

WHILE MYTHS LIKE THE CONQUEST of good over evil and the infinite resilience of the human spirit are so ingrained in our culture as to be almost endemic, so is a newer ethos: In Recovery We Trust. "Strikeouts and Psych-outs," a 1991 article in *The New York Times Magazine*, gives a thoroughly charming example of the blind faith many Americans have come to place in the practical powers of therapeutic pros.

> In the late 1980's, the troubled New York Mets took a step that was unusual even for that idiosyncratic franchise: The team hired a psychiatrist. While managers had long interpreted their players' performance in terms of baseball mechanics — hitting, fielding, throwing, running — the Mets' top management apparently decided it was time to probe the inner selves of players who had trouble throwing the ball back to the pitcher and managers who had trouble communicating with — and relating to — their high-priced charges. There were, of course, skeptics. "If we need a team psychiatrist, what's this world coming to?" asked Mets catcher Gary Carter. A coach for the L.A. Dodgers mused, 'What's a psychiatrist going to say? 'It's O.K. if you throw it away. I'll still like you'?"

If "In Recovery We Trust" has become American pop culture's national motto, it is no small irony that many of the Americans in dire need of psychological guidance are unlikely to seek it.

Hard data on the frequency with which survivors of human cruelty turn to mental health experts for help are lacking. Certainly Vietnam veterans and many sexual abuse survivors are pursuing post-traumatic therapy in record numbers. However, it is the nearly universal impression of experts in post-traumatic therapy that many trauma survivors remain loath to do so. Some survivors are reluctant to enter into the formal but intimate relationship that is fundamental to therapy. But many fear something more basic. They fear the talking. More specifically, they fear talking about trauma.

In his landmark 1987 book, *Psychological Trauma*, Dr. Bessel van der Kolk was one of the first to point out that "warding off the return of unresolved psychological trauma becomes a central focus in [survivors'] lives." Talking honestly and deeply about trauma and its aftershocks would, of necessity, require a survivor to discard this organizing principle of post-trauma life. Talking would invite the return of unresolved psychological trauma. Talking — and treatment — would involve pain.

This is not a fear to be blithely dispelled, for in the psychodynamic therapy practiced by most trauma experts, memories are navigated and pain is aroused. To survivors already awash in misery, the prospect is disheartening. Virtually no sane person would choose to experience the chaotic pain of trauma. Already traumatized people are understandably loath to reexperience it.

Unfortunately, the impulse toward self-protection requires survivors to shun more than the risks of therapy. It frequently demands that they dodge the perils of human relationships, as well. And, as Dr. van der Kolk further notes in *Psychological Trauma*, "avoiding emotional involvement further diminishes the significance of life after the trauma, and thus perpetuates the central role of the trauma."

Entering therapy is not the easy choice for some survivors that it apparently is for millions of Americans. However, considering that the alternative may be a life of emotional isolation, it is probably the most reasonable one. Dr. Raymond Scurfield, a psychiatric social worker who has spent a career helping war veterans, offers some solace when he advises survivors that, while post-traumatic pain "usually gets worse before it gets better" in therapy, "this appears to be a necessary step to work through what you have to work through, and it is only temporary." And, as many trauma therapists suggest to survivors, "If you can survive the experience, you can survive the talking."

Such assurances may be of some help to survivors when they are voiced by an already trusted therapist. But they probably are cold comfort when a therapist has yet to be found, or at the outset of therapy when the relationship between survivor and therapist is in its infancy. Fortunately, expert trauma therapists such as Dr. Scurfield offer newcomers to therapy more than platitudes. They structure therapy so that it usually begins not with deep memory exploration but with more ordinary matters such as education, diagnosis, and symptom control. Many therapists offer hypnosis, cognitive therapy, meditation, relaxation techniques, or medication to help survivors manage pain and thereby increase the competence with which they face the tasks of daily life and the courage with which they face the prospect of memory exploration. Most importantly, trauma therapists explain to survivors that therapist and survivor will jointly pace the exploration of traumatic memories, exercising mutual and cautious control over both acceleration and constraint.

Dr. Judith Lewis Herman works primarily with survivors of sexual abuse and family violence. In *Trauma and Recovery*, she explains that the therapist and survivor's joint responsibility in pacing memory retrieval is

Dr. Christine Dunning, a Professor with the Governmental Affairs Department of the University of Wisconsin in Milwaukee and a consultant to employers about their responsibilities to workers with job-related mental injuries:

"One aspect of mental injury safety programs is to simply inform people about emotional reactions to trauma so that, once they are involved in a traumatic situation, they know what to call what is happening to them and they know what remedial activities are available to them. But there's a lot an organization can do to develop a social support system among its workers that helps the workers avoid mental injury.

"For example: Generally administrators see an air crash as an opportunity to train their workers. They like to give everybody experience on the crash site. Well, I did a research study at a crash. An organization said, "Let's give everybody a chance to see what carnage looks like," and rotated new people into an air crash site every two hours, though some people worked all the way through. Interestingly, the group of people who worked only two hours had a higher incidence of traumatization.

"When an air crash occurs the insurance company of the airline has to pay police and fire departments for the time their workers were on the scene. Because of this, the departments keep very good records of who was on the scene for how long and what they did. We pored over these records and did some on-site interviews and some post-incident interviews. We found that the development of PTSD symptoms was linked to fifteen minutes' exposure to the carnage. In other words, once you were on the job for fifteen minutes, you were likely to need some emotional help. Through interviews, we found out why. It had to do with issues of closure.

"If you simply work a shift of a preassigned length, there's no closure. You come on the site, you're overwhelmed by the enormity and futility of the job. All you can think is, 'Oh my God, this is more than we can handle! How can anyone be alive?' You have no sense that you can have a positive impact and when you're pulled off the job at the end of your shift, you feel the same way.

"So a lot of the techniques that we use now are aimed at reducing feelings about the enormity of the event down to what the psyche can handle. One of the ways we do this is by telling rescue workers that they are only responsible for one small geographic area. 'There's a definite task that you're going to do. We won't make you stop until you've completed the task. And we're going to organize you in a way that while you're doing the task you will have emotional support from each other.'

"Another example: At most crash sites, you do a cordoned search. You line up every fifteen feet, eyes forward. You don't have the ability, except by yelling, to talk to anyone. You walk through the crash site. And most rescue workers, when they do that, don't even look down at the ground because they don't want to see feet or heads or anything. So they actually do it but they don't see. Well, we've gone to a matrix approach where you have a team of four to six people, depending on how big the geographic area is. They work together, with eye contact, with the ability to converse, in that small geographic area.

"They are self-governing. They decide when to begin, when to stop, how to organize the search in their area. It's easier to do the task well and to face gruesomeness if you can have some social support.

"Police officers and fire fighters need a feeling of mastery over the event as it's occurring and the feeling that they make a difference. They've been trained in medical procedures, extrication, rescue, and they are ready to help. But when they are sent to disaster sites, they don't do any of that. Mostly, they do body handling. So there's a sense of futility there. 'What are we doing here? Why are they asking me to do this?' That sense of futility is what we need to help them cope with as much as anything."

to err, if at all, on the side of caution, lest exploring trauma simply re-traumatize the survivor. "Patients at times insist upon plunging into graphic, detailed descriptions of their traumatic experiences, in the belief that simply pouring out the story will solve all their problems. At the root of this belief is the fantasy of a violent cathartic cure which will get rid of the trauma once and for all. The patient may imagine a kind of sadomasochistic orgy, in which she will scream, cry, vomit, bleed, die, and be reborn cleansed of the trauma. The therapist's role in this reenactment comes uncomfortably close to that of the perpetrator, for she is invited to rescue the patient by inflicting pain. The patient's desire for this kind of quick and magical cure is fueled by images of early, cathartic treatments of traumatic syndromes which by now pervade popular culture, as well as by the much older religious metaphor of exorcism." It is better to wait, Dr. Herman points out, until the traumatized person, "little by little, . . . regains some rudimentary sense of safety, or at least predictability, in her life. [In therapy,] she finds, once again, that she can count on herself and on others. Though she may be far more wary and less trusting than she was before the trauma, and though she may still avoid intimacy, she no longer feels completely vulnerable or isolated. She has some confidence in her ability to protect herself; she knows how to control her most disturbing symptoms, and she knows whom she can rely on for support. The survivor of chronic trauma begins to believe not only that she can take good care of herself but that she deserves no less. In her relationships with others, she has learned to be both appropriately trusting and self-protective. In her relationship with the therapist, she has arrived at a reasonably secure alliance that preserves both autonomy and connection."

With memory exploration proceeding in a therapeutic alliance marked by parity and caution, reexperiencing and making sense of traumatic pain is one of the prices of recovery for a survivor. Gratuitous pain is not.

Dr. Laurie Anne Pearlman, Research Director at the Traumatic Stress Institute in South Windsor, Connecticut, describes therapy as, in part, a process by which therapists help survivors build a base of safety, strength, and understanding that survivors draw on when remembering trauma. In so describing therapy, Dr. Pearlman also suggests why remembering and talking about trauma is important. Therapy includes "a fair amount of education. We explain that post-traumatic stress is a normal reaction to an abnormal event. People will come in the first session and say, 'I'm having nightmares and flashbacks and I want to kill myself.' I'll normalize that and provide a framework that helps people make sense of these frightening experiences. For example, over time, if there are other trauma-related difficulties as well, I might wonder with people whether their flashbacks might be representations of an experience from the past; not necessarily an accurate memory, but a partial representation or fragment, a feeling state. If so, those fragments may keep coming back in bits until we're able to piece together whole memories. Whole memory has pictures and a story line that explains what it's about. Flashbacks usually don't. I'll tell people pretty clearly what to expect from therapy: Over time and when you're ready we're going to talk about the traumatic memories, about your intense fear, and try to understand what they mean to you."

In *Psychological Trauma*, Dr. van der Kolk makes explicit the inverse relationship between remembering and painful symptoms that Dr. Pearlman suggests. "Once a patient can start remembering the trauma and is able to understand the connections between events and subsequent emotional experiences, there is a gradual reduction in the intensity and frequency of the intrusive nightmares, reenactments, or anxiety and panic attacks." He and Dr. Pearlman also make clear, however, that pain is not ameliorated simply by being reexperienced. While remembering trauma may be necessary to healing, regressing emotionally into a puddle is not. Talking about traumatic memories is not necessarily helpful in and of itself. Ordering the welter of impressions, incidents, and feelings that constitute psychological trauma into comprehensible form is what is helpful, for it gives survivors a sense of personal control where once there was none.

This Dr. Pearlman makes explicit in reassuringly conversational language. "I think survivors need answers to questions like, 'Why is it that my relationships have been so messed up all my life? Why is it that I can't stand myself?' The answers lie in traumatic events and experiences, and in the survivors' perceptions of them and themselves as the experiences happened."

While trauma experts agree that there is a cognitive benefit to memory retrieval and exploration, they also agree that healing lies on an experiential level as well. In therapy with a trauma expert, the historical experience of terror stripped of morality, sense, or comfort is supplanted by a more contemporary experience of terror eased by probity and insight. In the face of catastrophe a survivor feels abandoned by all sources of security. In therapy, this same survivor finds consolation and sanctuary. Abandonment is reversed and healing begins.

Memory exploration seems eminently sensible as a therapeutic technique when its process and purposes are described by trauma experts such as Drs. Pearlman and van der Kolk. But memory exploration in therapy has come under fire. The question, according to skeptics, is not whether exploration of relatively recent memories helps survivors understand their personal adaptations to human cruelty and reshape those adaptations now that the crisis of cruelty has passed. There seems little doubt that it does. But as Dr. George P. Ganaway, a medical consultant for dissociative disorders in the Adult Psychiatric Program at the Ridgeview Institute in Smyrna, Georgia, points out, memories recovered from events long past often have a "bizarre and exotic quality and [are retrieved in such] incredible quantity as to test the credulity of even the most empathic and open-minded therapist." The question at which skeptics have arrived, therefore, is about the value of rummaging for buried memories. More specifically, the question is whether even an artful attempt at rummaging can create memories of events that never occurred.

This is a volatile question, and one to which many people quickly adopt a partisan approach. Those who dare to recognize the fact of unmitigated human cruelty and to hold out to survivors the hope of recovery usually align themselves in solidarity with anyone claiming to be a survivor. While their position is laudable, it has its risks. First, uncritically accepting reports of cruelty may lead one to grossly over-determine the actual incidence of cruelty; over-determination may stretch society's capacity to believe and respond empathically to the breaking point. Second, false memories may implicate perfectly innocent people as perpetrators.

In opposition to those who risk over-determining the incidence of cruelty are those who underscore the potentially disastrous consequences of false accusations. They prefer to presume perpetrators innocent until proven guilty by something more conclusive than half-remembered descriptions of bizarre events. They probably under-determine the incidence of cruelty, but their position, too, is reasonable by virtue of shoring up indispensable Bill of Rights protections. It is also reasonable — though not necessarily wise or fair — by virtue of its function as psychological self-defense, an attempt on the part of its proponents to escape the truly intolerable expectation that humankind's seemingly limitless capacity for brutality places us all in peril.

Survivors need to find good therapists, and the issues raised by the polemic about disinterred memories are central to therapy. Skeptics' criticisms are largely based on sound research that points to ways in which even someone claiming to be an expert trauma therapist can irresponsibly and inadvertently revictimize survivors. Some survivors contemplating therapy fear just what the criticism implies.

Those fears need to be addressed. Abundant research has shown that adults who were victimized as children are virtual sitting ducks for further abuse. Moreover, a history of childhood victimization weakens an adult's psychological resilience to trauma. For any survivor of adult trauma who remains continuously off keel, there is at least a reasonable chance that therapy will exhume memories of long-forgotten childhood trauma. Because of this, any widely-discussed research merits — even demands — truly open-minded examination by survivors, their friends and family, and their therapists. Searching for value in the harshest of criticisms can, in fact, reassure survivors and those who care for and about them that the ground occupied by expert post-traumatic therapists is morally, theoretically, and practically quite defensible.

Scrutinizing the body of research concerning the credibility of disinterred childhood memories requires one to understand something about memory. Research over the last century has led investigators to believe that the popular conception of memory is grossly in error. Memory is not at all like home movies. A person doesn't mentally record images as they happen and play them back later in reliable sequence and focus. Rather, a person actively constructs memory as she remembers it. Furthermore, memory is made up of experience, the interpretation of which a person actively constructs as she experiences it.

Every time a person sees a tree, she does so in relation to the memory of the trees, tree-like objects, and non-tree-like objects she saw before. Not one of her perceptions is pure; all are contaminated — indeed, defined — by memories. Likewise, not one of her memories is pure. All are informed by an elaborate set of experientially-based expectations. Memory corrupts experience, and experience corrupts memory.

Perhaps more significantly to people concerned about the psychological aftershocks of trauma, emotions play some role in determining the memories to which a person will compare a new experience and the expectations with which she will interpret new memories. In other words, emotions distort memory both as it is encoded and as it is retrieved. And the degree of distortion is determined, in large part, by the intensity of the emotion at play. A person's most "memorable" moments are memorable, by definition, because of what she brought to the experience and what she brought to the remembering.

"Traumatized persons must come to terms with their pasts," writes Dr. Richard P. Kluft, Clinical Professor of Psychiatry, Temple University School of Medicine, and Visiting Lecturer in Psychiatry, Harvard Medical School. "However, their pasts are encoded in memory. Trauma distorts the memory process. Were past perceptions encoded accurately?

. . . Were the memories retained without contamination or alteration, or have they become adulterated? Has their retrieval been optimal, or has it occurred under circumstances that may possibly influence what is 're-trieved'? To what extent should we regard the possibility of contamination as a probability in the absence of data that points one way or the other? Furthermore, what are we to make of much of what is retrieved?"

The formulation relied on by trauma experts to resolve the question of the credibility of disinterred traumatic memories is rather tidy. By and large, rather than tackling this unanswerable question head-on, they draw a distinction between narrative truth and historical truth, and maintain that a knowledge of either has therapeutic value. Although trauma therapists are considered by some traditionalists to be the gadflies of modern psychiatry, in taking this creatively nonjudgmental position on the veracity of traumatic memories, trauma therapists have raised the ire of not even the most ardent traditionalists. In fact, they stand squarely in theoretical center field.

From Freud's time on, psychotherapists have assumed that narrative truth includes perception, emotion, and sensation born at the time of the event, and incorporates additional errors introduced by factors such as the passage of time and a therapist's fumbling. As such, narrative truth is neither precisely accurate nor unequivocally false. Historical truth, on the other hand, is less messy. It is the complete record of events as they happened. Its beauty lies in its precision. Its flaw is that it is usually anyone's guess.

For example, a twenty-six-year old man's narrative truth may include an episode from when he was four. He remembers ropes on his arms and legs, and his face being pushed into the carpet. He remembers screaming in pain. He remembers being unable to see his abuser, or even to know precisely what is happening to him. He remembers a television set blaring. He remembers thinking he is being branded in the posterior, rodeo-style.

Should this memory disturb the young man, part of his work with any good psychotherapist would be to refine these sensory images into a more elaborate narrative truth making logical sense. The man might process these fragments as follows: Because he was frequently left in the care of his alcoholic and violent father, he comes to believe that the assailant was his father. His therapist, trying to help him recover as much of the experience as possible, says, "I know you can't see anything but carpet. I know you are screaming so loudly that your own voice and the TV are all you can hear. But do you smell anything? At any point during the assault do you smell anything unusual? Smoke? Incense? Semen?"

The adult survivor leaps at this proffered clue: Yes. Semen. Searing posterior pain. He was raped by his father.

Who knows? He may have been. And he may not have been. In reworking the remembered fragments he has attempted to alight on historical truth. At best, because an incomplete set of verifiable details are available to him, he has only hovered above it. Most therapists of any theoretical persuasion would assume as much. An admittedly sweeping generalization, however, is that a therapist inexpert at post-traumatic therapy would be more likely than a trauma therapist to protect himself from the unspeakable truths of the young man's tale by holding the bulk of the tale as a clue to the tale teller's pathology, wondering privately, for example, why the young man insists on clinging to a self-concept of "victim." A good trauma therapist, on the other hand, would probably find most significant that, as a young boy, the survivor was shamelessly and violently abused in some way by someone. The trauma therapist would understand that the survivor's private experience of abuse requires attention. The trauma therapist would help the survivor examine his subsequent life problems and achievements in light of the aftershocks of being brutally hurt, intimidated, and humiliated. The trauma therapist would hold in mind that, regardless of their individual veracity, the remembered details and the story the adult survivor imposes on them help the adult survivor order into comprehensible form the impressions, incidents, and feelings that make up this incident of abuse and possibly an entire childhood of abuse. They help him understand a lifetime of preparing for and overreacting to threat. They give him a much-needed sense of personal control over trauma's emotional aftershocks in his life today.

All this being said, historical truth is not irrelevant, certainly not to the judicial system and certainly not to people who feel they have been preposterously accused. And the incredibility of some of their memories has not escaped survivors. On the contrary, the surreal quality of those memories convinces many survivors that they are not traumatized but crazy. The memories of this twenty-six-year old man, for example, might not stop at being raped by his father. He might eventually also remember being raped by both parents, or perhaps by groups of parents; perhaps not only by people but by beasts; perhaps not only by beasts but by Satan himself. For survivors like him and for those they accuse, questions of veracity are especially pressing. Are such memories gross distortions of the truth? If so, what causes such elaborate memory distortions when there is no attempt to deceive? If recovered memories can be anywhere from mildly to wildly inaccurate, what are the implications for therapy? For a survivor's relationship to the supposed abuser? What is the value of weaving such inaccuracies into one's life history?

The results of laboratory experiments about the reliability of eye-witness testimony begin to offer some answers to these questions. The answers are intriguing. For example, skeptics of the field of post-trau-matic therapy charge that a trauma therapist's questions can implant false memories of trauma. Eyewitness testimony experiments suggest that skeptics are right. Eyewitness testimony experiments have consistently demonstrated that biased questions can prejudice a witness's answer. For example, the impartial question "Did you see a gun?" can lead eyewit-nesses to a crime to remember a gun where there was none. And a lead-ing question such as "*Didn't* you see a gun?" steers not just some but many eyewitnesses into inaccurate reports.

Therapists practicing post-traumatic therapy have an informed bias. They believe that traumatic memories are sometimes so deeply sup-pressed that they are not readily available to the survivor's awareness. When these therapists see a client with no conscious memory of trauma but with some of the post-traumatic symptoms — for example, anxiety, depression, suicidal thoughts, dissociative habits, hypervigilance, sleep disturbances, concentration difficulties, self-loathing, nightmares, flash-backs, or problems with intimacy or addiction — they hypothesize that a buried trauma may lie at the symptoms' root. They begin to ask ques-tions, and herein lies the danger.

Even a seemingly innocuous inquiry (for example, "This anxiety, these fears about sex, are not necessarily pathological. For many people, they are born from experience. Do you think it is possible you were ever sexually abused as a child?") is not necessarily impartial. Predicated as it is in the disclosure that fear of sex might be rooted in childhood sexual abuse, the question is as loaded as a bombshell.

Admittedly, a direct question about sexual abuse can be asked with-out introductory remarks tying fears of sex to forgotten childhood sex-ual abuse. But even so, such a question insinuates a correlation between adult problems with intimacy and childhood sexual abuse and as such is inherently biased. And it is possible that no amount of careful shearing away of suggestions by a therapist can entirely correct that bias.

Hypnosis is often used during memory retrieval in post-traumatic therapy, partly to facilitate recall and partly to help survivors tolerate the emotional impact of remembering. As part of their assault on the pre-cepts of post-traumatic therapy, skeptics cite research about the distort-ing effects of hypnosis on memory. And again, the objections they raise are intriguing.

Laboratory experiments clearly and consistently demonstrate that, as a group, hypnotized subjects report more memories and more vivid memories than subjects who are not hypnotized. Hypnotized subjects do not, however, report more accurate memories. On the contrary, hypnosis seems to amplify the distorting effect that leading questions have on memory reporting.

For example, Dr. Elizabeth Loftus and researchers at the University of Washington in Seattle introduced complex, credible, but entirely false episodes into the memory of young subjects simply by asking leading questions such as, "Do you remember the time when, at the age of five, you were lost in a shopping mall?" At Carleton University in Ottawa, the late Dr. Nicholas P. Spanos used leading questions with hypnotized subjects to successfully introduce elaborate memories of past lives — memories that the experiments' subjects frequently continued to accept as true regardless of how preposterous they sounded.

At first glance, the implications of the studies by Loftus and Spanos seem alarming, so much so that skeptics of post-traumatic therapy frequently lob leading questions and hypnosis data as dialectical grenades of first choice. Likewise, to even mention the names Loftus and Spanos in survivor movement circles without simultaneously sneering can be tantamount to taking one's life into one's hands.

Reasonable people, however, need not leap lustily into the fray. Drs. Loftus and Spanos's data are astonishing. The data on eyewitness testimony seem only mildly less so. This does not necessarily mean, however, that memory retrieval has no place in therapy or that hypnosis has no place in memory retrieval. What it does mean is that memory retrieval must be responsibly paced and conducted. What it does mean is that, just as a capacity to empathize with unspeakable truths distinguishes trauma therapists, an ability to responsibly conduct and pace memory retrieval and to help survivors carefully interpret disinterred memories distinguishes competent trauma therapists from incompetent ones.

Some overzealous therapists undoubtedly do help clients misinterpret memory. This can create enormous problems for therapy clients and for their implicated perpetrators. Unfortunately, as experimental data suggest, it probably doesn't take much bumbling on the part of a therapist to lead a client astray from historical truth. Confabulation and reporting biases seem to be in the nature of memory retrieval. However, where an incautious therapist rushes in to root out memory and then sanctify every aspect and implication of the memories reported, expert trauma therapists tread more cautiously. Acutely aware that the form of the question may contaminate what is remembered, most therapists expert in post-traumatic therapy are exceedingly careful about how they phrase their questions. In initiating hypnosis, expert trauma therapists avoid using provocative phrases like, "You will remember every trauma as it happened!" that can lead to very creative memories. And when a line of inquiry produces traumatic memories that stretch the limits of either the therapist's or survivor's ability to believe, an expert therapist can help the survivor examine what functions distortions in memory may have served the survivor both when experiencing trauma and when remembering.

Dr. George Ganaway of the Ridgeview Institute articulates the responsibly cautious stance of post-traumatic therapy regarding the accuracy of memories when he writes, "No matter how compelling seems the need to validate every traumatic memory in the service of promoting a healing experience, it must be kept in mind that the patient has on the deepest level, deeper than the transference wish to be believed, protected, and nurtured, entered into a therapeutic alliance with the good faith and expectation that the therapist always will remain firmly grounded in reality, and will help the patient carefully sift through the mixture of fact, fantasy and illusion, eventually to settle on what the patient must decide is his or her final truth."

With vigilance, the problem of contamination of a client's narrative truth with a therapist's expectations might be no less serious than it is in any form of therapy. For, as social psychologist Carol Tavris drolly observed to the *New York Times,* the quandary is ubiquitous. "[P]eople in psychoanalysis have Freudian dreams, people in Jungian therapy have archetypal dreams, people in primal scream therapy remember being born and people in past-lives therapy remember being Julius Caesar (or whoever)."

Unfortunately, the matter is not so blithely settled. While contamination is not unique to post-traumatic therapy, it is true that the memories of some people are more easily corrupted by a therapist's questions than those of others. Experts in post-traumatic therapy, such as Dr. Ganaway, readily acknowledge that people who, as young children, experienced ongoing or systematic human cruelty are among the group of people whose memories may be easily corrupted. This is because many adopted dissociation as a response to trauma and incorporated it at an early age into their lifelong behavioral style. And dissociation, a sometimes trancelike change in memory, identity, awareness, and volition, is widely considered by experts in the field of research about hypnosis and memory to be a form of autohypnosis.

In fact, Dr. Ganaway suggests that when survivors dissociate they are, in effect, "moving in and out of hypnotic trance states, no matter what the therapists' intent may be regarding the use of hypnotic techniques." Observing that people who use dissociation as a psychological defense are actually more easily hypnotized in laboratory situations than other clinical groups, Dr. Ganaway also notes, "Further compounding the risk of inaccuracy of memories . . . is evidence that high hypnotizables feel more compelled than low hypnotizables to fill in memory gaps with confabulated fantasies when pressed for details. . . . These data suggest that . . . [such] patients should be considered at high risk for contamination by pseudomemories in the hands of therapists who unwittingly or not, verbally or otherwise, cue them to respond to the therapists' expectations or needs."

The very people reporting histories of extreme abuse are probably the people most likely to confuse reality with illusion. This has been acknowledged by Dr. Ganaway and by experts throughout the field of post-traumatic therapy. Oddly, this acknowledgment has not been co-opted by skeptics of post-traumatic therapy and used to fuel the debate. Skeptics' failure to do so is probably not due to negligence, however. Instead they may simply have recognized that exploiting the acknowledgment that the most bizarre memories do not always reflect historical truth would catch them in a polemical dilemma.

By their very silence, even skeptics of post-traumatic therapy seem to concur that, grotesque as some of the tales of extremely dissociative people may be, these tales are not completely confabulated. Post-traumatic therapy has not imposed scars on otherwise clean psyches. Rather, long-term, catastrophic, and inescapable abuse has stripped some people of their ability to create a credible narrative of themselves. The particulars of some stories may be wrong, even fatuously so; but the essence of those stories—"The world is not safe; I have been reduced, destroyed"—is dead right.

There is an unsolvable flaw in historical truth: It is unknowable. The unsolvable flaw in narrative truth is that, for anyone, it is biased by many factors, including suggestions from other people. What is clear from experiments concerning hypnosis and memory is that if one believes that hoodlums carry guns, given the right cues and conditions, eyewitnesses to a crime can remember a gun where there was none. If one believes in reincarnation and sees oneself as having a certain under-recognized majesty, given the right cues and conditions, one can probably remember being Julius Caesar. If one believes that childhood sexual abuse is epidemic and one felt victimized as a child by insensitive adults, given the right cues and conditions, one can probably remember being raped as a four-year-old, perhaps not by a stranger but a parent, perhaps not only by a parent but by groups of parents, perhaps not only by people but by beasts, perhaps not only by beasts but by Satan himself.

This conclusion is troubling. It has been reached by skeptics of the field of post-traumatic therapy. But it has also been reached by post-traumatic therapy's most ardent advocates. The difference between the skeptics and the advocates is this: Skeptics take the evidence about bias and confabulation and disbelieve survivors out of hand. Advocates weigh the evidence about bias and confabulation against what they know about themselves.

Advocates know that survivors' testimony about abuse makes them, the listeners, angry and fearful. When they become angry and fearful, they remind themselves that almost no cruelty is outside the realm of possibility. And they remind themselves that if dissociative people are the least credible, this may be because they were the most severely abused. Not only do their trauma-born dissociative habits have them wandering in and out of hypnotic trance; these same habits infect their truth-telling style, making them seem wooden, unreliable, even hallucinatory. Doubting such people is far easier than believing.

Advocates also weigh the evidence about bias and confabulation against what they know about survivors' fear, shame, and self-blame. They know that discounting stark evidence is inescapably human, and that, because survivors are only human, they sometimes discount stark evidence about their own lives. Advocates know that because the truth can be so difficult for survivors to face, their stories may change with each telling. They know that the shifting sands of survivors' tales can make the stories seem crazy; even worse, they can make the survivors feel crazy. And advocates for survivors know that feeling crazy may be easier for a survivor than accepting the full reality of what transpired.

Advocates for survivors know that even the tales that are clearly untrue are not to be derided. Instead, listeners should find them the most chilling tales of all. This position is well articulated by Dr. Ganaway, who explains that outlandish memories can "represent dissociatively mediated distortions and fantasies created in an effort to achieve mastery and psychic restitution in the wake of genuine and factual trauma of a more prosaic (but not necessarily less heinous) nature." In other words, the truth of some survivors' tales is so harrowing that rather than construct a narrative truth approximating reality, they create grotesque decoy memories, thus terrifying themselves perhaps to the point of madness but handily resolving for themselves memory fragments implicating, for example, a parent as predatory. If Dr. Ganaway is correct, we cannot find comfort in discounting even the most incredible of survivors' tales. Rather, the tales we feel most comfortable belittling as patently untrue are the ones we should find most disconcerting; the historical truth may be far more sinister than the decoy.

Finally, advocates know that there is a yet larger danger than revictimization in tuning out the tales survivors tell. Sometimes the most preposterous tales of atrocity are true. Witness the Holocaust. Witness Bosnia. Had anyone in a position to act given even a smattering of belief to early survivors' tales, genocide, ethnic cleansing, and rape as military bludgeon might been greatly impeded.

The answers to questions of veracity are too costly to be decreed by popular vote derived from prejudiced debate. As a society we need to understand that, while not every memory is credible, not every denial is factual. We need to think about the consequences of human cruelty clearly and about our obligations to both survivors and alleged perpetrators. This is not to say that people on either side of the argument should refrain from emotion or bridle their passion. Outrage is necessary; it can fuel social change. But if we value a society of order and decency, even righteous anger must be tempered. By remaining clearheaded, we can inform our speech with analysis, not just attitude. We can become activists on behalf of our beliefs, not just acolytes of them.

* * *

Six weeks after I first met Madeline Goodman, I returned for a second visit with her and her therapist. At the time of this second visit, Madeline had been in post-traumatic therapy for about seven and a half months, talking about her memories of incest and of the gang rape, and exploring how the aftermath of incest and rape influences her present behavior. Over the past months, Madeline had insisted that memory exploration proceed at a more accelerated pace than her therapist would have preferred. But Madeline seems to have been up to the task of intense memory exploration. Her recovery to date has been remarkable. She seems much less dissociative than she was only six weeks before. Her therapist says that seven months ago, Madeline spent most of each session looking at the floor, seeming forever caught up in the experience of trauma. Today she seems quite present. She has a very easy, happy manner as we go over the transcript I made of our previous meeting. She offers corrections and additions to the transcript.

Then Madeline turns to her therapist, saying that she would like to discuss a certain memory she has retrieved. Immediately, her natural beauty, which is readily apparent when she feels confident, becomes completely obscured by fear. I am struck by the difference in her appearance. Fear distorts her facial features and seems to transform the way she moves. The athletic grace of the self-confident Madeline is completely gone. Although she doesn't seem to have dissociated psychically, she does seem changed.

A reminder is in order here. During the most brutal part of a night in which Madeline was raped by twenty-seven men, the rapists physically stopped her from screaming by putting a sock in her mouth. The sock obstructed Madeline's breathing. In order to stay alive she had to get them to keep the sock out of her mouth. To accomplish this, she agreed not to make noises that could be heard. But in order to mentally endure the rape, she had to scream. As a compromise of sorts, Madeline timed her screams to coincide with an intermittent fog horn.

Madeline: "Last night I had a nightmare about the rape. And then this morning I had to take my dog to the vet's and that place is real close to the bay, and it was really foggy and the fog horns started to blow and it was uncomfortable for me. I could still talk to the vet, but I got afraid."

Therapist: "Is there anything you've found that helps, like talking to yourself or taking deep breaths or grounding yourself where you are then?"

Madeline: "I had the dog in my hands and I think that helped, because I care about the dog a lot. I haven't really figured out a way of calming myself down completely, but I think when I become conscious of my breathing in and out, that seems to help. [Long pause.] Remember the time I thought the ant creatures from outer space were in my room? I was scared because I thought it was proof that I was crazy and you showed me that this 'memory' was my mind's way of telling me that something was not right, and there's this alien force in me, controlling me. And as soon as you said that it made so much sense, and it gave me so much relief, because that's the way it is, that's the way my mind was working."

Therapist: "But you had spent much of your life being afraid that things like that were a sign that you were crazy, instead of knowing, or ever being told, that the way your mind worked made sense if you just understood the context."

Madeline: "I wanted to talk today to you about a memory. I think I brought it up before about that ESP sensation while I was in the shower. I got the sensation of a train coming. I was about fifteen years old, I was in the shower washing my hair, a train is coming, and someone's thinking about me a lot, and that's coming through in my mind as an ESP. I don't know who it is who's thinking about me, and they're asking for help, and then suddenly it stops and it's over. Then I get the paper in the

Madeline's therapist:

"Madeline 'remembered' that a flying saucer had landed and that alien creatures that looked like ants had come into her bedroom at night and put things up her nose. She was sure this had happened and she was very worried about telling me because she was afraid it would make me think she was crazy. As we talked about it, we came to understand that it was a way of remembering, at a time before she could allow herself to remember, that something alien and horrific had come into her world and changed things forever. We talked about the image of something being put up her nose as a displacement of an image of a rape. The alien beings were about the loss of what was familiar to her at the occurrence of the rape and it was as though what happened was so alien that it made her feel alienated from everyone. She talked about walking around school and everyone pointing to her, "That's the one," as though she were an alien from outer space. As we came to understand it not as a psychotic delusion but as a way of holding a memory she was not ready to face, she became fascinated and delighted with the resourcefulness of her mind. She calmed down enormously and was delighted in her ability to survive. And it really was wonderful."

morning and I see where a friend of mine has put his head on the tracks until the train came and decapitated him. But now when I think back about it, I see myself younger, I see myself with about four other kids my age running along the railroad tracks, and I see a football shape coming over and it has eyes on it. And it's shooting across in the air about thirty feet, swinging towards us. And I'm not sure if I was there when my friend died or not, but very likely if that did happen around dusk it seems that I could have been. I think one of the kids I was with dared my friend to do something like that and because he was taking LSD, I think, he did it."

Therapist: "So you may have witnessed...?"

Madeline: "I think that was his head zooming by! I remember my friend Margo hollering 'Run, run!' and we all ran away. I never made a connection."

Therapist: "That seems like a really frightening memory."

Madeline: "I'm not sure if it is a memory. I'm not sure."

Therapist: "When did that image come to you, that image of the kids, and seeing the head?"

Madeline: "It was last night."

Therapist: "What feelings came with that?"

Madeline: "Confusion. Because I didn't know he was going to do that."

Therapist: "Do you think that you were there when he was dared?"

Madeline: "I think I was there only like three minutes prior to when he was dared. I think the kids were razzing him a long time before I even showed up. But I thought it was a football. 'What's that?' I thought it was a football. And Margo said, 'Run, run!' I think she knew exactly what it was. Margo lives just a few towns over. I can get in touch with her, but whether she'd tell me the truth or not I don't know. Because Margo was also at the gang rape. I remember seeing her walk by me as I was getting injected with the drug. The papers listed the rape as a conspiracy, so I don't know how much she was in on it, and she was neighbors with the pregnant girl who took me. I don't know why these people would be mad at me. I don't know why they would pick on me. I was not a vicious kid. I was always nice."

Therapist: "Is remembering Margo at the gang rape a new memory?"

Madeline: "Not one that I trusted, so I wouldn't bring it out. Similar to how I feel today. I don't dare trust this memory, because I'm so searching for truth. And I'd hate to find out that, 'Hey, that is not a memory.' That would kind of like mean I'm insane, I think. If you can't trust your memories, I mean, where are you?"

Therapist: "Memories are very complicated things. There's a reason for each memory, and there's always a kernel of truth in it. But we shape memories over time. It's not unusual for a memory to be a screen memory, which means that you can put together different events into one. That doesn't mean the memory is a lie. It's a condensation. It's like shorthand. But it's only over time that you start to sort screen memories out and know that about them. Sorting them out is a matter of taking seriously what you remember and looking at the images, looking at the pieces. Yeah, they may shift and sort themselves out over time. But that doesn't mean you're crazy. That's just how the human memory works.

"You're sorting out some complicated things right now. A memory of the sensation in the shower, of what it felt like to read the account of someone you knew who had committed suicide by putting his head on the railroad tracks and being decapitated, of a scene of a head flying through the air, of kids razzing and teasing and verbally taunting and tormenting someone. [Madeline's eyes fill with tears.] You look like you're feeling sad."

Madeline: "Well, when I think of that dog that got burnt the night I was raped. . . . I feel worse for the dog than I do for myself, even though they left me for dead."

Therapist: "That dog was even more helpless than you were."

Madeline: "Yes. And the way they—that one girl was over there trying to calm it down, putting her hands all over it, and then the dog's getting drenched with the gasoline and they're patting it in to make sure it's saturated in. The dog wagging its tail, it likes all the hands on it."

Therapist: "That's a cruelty that you're familiar with, a cruelty that masquerades as affection. Abuse that masquerades as affection."

Madeline [Crying]: "It is, it's a trick, a terrible trick."

Therapist: "And you've been tricked." [Madeline cries for a while.]

Madeline: "I went to the city library and did some microfilm research, hoping to find the headline that actually flashed into my mind when I first remembered."

Therapist: "Which headline?"

Madeline: "In my mind, like a flashbulb going off, and it said 'Rapists at Large'—that's all I got. I saw it in big, bold type. But there was no such big headline! Just a small one. I guess I saw in my mind the kind of headline I felt the rape deserved."

Therapist: "Yes. It may be that the day that headline was in the paper those words jumped out at you, so in your mind they were big and bold. The headline screamed at you when you read it, and although even then you didn't consciously remember being at the rape, some part of you recognized it. So what you may be remembering is an emotional response to it that translates it into the appropriate type size."

Madeline: "Memory is amazing! That is something."

Therapist: "Well, it involves feelings. And when you put together how you feel about something with the facts, it has a very particular tone. It's not just any old memory, it's the memory and what it meant to you."

Madeline: "Well, I had no idea that memory involved so many feelings, that memory connects with feelings. But of course!"

Therapist: "When you've had a traumatic event, your memory gets broken into different parts. What you had to do to protect yourself during and immediately after the rape was split your memory apart. Your body was in intense pain, and your feelings were so powerful that they would overwhelm you. So you buried both your physical pain and your emotions."

Madeline: "When I began to remember, my anus and vagina — in fact my whole torso — hurt for probably six weeks. I was careful to sit down gently. I think even seeing you, I had trouble walking. And I never remember ever having that before. Even the next day following the rape, I don't remember being in any pain at all."

Therapist: "You were still in shock."

Madeline: "It is better knowing, it is better having my memories. It's better because my history makes so much sense — why I was sexually dysfunctional, why I was into drugs so heavily, alcohol. It makes so much sense. I mean, this is a way of escape and not ever dealing with what's bothering me. It makes so much sense. My whole life makes sense now. The 'How come,' the 'Why.'"

Therapist: "Paradoxically, as well as being a way of escaping what happened, it was also a way of remembering. I remember early on when we talked about how having a lot of different sexual partners and relationships that were not caretaking in effect repeated the rape over and over. And it was like, although you didn't remember the rape, your body was trying to master it in some way. I think the same with the drugs and alcohol. Yes, you were trying to deaden feelings, but you were also putting yourself into an altered state of consciousness, perhaps trying to master the altered state of consciousness you were forced into by being injected by drugs against your will."

Madeline: "That's amazing, that my mind was screaming out like that to me in those ways."

Therapist: "I think that's been under-recognized, that the paradox about symptoms and ways of coping is that they're usually *both* — ways to escape and ways to remember and reenact."

Madeline: "It's the mind's way of surviving and of coping. So I don't go insane. I think I did a good job."

Therapist: "You have survived. And you're not insane."

* * *

About the time of America's revolutionary war, Franz Anton Mesmer, an Austrian physician working in France, believed that by passing magnets over the bodies of people who had imbibed a liquid laced with iron, he could cure anything that ailed them. His doctrine: "There is only one illness and one healing." At some point during the cure ceremony, Mesmer's patient would convulse in frenzy, slip from frenzy to deep sleep, and then awaken to find physical ailments much improved. Eventually Mesmer found that metal bars were superfluous to the rite. In the context of a streamlined but highly ritualized cure ceremony, Mesmer's touch alone could heal. Mesmer explained this feat by claiming that all people were filled with a mysterious fluid called "animal magnetism." In sick people, the fluid was less equally distributed in the body than in healthy people. Mesmer's own magnetism, which he held to be impressively compelling, could realign magnetic imbalances in sick people.

The animal magnetism of Mesmer's pupil, Amand-Marie-Jacques de Chastenet, the Marquis de Puységur, seemed equally impressive. In fact, de Puységur claimed an animal magnetism so strong that he could effect cure simply by talking. In the midst of the talking ceremony, the patient would fall into what de Puységur called "magnetic sleep," in which the patient could diagnose his or her own disease and prescribe his or her own cure.

Whatever their methods, Mesmer and de Puységur did seem to be mesmerizing patients, if not into good health, at least into symptom remission. But their cure-all claims met with much skepticism — so much so that the French government called together an official investigative commission on animal magnetism. The commissioners included Benjamin Franklin (residing in France at that time as an American diplomat) and the French chemist Antoine-Laurent Lavoisier. The commissioners observed cure ceremonies and concluded that there was nothing particularly magnetic or curative about mesmerizing. On the contrary, whatever cures the mesmerizers had effected had undoubtedly been imaginary.

Of course, the esteemed commissioners were probably right in dismissing the curative powers of metals. They were also right to call what they had seen imaginary, if what they meant by the term "imaginary" was something along the lines of "centered in the mind." They were less than astute, however, if they equated the imaginary with the fictitious, for what the commissioners had observed, perhaps without realizing it, were the very real curative powers of the mind. They had watched the mind anesthetize pain. When they saw it violently and abruptly induce physical purgation and then ease the body into calm, they undoubtedly saw the mind banish substantially debilitating symptoms.

The commissioners are to be forgiven if they did, indeed, fail to realize that the illnesses they saw cured were centered in the mind, that psychogenic illnesses can genuinely cripple, and that a cure that mends the psychic rift causing the illness is not itself fictitious but powerfully real. Mesmer's time predated any significant scholarly thinking about mental illness or health by more than a century. But it is still somewhat ironic that the investigators conducting history's first scientific inquiry into the curative powers of metals ended their investigation without expressing astonishment at the evident curative powers of the mind and, of course, of hypnosis, for it was undoubtedly the sometimes ritualistic but always enchanting quality of the mesmeric ceremonies that suggested precisely to the patients' minds the cures they needed to effect. Dismissing claims about the curative powers of metals without commenting on the evident curative powers of the mind was tantamount to walking out of a barn on fire and reporting only the suspicious absence of ice.

Eventually de Puységur himself realized that patients' recoveries had less to do with the magnetizer's magnetism than with the magnetizer's will. But despite de Puységur's defection from the ranks of the mesmerists, and regardless of the opinion of France's official commission of inquiry, the next century saw French physicians again mesmerizing patients.

In the early 1800s, the induction ceremonies of Mesmer's loyalists presaged the carnival cliché of hypnotism popular today. The mesmerizer began the ceremony by interminably swinging a nickel before the patient's eyes. Because a successfully mesmerized patient could experience major surgery as painless, the loyalists believed they had finally proven the existence of animal magnetism. However, while observing a physician mesmerize a patient, the editor of the London medical journal *Lancet* surreptitiously switched a lead coin for the mesmerizer's nickel one. Because lead is virtually nonmagnetic, once again it became evident that all the talk of magnetism was nonsense. This time, however, the scientific elite caught on to what they had seen: the will power of the magnetizer, the suggestibility of the patient, and the rapport between magnetizer and patient.

Over the next several decades, inquiries into the power of suggestion were considered scientifically legitimate, with investigators coining the term "hypnosis"—after Hypnos, the Greek god of sleep—to divorce their work from the now debunked work of Franz Mesmer. These decades were a time in Europe of fledgling but intense interest in physiology, pharmacology, and neurology. These decades also saw the beginnings of scholarly inquiry into whether psychological processes could be distinct from physical ones. Psychology, however, was still a bit of an outlaw study. At that time, nearly all thinking people weighed in on the side of the physiological in the debate of psychological vs. physiological explanations for behaviors and illnesses.

Jean-Martin Charcot, a Parisian and the world's leading neurologist, was no exception. But he was a highly curious man, and he was loath to allow his own prejudices to cloud his scientific judgment. During the 1860s, Charcot was appointed chief physician in one of the largest sections of Paris's Hopital Salpêtrière, a medical poorhouse for women. There, Charcot had an unparalleled opportunity to study hundreds of neurology patients. Some had rare or unknown neurological diseases and functioned as an invaluable resource for his neurological observations. But even Charcot had to admit that some seemed to have no organic disorders whatsoever; he believed that their strange behaviors, instead of being organically rooted, mimicked the symptoms of common diseases and convulsive disorders. Curious about how his patients had come to such a state of affairs, Charcot placed these women under hypnosis and asked them about the roots of their illnesses. And almost routinely, they explained that they had been either thoroughly and constantly beaten or thoroughly and constantly sexually abused, sometimes as adults, but almost always as children.

Two decades later, Charcot used the understanding he gleaned about trauma and illness from the women of the Salpêtrière in resolving a dispute involving railway companies and their insurers. In the 1880s, railways proliferated, criss-crossing the Western world. Railway accidents became increasingly common and an enormous international hue and cry was being raised over whether financial compensation was owed people suffering "railway spine" and "railway brain," since often no muscular, neurological, or bone damage could be found.

Charcot entered the debate, claiming that both sides of the argument were right and both were wrong. True, some people with railway spine and railway brain showed no detectable signs of neurological, muscular, or bone damage. However, one could not assume that such people were willfully malingering. He compiled his argument and evidence as follows:

First, Charcot compared the symptoms of the hysterical paralyses he had observed in abused women at the Salpêtrière with the symptoms of paralysis he observed in three men whose disabilities followed a traumatic accident but in whom no relevant neurological, bone, or muscular damage could be found. Charcot identified an exact symptom match between the two groups. At the same time, Charcot was able to point out clear differences between the symptoms shared by the three men and the abused women and those of people suffering paralysis clearly caused by an organic lesion.

Next, Charcot went so far as to experimentally and exactly reproduce the three men's traumatic paralyses in subjects placed in hypnotic trance and to reverse the hypnotic paralyses hypnotically. At the time, hypnosis was considered to be one of the few indisputably psychological phenomena. If debilitating physical paralysis could be hypnotically induced, Charcot suggested, perhaps railway brain and railway spine could be physical manifestations of legitimate psychological injuries.

To test this suggestion, Charcot next took it upon himself to demonstrate how psychological injuries might result in debilitating physical manifestations. He chose healthy subjects who had before proven easily hypnotizable. While they were in trance, he suggested to them that once out of trance, a mere slap on their backs would paralyze their arms. When they were brought out of trance, the experiment's subjects were unable to recall Charcot's hypnotic suggestion. But once they were slapped on the back, their arms became paralyzed. This, in effect, demonstrated that a psychological factor operating completely outside a person's conscious awareness could cause real functional paralysis.

In concluding his experiments, Charcot speculated that the nervous shock following traumata such as a railway accident might place some people in a state of permanent somnambulism. For such people, a stressor as apparently insignificant as a slap on the back might produce quite significant impairment, even in the complete absence of organic injury.

Charcot had not joined the debate simply to clarify matters for the railway and insurance companies. He had entered as a scholar, intrigued with a question about nosology, or the classification of diseases. Were there three types of paralysis, as commonly thought (traumatic, occurring in the aftermath of a trauma such as a railway disaster but in the absence of clear evidence of neurological, bone, or muscular damage; hysterical, as seen in women reporting histories of extreme childhood abuse; and organic, clearly resulting from a neurological, bone, or muscular problem)? Were there four types (traumatic, hysterical, organic, and hypnotic)? Or were there simply two (organic and traumatic/hysterical/hypnotic)?

Charcot suggested that there were simply two types of paralysis, and that traumatic, hysterical, and hypnotic paralyses should be grouped under the rubric "dynamic," for all three, he said, seemed psychologically rooted and all three, he predicted, would consistently prove psychologically mutable. But although he had single-handedly demonstrated that psychological pathologies could be distinct from physiological ones, to the very end, Charcot remained studiously uninterested in the prospect of a dynamic, therapeutic psychology. At what seems to have been his finest moment, Charcot walked away from his line of inquiry.

Fortunately, at least two of his students—Pierre Janet and Sigmund Freud—did care about psychological treatments for psychological problems. Exploring the nature and many manifestations of disorders they suspected were dynamic, each man eventually devised lasting cures counteracting those disorders' real-life causes.

Pierre Martin Janet began his professional life as a philosopher. He became a neurologist under Charcot's tutelage and eventually headed Charcot's laboratory of psychological research at the Hopital Salpêtrière. Here he found deranged patients with the by now predictable tremors, tics, and paralyses. But by talking at length with these women, Janet also noticed that many appeared to have developed more than one well-established personality, each with a discrete life history sometimes unknown to the other personality or personalities.

At that time, the popular scientific view of memory proposed that memories were retrieved through the association of related ideas. To explain the parallel life histories and amnesias that he observed in women with multiple personalities, Janet coined the term "dissociation" and wondered about why a person might not be able to associate certain ideas into memories. Simply talking to his clients gave him the answer: They had been abused in ways too horrible to either fully experience or dare to remember. Janet used hypnosis to help patients associate dissociated ideas, put the memories into words, and experience the painful emotions associated with the memories.

Janet found that by helping patients dissolve dissociative barriers he could not only relieve tics, tremors, and paralyses, but help them function as a single personality. In so doing, Janet effectively combined Mesmer's chicanery and Charcot's nosological observations into a clinically useful basis for treatment.

Being a modest and scientifically cautious man, Janet never expanded his theories on dissociation to encompass a larger psychology. This Freud did, basing his early theories, in large part, on the work of his colleague, Josef Breuer.

Breuer was an eminent Austrian physician who had treated a young woman, Anna O. This young woman exhibited a familiar battery of hysterical symptoms: paralysis of three limbs, disturbed sleep and a revulsion towards food. Furthermore, Anna O. seemed possessed of two distinct states of consciousness. One of her personalities was depressed and anxious but socially ordinary; the other was wayward, rebellious, and unpredictable. Breuer hypnotised Anna O. to help her recall what for her were traumatic memories about nursing her father through his fatal illness. He then used what Anna O. nicknamed the "talking cure" to help her grapple in a non-hypnoid state with her emotional responses to those memories.

In 1885, having been thoroughly briefed by Breuer about the Anna O. case, Freud arrived on Charcot's doorstep, proposing to talk with Charcot about the long-term psychological impact of childhood trauma and the therapeutic possibilities of Breuer's "talking cure." Charcot was far more interested in categorizing patients' symptoms than in curing them. In his four months at the Hopital Salpêtrière, Freud didn't succeed in interesting Charcot in his line of inquiry. But he hardly walked away from his time at the Salpêtrière empty handed. Rather he brought with him a body of information about dissociation, hypnosis, and post-hypnotic suggestion.

Combining what he learned from Charcot and Janet with what he had learned from Breuer, Freud gave birth to modern psychoanalysis. He staunchly held that psychological processes can be distinct from physical ones; that myriad secrets can lie behind manifest physical or emotional symptoms; that rapport between therapist and client can create a suggestibility in the waking state that is as curatively powerful as that in the hypnotic state; and that while trauma can cause emotional harm, remembering can heal.

Although Anna O.'s wayward personality had some fairly bawdy behaviors, the ever-proper Breuer had never asked his famous patient about the possibility of sexual trauma in her past. But inspired by the findings of Charcot and Janet, Freud did vigorously ask his own patients about links between adult hysteria and childhood sexual trauma. Making deliberate inquiries into the deeply private pasts of his patients, he found that a remarkable number of traumatic memories concerned very early sexual experiences.

In 1895, Freud and Breuer together published *Studies on Hysteria*, which introduced a theory of trauma-driven dissociation. It was poorly received in the medical world, and Breuer seemed not only embarrassed by the book's failure but increasingly uncomfortable with the far-reaching conclusions that Freud was beginning to derive from his blunt questions about sexual pasts. Breuer was willing to concede that "sexuality is one of the great components of hysteria." But he recoiled from Freud's insinuations that sexuality might be hysteria's essential component.

This, however, was the very idea that Freud was formulating. At an 1896 meeting of the Society for Psychiatry and Neurology in Vienna, Freud presented a brilliantly argued paper, "The Aetiology of Hysteria," in which he presented well-marshalled evidence that the symptoms of hysteria are a direct result of childhood sexual trauma. The paper was not only frostily received; it was lampooned. The chair of that evening's meeting called it a "scientific fairy tale."

If European intelligentsia had been able to tolerate Charcot's, Janet's, and Breuer's polite speculations that hysteria can be based in childhood trauma, no one, not even Breuer, could stomach Freud's insistence that childhood trauma is always sexual. For considering the prevalence of hysteria among middle and upper class women (and among the families of eminent doctors and neurologists), Freud's theory implied volumes about the sexual deportment of his friends.

At first, Freud's response to the general intellectual boycott of his ideas was one of defiant rebelliousness. But as Breuer, too, withdrew his support, Freud was deprived of his cherished friend and partner in curiosity. Although he never succeeded in retrieving Breuer's friendship, Freud eventually softened his rebellious stance. In a letter of September 21, 1897 to his friend Wilhelm Fliess, he announced that most of the childhood rapes his patients had reported to him were probably fantasies. Indeed, he expressed astonishment at ever having believed that sexual perversions in adults could be common.

Correspondence between Freud and Fliess shows that for a while after his September 21, 1897 letter, Freud waffled about the extent to which he believed his patients' stories of childhood sexual abuse. Then, in 1898, Freud began formally inching away from the position he had taken in "The Aetiology of Hysteria." He published a paper, "Sexuality in the Aetiology of the Neuroses." That paper defended his rigorous investigation of the sexual lives and pasts of patients. But it failed to make any definitive declaration about whether memories of childhood sexual experiences are real or imagined.

Regardless of whether and for how long Freud toyed with the idea that his patients may have been right about themselves and their pasts, it is undeniable that Freud became progressively more entranced with the idea that adult hysteria resulted from adults' internal fantasies as children. In a 1905 publication, *Three Essays on the Theory of Sexuality*, Freud decidedly relegated his female patients' reports of rapes by their fathers to the realm of fantasy. He attributed those fantasies to an excess of sexual affection on the part of the child for the father. Thus, *Three Essays on the*

Theory of Sexuality proposed that hysteria is an effect of children's thwarted lust for adults and not an effect of adults' unthwarted lust for children.

Clearly, *Three Essays on the Theory of Sexuality* constituted quite a recast of psychoanalysis.

Ultimately, Freud and his direct intellectual descendants expanded Freud's morally questionable but socially acceptable Oedipal theory into an elaborate general theory of the mind that identified every mental disorder from manic depression to fear of snakes as a disguised representation of an unpleasant and unrealized fantasy. While Freudian metapsychology has proven clinically useful for many, many people, it overlooks the possibility that while some imagine their injuries, others have injuries that are quite real.

What Janet called dissociated, Freud called unconscious and repressed. What Janet called traumatically-rooted, Freud called neurotic. Janet assumed that the therapy helpful to trauma survivors would not necessarily be useful in a watered-down version to everyone. Freud, on the other hand, seems to have overgeneralized. In the early part of his career, he assumed that the only significant psychological trauma occurs in childhood and, furthermore, is always sexual. Both empirical evidence and common sense suggest that he was stretching a point. Then, later in his career, Freud assumed that therapy helpful to people whose troubles are not trauma-driven would work for trauma survivors as well.

It hasn't. Unless the therapist incorporates into clinical practice a recognition of and appropriate response to the ongoing devastation that can be wreaked by real-life trauma, conventional therapeutic approaches are disappointing in the treatment of emotional disorders born of traumatic stress. And they are virtually worthless in the treatment of the multiple personality phenomenon studied by Janet and Breuer.

With the waxing of Freud's theories came the waning of serious investigation into dissociation and into the phenomenon of multiple personalities. As the years progressed, more often than not, adults experiencing mental health problems because they had been repeatedly and sadistically traumatized as children were misdiagnosed, for example, as schizophrenic, manic depressive, or epileptic. Some were treated with pharmaceutical weaponry that was brutally off the mark.

In 1980, at the same time that the American Psychiatric Association's *Diagnostic and Statistical Manual of Mental Disorders* (3rd ed.) first incorporated post-traumatic stress disorder as a distinct diagnostic entity, it also braved distinguishing multiple personality disorder (MPD) from the mental disorders with which it had long been confused. (The 1994 *Di-*

agnostic and Statistical Manual renamed MPD "dissociative identity disorder." However, "MPD" is still the most common way in which therapists and, indeed, people in general refer to multiple personality disorder.) Shortly after the publication of the 1980 manual, the National Institutes of Mental Health released the results of a retrospective survey of one hundred people diagnosed as having MPD. Ninety-seven percent of the survey's respondents reported experiencing significant, ongoing physical or sexual trauma in childhood. More than three-fourths of all respondents reported sexual abuse that was incestuous and often sadistic.

MPD was once considered extremely rare. During the 1950s, Eve White, whose story was told in the book and movie *The Three Faces of Eve*, was thought to be the only living person with MPD. But a 1989 survey of the general adult population of Winnipeg, Manitoba suggests that MPD affects as much as one percent of the adult population. And over the past decade or so, MPD has come to be recognized as one of the most serious of the emotional disorders. Suicide attempts are common, as are self-mutilation, drug and alcohol addiction, and criminal violence.

Fortunately, recent clinical data have demonstrated that MPD is highly treatable. The success of treatment seems directly tied to the therapist's understanding that symptoms of MPD are the ingenious and indefatigable remnants of a childhood spent doggedly inventing ways to survive.

Sadly, even though MPD appears to be highly treatable, many therapists fail to diagnose MPD, even in clients showing clear diagnostic clues. Their judgment may be clouded not only by prejudices about violence and its victims but by conventional misconceptions about MPD.

Contrary to popular belief, most people with multiple personalities are not Dr. Jekyll/Mr. Hydes. In fact, dual personalities warring out a classic struggle between good and evil are the exception to the rule. Much more common is a multitude of alternate personality states (usually referred to as "alters") that recurrently exchange control over an individual's behavior. While some alters may be malevolent, most are simply frightened. While some may wage war, most actively and furiously preserve a metaphorical ceasefire. Created through a sort of self-hypnosis at the moments of abuse, many alters initially function as sacrificial lambs, absorbing terror so that the psyche of the child suffering the abuse can continue to function. Years after the abuse has ended these alters continue to come to the fore during times of imagined or real threat. They wage peace, laboring to protect themselves, each other, and the core psyche from current threats and from the memories of long-ago abuse.

The *Diagnostic and Statistical Manual*'s description of MPD makes the

"300.14 Dissociative Identity Disorder (*formerly* Multiple Personality Disorder)
"*Diagnostic Features*

"The essential feature of Dissociative Identity Disorder is the presence of two or more distinct identities or personality states (Criterion A) that recurrently take control of behavior (Criterion B). There is an inability to recall important personal information, the extent of which is too great to be explained by ordinary forgetfulness (Criterion C). The disturbance is not due to the direct physiological effects of a substance or a general medical condition (Criterion D). In children, the symptoms cannot be attributed to imaginary playmates or other fantasy play.

"Dissociative Identity Disorder reflects a failure to integrate various aspects of identity, memory, and consciousness. Each personality state may be experienced as if it has a distinct personal history, self-image, and identity, including a separate name. Usually there is a primary identity that carries the individual's given name and is passive, dependent, guilty, and depressed. The alternate identities frequently have different names and characteristics that contrast with the primary identity (e.g., are hostile, controlling, and self-destructive). Particular identities may emerge in specific circumstances and may differ in reported age and gender, vocabulary, general knowledge, or predominant affect. Alternate identities are experienced as taking control in sequence, one at the expense of the other, and may deny knowledge of one another, be critical of one another, or appear to be in open conflict. Occasionally, one or more powerful identities allocate time to the others. Aggressive or hostile identities may at times interrupt activities or place the others in uncomfortable situations.

"Individuals with this disorder experience frequent gaps in memory for personal history, both remote and recent. The amnesia is frequently asymmetrical. The more passive identities tend to have more constructed memories, whereas the more hostile, controlling, or "protector" identities have more complete memories. An identity that is not in control may nonetheless gain access to consciousness by producing auditory or visual hallucinations (e.g., a voice giving instructions). Evidence of amnesia may be uncovered by reports from others who have witnessed behavior that is disavowed by the individual or by the individual's own discoveries (e.g., finding items of clothing at home that the individual cannot remember having bought). There may be loss of memory not only for recurrent periods of time, but also an overall loss of biographical memory for some extended period of childhood. Transitions among identities are often triggered by psychosocial stress. The time required to switch from one identity to another is usually a matter of seconds, but, less frequently, may be gradual. The number of identities reported ranges from 2 to more than 100. Half of reported cases include individuals with 10 or fewer identities."

From *Diagnostic and Statistical Manual of Mental Disorders,* 4th ed. (Washington, DC: American Psychiatric Association, 1994) pp. 484-485.

disorder seem a bit fantastic. But as a theoretical construct, MPD is really quite uncomplicated. Dr. Colin Ross, President of the Colin A. Ross Institute for Psychological Trauma and past President of the International Society for the Study of Dissociation, reduces the baroque clinical description of MPD to a construct haunting for its simplicity: "MPD is a little girl imagining that the abuse is happening to someone else."

The theoretical construct for post-traumatic therapy for MPD is as elementary as Dr. Ross's construct for the disorder. Therapist helps survivor gently strip alters of their self-protective functions by revealing to all alters the very secrets individual alters struggle so furiously to keep. Encouraging cooperation among alters allows the many alters to eventually merge into a single, integrated self capable of handling the stresses of life.

Memory retrieval paced jointly by therapist and survivor is a distinguishing characteristic of post-traumatic therapy for any trauma survivor. But with MPD, memory work takes on an added dimension. While assembling whole memories from fragments is in the nature of any post-traumatic therapy, scavenging across alters for fragments is not. In MPD, the memory of a traumatic experience might be sequestered by a single alter. The other alters may not only be amnesic for the sequestered memory, they may be entirely unaware of the existence of the sequestering alter. Worse, fragments of one memory may be retained by several hidden alters. One alter might, for example, hold visual details. Another might hold emotional reactions. Still another alter might hold the desire for revenge.

Skeptics clamor that, rather than being a clinical entity rooted in childhood trauma, MPD is an artifact of post-traumatic therapy. Overly zealous therapists, they argue, encourage deeply troubled and highly suggestible people into fabricating gothic memories and "losing control" over their actions in order to meet their therapist's expectations. Advocates of post-traumatic therapy counter with a less elaborate argument: There is great clinical utility in the theoretical stance grounding MPD in real and overwhelming childhood trauma. When the unspeakable truths of people with MPD are held suspect and they are treated with strictly conventional psychotherapy, most fail to get better. When, because of their auditory and visual hallucinations, they are treated with anti-psychotics, most get worse. When treated with compassionate post-traumatic therapy, however, most meet the therapy's emotional and integrative goals.

Throughout the 1980s, Dr. Richard Kluft, then at the Institute of Pennsylvania Hospital, published detailed studies of his MPD caseload. In 1984 he analyzed treatment outcomes of 123 cases. Eighty three people were able to integrate alters completely. An average of 21.6 months was necessary to bring about integration. These data stand in stark contrast to statistics reported by the National Institutes of Mental Health. In a retrospective study the NIMH found that people with multiple personality disorder floundered for an average of 6.8 years in the mental health system when treated with therapies appropriate for depression, schizophrenia, schizoaffective disorder, manic depression, and temporal lobe epilepsy. At the end of mistreatment, most people still suffered from sometimes crisis-level distress and disability.

It is, of course, a pedagogical error to infer a medical disorder's cause from its treatment. But whether a mental disorder's cause can be inferred from its treatment remains open to debate. Intuitively, it seems that it can. Janet, Breuer, and even Freud seemed to have believed so.

In the end, of course, the question is moot. In psychology, the merit of a therapy lies not in its ability to define the problem but in its ability to fundamentally improve the quality of a person's life. It remains to be proven definitively that MPD—or any constellation of dissociative symptoms—is a defensive reaction to a childhood of elemental terror. But a large body of clinical data has rendered undeniable the understanding that dissociative habits can be learned and unlearned, that the past can be confronted, and that memories can be mastered.

Skeptics of the ideas of MPD and of post-traumatic therapy for MPD have posed provocative questions. Rather than dismissing their questions with hostility, advocates should perhaps welcome them. For, once welcomed, they can be addressed. Skeptics cite as suspect a recent profusion of diagnoses of MPD, the ballooning number of alters encountered and reported by post-traumatic therapists, the preposterous quality of the tales of many people diagnosed with MPD, and the finding that clinical cases of MPD appear between five and nine times more frequently in women than in men.

The diagnostic explosion of MPD may partly reflect naive enthusiasm in some therapists. But it may also reflect the fact that more therapists than ever before are aware of trauma and its aftershocks. Some therapists do seem to be striving to best each other in the numbers of alters they can report. And, indeed, some therapists may themselves be confabulating. But now that serious attention to the phenomenon of dissociation is no longer universally frowned upon, an ever increasing number of therapists may simply have become very good at diagnosing MPD and at discerning when one alter has "left" and another "arrived." Tales of trauma can be outlandish; sometimes they are clearly preposterous. But it may be true that some people's most outlandish memories are elaborate decoys, screening away from consciousness an understanding that more prosaic violence occurred closer to home. And it may also be true that memories of bizarre forms of cruelty such as ritual cult abuse sometimes reflect fact; crime statistics and newspaper stories have amply demonstrated that some members of our society are surprisingly sick. Clinical cases of MPD may be five to nine times more common in women than men. But it could be that "the clinic" is not where men with MPD go. Some alters are sadistically malevolent. And in general, women turn to mental health services far more frequently than men. While "the clinic" is where women with sadistic alters seem to go for help, maybe men with sadistic alters go someplace else. Maybe they go to prison.

8

YOLLA HOGAN IS COMPLETING HER surgical residency at a major teaching hospital.

Yolla Hogan: "I'm probably like lots of trauma survivors in that I've had several therapists. I guess an overview of my trauma history would be that there was sexual abuse and physical abuse by my father when I was a youngster, which I then suppressed. I probably developed multiple personalities from the time of early physical abuse, at about age two and a half. But I didn't really come to an awareness of my multiplicity until fairly recently.

"The first time I went to therapy I was maybe twenty-two. My therapist probably had no idea what the hell was going on because it looked so straightforward: a bright medical student who is depressed because her brother died. My presentation is very functional and not at all dissociative.

"That was some years ago. People didn't know a lot about dissociation then. My therapist didn't realize how dissociative I was. But I remember finding myself places and not knowing why I was there, finding myself in bed with somebody who I didn't remember having gone to bed with.

"When I look back, I think that although I was dissociative the alters weren't 'out' much. So mostly what people saw was a very competent, worldly person. It's a not unusual MPD picture. You don't read about it much because it's not very dramatic.

"So my therapist was simply trying to do 'identity' stuff with me. It was the kind of therapy that a lot of women get in their early twenties to help them figure out who they are. But it didn't work much for me. I was getting more and more scattered and sending out signals that my therapist wasn't seeing. I still had no memory of what had gone on with my father. I didn't stay in therapy long.

"A year or so later I fell in love, got married, and was happy for a while. But eventually my husband and I decided that we couldn't make it together. When my marriage broke up I was pregnant.

"I had always been a little heavy but I'd lost a lot of weight right before getting pregnant. I'd saved some money, which was something I'd never been able to do. I was happy in school and thought I was in my marriage. Then everything fell apart. With the pregnancy, I'd had to leave medical school. The money I had saved got tied up in baby and pregnancy expenses. Then the pregnancy got complicated and I had to go on bed rest. I gained a lot of weight. So, near as I could tell, I had lost almost everything in order to have this baby.

"So I went to see a psychiatrist. I should have known he wasn't for me when he sat behind his desk looking very stiff and uncomfortable. I was *very* pregnant. When I told him how depressed I felt he told me that I was a Type A personality and needed to relax. He said I was too tied up with the concept of time. Well, any pregnant woman is! 'How many weeks is it?' 'How long before the due date?' I left and didn't come back.

"I had a son. When he was about eight or nine months old I had to go back to work. At that point I became really depressed and went to see a psychologist. I've since seen his notes. It was interesting. At the first meeting he thought I was bright, I was grieving the loss of my marriage, and I was tired from being up with the baby at night and from nursing. And he said I was seductive.

"I did therapy with him for about a year and a half. I was not able to seduce him. I do remember trying to. It was very helpful to have someone who would not cross that boundary, although it was always part of the conversation. And who thought I was a neat person and was very positive about my parenting.

"I told him that I was a puppet that was being pulled by other components, other parts. For example, there was a part of me who wanted to do nothing but mother the baby and a part of me who wanted to have a career and earn money. But he never bought the 'puppet' part because I didn't seem wooden to him. He thought these were just feeling states and that I was really an intact person. But what I was describing was that there was no core person.

"Eventually I left therapy. He felt I left early. I remember fleeing therapy and not knowing why. Now I think it had to do with the fact that we had started talking more about my relationship with my father. He was alive at that time. He was also still crazy. At one point I was telling my therapist how my father still sent me pages from *Playboy*. In fact, my father had shared *Playboy* and *Penthouse* with me from the time I was very little. That was one of the first things I learned to read. And my therapist was saying how inappropriate that was, and that it still continues. 'How at thirty-odd years old are you still having *Playboy* come to your house from your father?' It had never occurred to me that I could stop that. So then came the question of responsibility. How responsible am I for my crazy relationship with my father? We were also talking about the fact that I was raised Catholic. And he said, 'What does the Church say about when you are responsible for your own acts?' And I said, 'Six. You are responsible for your own acts when you're six.' And what happened was that my alters viewed this as, 'This person's going to think we were responsible for everything from age six on. So we're not safe here and we've got to get out of here.' That's I think what happened. All I knew was that all of a sudden I wanted out of therapy. What he interpreted it as was that we were getting too close to the 'father stuff.'

"Anyway, I fled therapy. But I was really OK by that point. I was about to graduate medical school. I was doing OK with my son, money was sort of straightened out. And I was pretty stable for a while. And then I started thinking about specializing in psychiatry. I called up my therapist and said, 'I need to be in therapy again because learning about mental illnesses is really hard for me. I think I'm an incest survivor. I feel like an incest survivor but I don't remember anything.' And he said, 'No,' he didn't think I was, but I did have an inappropriate father. And it would be a good idea to be in therapy. But at this point he felt that it wouldn't be a good idea to work with him. I'd had some social connections with him. And so he referred me to a colleague of his, whom I saw for two years.

"One of my early clues about my multiplicity was that I would write letters to this therapist when I thought he had made a mistake in therapy. I would leave the session, go home. I thought *I* was writing a letter. But often one of my alters would write the letter telling him that he had been wrong. The next time, I would go back and he would always have the letter in his pocket, sticking out so I could see it. And he would always say, 'Thank you for letting me know what I had done, how I made a mistake.' And sometimes I wouldn't know what was in the letter.

"My father died when I was in therapy with this man and I remember almost nothing for the year after my father's death. Almost nothing about school. I remember a lot about my son. Apparently I was alert in my parenting. I was very active in his day care and was on the board. But I was having a lot of nightmares.

"This therapist was older and very understanding and non-flapped by my incredibly punitive alter—he thought it was only a 'persona,' a feeling state or tendency on my part that was an internal representation of my father.

"My father was very bright. IQ was tested in the 160s. And he was also pretty crazy. He did not like women. He told me that women were incapable of logical thought: men were chefs, women cooked. Men were artists, women knit. These kinds of things. In fact, he brought me charts of IQs for women and IQs for men and showed me how the peak IQ for women was higher, but the scale for men was actually—I've gone back and found that study and, methodologically, it was incredibly flawed.

"He showed me all sorts of 'scientific' evidence that women couldn't succeed. I wanted to be an anthropologist. He informed me that women couldn't be anthropologists. And I said, 'Well, Margaret Mead's an anthropologist,' and he said, 'She's not a real woman because she's been divorced and she never took good care of her kid.' The message from my father was: Be a real woman and be a wife and take care of your kids. You can't do those other things. And I said, 'Well, I get straight A's in school. I get straight A's in math, and straight A's in science.' And he said, 'Yeah, but you're being taught by women. You're not really being taught.'

"There was a huge message that I could not be bright. He liked that I was little and sweet, and there was an alter that came forth to do those kinds of things with him. But he was tremendously threatened by any part that was in any way accomplished. And he worked hard to undermine me. Ultimately, it became really hard for me to feel or be successful. When I do well I often have a rush of how awful I am. I feel torn apart inside when my punitive alter gets really churned up. And paralyzed. It makes me unable to think, unable to move, not want to talk to people at all. All I want to do is be quiet and not move much, wait for it to go away. Which I suspect was an element of the abuse, also, that there were times during the sexual abuse . . . I suspect my father was multiple. He had me call him by different names. Different names corresponded to different speech patterns of his and corresponded with different kinds of activities that he wanted sexually. There were times when he was actively psychotic. He was hospitalized several times when he was very violent. Part of his violent episodes were to tell me how awful I was and how dirty I was and how I deserved this kind of stuff. So I think as I did anything to succeed, that stuff got really churned up and there was just a sense to be quiet and stay still. Don't say anything. Don't move. Don't do anything until people's attention goes someplace else. And then just stay there a while longer until you know nothing is going to happen and then kind of creep out and do the least amount you can as quietly as you can.

"My therapist was really good at managing my self-loathing and guilt. He was incredibly gentle. He let me express my punitive part and then he talked about its function. He saw the punitive part of me as a protective mechanism. And it was the most useful gift he could have given. Because it was totally non-blaming and totally accepting and in no way arguing with what I was saying.

"This was all well before psychotherapists were talking much about multiplicity. Both of these two therapists I just told you about now do a lot of work in multiplicity. And I think they probably knew a lot about trauma back then but they didn't put it together. I didn't look 'border-line.' I had no scars on my wrists, I wasn't in hospital, I didn't tell them crazy stuff. But then, nobody once asked me if I heard voices. I'm just not the kind of person you would ask that question of. And if they had asked it I would have known enough to say, 'No,' because I wouldn't have wanted to be tagged 'schizophrenic,' which is something my father was sometimes tagged. I was afraid of being schizophrenic and I was afraid for my boy.

"I still didn't have any memories of the abuse. I ended therapy with that man because I was doing fine. Doing well in medical school. I was no longer as spacey. And basically I felt that things were OK.

"But once I started my internship I started having a lot of night terrors, waking up in the middle of the night, being very frightened, all that kind of stuff. And then I started having full-blown memory retrieval of abuse.

"It came back so powerfully. It was flashbacks off and on all day long, so I was really agitated and confused. I was hearing voices, I was hearing screaming. I was so hyper. I was afraid of sleeping because I did-n't want the night terrors and so I was sleeping a couple of hours a night. I was afraid for my son. I was getting more confused. I knew I wasn't OK. And from the studying I had done back when I was toying with the idea of a psychiatric specialty, I knew I was acute PTSD.

"I wanted to get on top of this stuff. So I went back to my last ther-apist. I told him what was happening. What he said was, 'You're reen-acting the sacrificial lamb role that you've played in your family all your life and you don't need to do this.' Which was true to some degree but it was not useful to me because, first thing, somebody had to get me a good night's sleep and tell me how to manage flashbacks. I didn't need interpretations of why it was happening now. I needed somebody to keep me together. So I said, 'This isn't useful to me' and he said, 'I can see it's not useful. This is what you need to do. You need to go see your family physician and get on something to help you sleep. You need to have somebody stay at your house for the next few nights because you're confused at night. And you need to find another therapist, and I think you should see a woman.' So I went to the family physician and got something to help me sleep. Had a friend come and spend the night with me for a few days. And I called around for three days before I could find any therapist who would take me because everybody was thinking that I should be in hospital, and I didn't want to be in hospital. I didn't need to be in hospital. I had lots of supportive friends. I just needed somebody who could accept my insurance, who wasn't associated with the hospital I was interning at, and who could help me figure out what was going on.

"I started with a woman therapist who had done a lot of this work. Settled down the flashbacks. I saw her three times a week for about ten weeks and then cut back to once a week for about a month and then stopped for a while. As far as I was concerned, I was now on top. The memories had stopped coming. I needed to concentrate on my internship. I went back to see her the following summer when my schedule was lighter and I did another piece of work for six or seven months. That was really concrete. Processing the flashback material. But I would come in and say that I knew what I was going to talk about but now I can't remember. She would comment about my being dissociative. But she didn't know about multiplicity. And again, I don't look 'multiple.' I come across really intact and, if anything, I've had a hard time convincing people of how hard a time I'm having.

"Eventually we finished therapy. But then I began having a different set of flashbacks. This time they were the violent ones. Before they were straightforward blow jobs. These were blow jobs with guns. It was a lot more traumatic. I had a good friend who was a therapist. And I would wake up in the middle of the night and find myself on the phone with him and not know who I was talking with. It was like, 'Hello? Oh, shit, I hate when this happens.' And what was happening was that a young alter of mine was coming out. She had seen me call his number before. So even though she didn't know numbers she could dial his number on a punch phone because she had memorized the pattern of buttons to push. And she would call him up in the middle of the night. She calls people by titles. She calls herself The Little One. She called him The Man That Helps. She calls my current therapist The Lady Across the River because I have to drive across the river to see her.

"The Little One would call The Man That Helps and tell him that another flashback was coming and he had to help. And she would narrate horrible abusive episodes — guns and rapes and beating up type things. Then she would say, 'OK, that's it! I need to get back. I can't be out any more.' And she would pop out and then the one who would be there would be the one who had sustained the abuse. The Little One called her The Then One. The Then One would talk to my friend briefly but that alter didn't like being out much. I don't know what it was like for my friend, but can you imagine getting these kinds of phone calls at twelve o'clock at night?

"My alters didn't have much information about my external world. They just knew that it was becoming increasingly important for me to know about them and they were trying to get my friend to help me understand that there was a whole crew back there. My friend knew it was me when I called. Once after talking to my alters he said, 'I have to talk to Yolla.' And they said, 'No. She doesn't like to hear from us.' And he said, 'No. I really have to call her. Is there a way that I can talk to Yolla right now?' And they hadn't done this before. And finally, he said, 'If I count backwards from five, when I get to one, could Yolla be there?' So he did, 5, 4, 3, 2, 1, and the next thing I know I'm on the phone, 'Hello?' And there he is, and he says, 'Do you realize that you've called me?' And I say, 'No, I don't realize that I've called you.' 'Do you realize that you've had a flashback?' 'No.' I didn't realize any of this stuff.

"And I was freaked. I was very upset that I was calling a friend in the middle of the night. I was very upset that there were parts of me that were having any effect in my real life at all. And I was incredibly embarrassed. I couldn't face him for days afterwards.

"Well, this happened every three or four months over the course of a year. Finally my friend said, 'You really need to go see a therapist. And we have to wonder about multiplicity.' And I said, 'But I'm not multiple. I have no access to these folks any other time. I think they're only event-bound. I think at the time of the events I split apart and when the events come back the events come back split apart. I don't think the Little One and the Then One exist outside the events.' So we both thought that sounded pretty good and we stayed with that thinking for a while.

"The flashbacks would come and then I wouldn't remember anything for a day or so. But I got better at remembering so that finally by the next morning I could recall most of the previous night's flashback. But now I'm left with this information, for instance, that I got pregnant by my father. That I had an abortion and because he had attempted to medicate me before I went I started to vomit, so they couldn't use anesthesia. And they did it while I was awake. What am I supposed to make of this? So this happened over about a year and my friend kept saying, 'You've got to go see a therapist.'

"He was right. I did have to see a therapist. But I kept thinking, 'As long as I can handle this OK, I don't want to see a therapist.' I didn't have any insurance any more. I was mired in my internship and I *needed* not to be distracted by all this. And I didn't want to go into therapy and have it there all the time. This only came up every three or four months. Every three or four months I'd blow two weeks. If he could live with it I could live with it and I didn't want to go into therapy. But it was becoming more and more clear that this wasn't going to work and it became difficult in my relationship with him.

"So what finally happened was one day I got a phone call from my attorney's office saying my new will was ready and would I like to stop by and sign it. And I had no recollection of contacting them in any way. So I said, 'No. Why don't you send it over and I'll check it out and get back with you.' When I hung up I was really upset to think that I was doing anything that I didn't know about and that had anything to do with a will. The will arrived, and there were major changes in the will that made it seem like I knew I was going to die pretty soon. And I decided I needed to see a therapist.

"I called a new therapist—the therapist I'm seeing now—because everybody I had seen so far was basically psychodynamic. And I didn't want any more interpretations of how I was drawn to charismatic men. I needed somebody who knew something about trauma and who wasn't going to be freaked out about trauma. I didn't want to have to worry about my therapist. I needed somebody who was going to be OK with whatever material I needed to bring and who would let me call as many shots as it was appropriate for me to call, again without necessarily interpreting the material or my presentation of it.

"I had heard about the therapist I'm seeing now because she taught a course about trauma at the medical school I attended. I'd gotten her syllabus and she had read all the literature that I'd read. So I called her up and we met. I later asked her when did she know that I was a multiple. She said that I had told her the first session and I don't think I necessarily had but I think I came in and talked about the lawyer's office calling and that I had these separate little people who hopped out during traumatic memories but I didn't think I was really a multiple. And she was cool. 'Yeah, it's all within the trauma spectrum, you know. Trauma goes over a range and you're in the range somewhere.' And I said, 'OK, that's cool. That's exactly what I needed to hear.'

"Then she went on vacation for a month. And the month she was gone my alters came out all over the place. The journal I kept has at least four different handwritings in it, telling of some of the rapes that were oral rapes. My father would get turned on by terror. So he would sometimes orally rape me with a gun. And if I wouldn't open my mouth he would fire the gun next to my head to make me scream. And when that memory came back I couldn't stand having anything in my mouth. So the month she was gone I had all these different handwritings in my notebook. I had stopped eating. Then she came back and I calmly asked, 'Did you have a good trip? I'm glad you're back.' And just as calmly she says, 'Oh, let's try a little hypnosis.' And as soon as I got into trance, there was the whole crew of alters right there. And it was like they were all whispering to each other, 'Should we tell her?' [Yolla laughs.]

"When I told her she wasn't very flapped. I would say things like, 'Do you think I'm a multiple personality disorder?' and she'd say something like, 'Some people might assign that diagnosis. It's certainly on the range of trauma, issues with multiplicity.' She just wasn't flapped and that was real useful.

"I still had a part that was pretty sure I was going to die on a particular date. And I knew from the studies I had done in psychiatry that my lethality was really high because I was so detached and I seemed so determined. And I appreciated that my therapist didn't get overly or underly upset about the date I was supposed to die. She was just steady.

"Not too many of my alters have come out in therapy sessions. The one who called herself The Little One has come out a couple of times. When she came out here in my therapist's office, as we were switching I would let her know that she was not to gesture or talk young. I would give her all these directions about how she could come out. So it's not like she was fully out here fooling around, she was out here under pretty close constraints. That made it a little easier for me to come back again, because the switches were not as traumatic and complete. There was more mushing.

"When the alters would come out—well, there were degrees of coming out. It's almost a spatial sense. Some alters were far, far, back [gesturing behind her head] and they had almost no access to anything that happens in my real, present life. And there were some that were closer, in intermediate space, that could come forward into awareness without actually being 'out' and in control. And they became more accessible as I learned I was a multiple and I became curious about working with my alters. I accessed them more frequently. In my therapist's office they came out sometimes in drawing work. A switch would be facilitated and I would look at the drawing and not know that I had drawn it and not know exactly what it would mean. There were also times when I knew a change had taken place and I wasn't exactly sure what had happened and my therapist would ask me if I wanted to know. But I was aware, mostly physiologically, when I had changed. There were two alters with definite differences in body temperature. And after those switches I would be left with the physical sense of the other one having been there. So it was more like walking into a room and smelling someone's cologne or being aware that someone had just left.

"It took a lot of work for me to able to switch here with my therapist. Can you imagine how embarrassing or humiliating it might feel to step back and let all kinds of parts come forward that don't feel like me that aren't particularly attractive or how I want to come across? And to trust that my therapist is going to be able to handle it and know what to do? And that I can come back and still face her after there's been a switch like that? And I don't think I was particularly outrageous. If anything, I was really constrained. But it was still difficult even to allow her to hear a different voice pattern or to have one truly be allowed to talk to her in a straightforward way.

"Outside of therapy, I think only two people in my life have noticed a switch. One is the man I'm married to, Kurt. The other person to see my alters was Guy, my friend and sexual partner for thirteen years before I met Kurt. He didn't necessarily know I was a multiple. He just knew very well how to accommodate my multiplicity.

"If my breathing changed or I seemed a bit frightened, Guy knew to call me by name and to make eye contact with me and then I would be fine. Guy knew early on that I had been raped as an adult, so when I said, 'I don't like being touched in this way,' or, 'I don't like to be grabbed in this way,' he heard that and it was never an issue. He was always careful. If my voice changed in the time that we were together, well, it's not unusual. Sexual activity can be playful. I'm not so sure he knew he was fooling around with a very young one. I think if I'd told him that he'd probably have been pretty freaked out. When I finally sat down and said, 'Look, we're talking about multiple personality disorder,' Guy was kind of thoughtful. I said, 'If you were to take guesses at what the alters might be like, whom have you known?' and he accurately described about five. And when I asked him what his experience of all those alters had been he said he'd just kind of seen the various aspects of me as my reactions to having been sexually assaulted.

"I don't think Guy was particularly freaked by learning I was a multiple. I think he was more concerned when he realized he had been fooling around with an alter that was young. I think that gave him some, 'Oh my God, what does this mean?' moments. But I think if anybody had ever interviewed him after we had spent an afternoon in bed and somebody said, 'Have you been fooling around with a five-year-old?' that would not have been his experience of the event. He would probably say that we had gotten silly or that playing cards was part of our time in bed.

"Actually, one other person has experienced me switching: my son. When I learned I was multiple, I read the literature, *all* of it. There was an article on the incidence of psychiatric disorders in the children of multiples. And so I went and talked to people who know me as a mother. 'Does my son seem OK? What is going on?' They thought that he was OK. But one day, it was very painful to do it, I asked him. I said, 'It's pretty clear that what happened when I was overwhelmed as a child was that parts of me became separated, and that probably exists in some way still. Have there been times when I've seemed not like myself? Or have there been times when I have frightened you? Are there things that have happened that have confused you?' And he was able to relate several events. One was when I slipped on ice and shattered my leg and was screaming in pain. People ran over to help me. I saw the look on my son's face, which was shock and horror. And I switched so that I had no pain. The very competent Other One came forward and said, 'OK, we have to go to the hospital.' Very calm voice. 'OK, go get the fishing gear.' What scared him was not my screaming. What scared him was the switch. Why, if I had a leg that was shattered, was I looking so calm and talking in this kind of voice? The friends who were there helped him understand that this was a shock reaction, that I was OK and that I *would* be having pain. He didn't have a context to understand my calmness in.

"A couple of other times, I screamed at night and he has awakened when I screamed. And what he does is get up and if I'm awakened I come back as myself. I don't think that's happened a lot, but I think it's happened a couple of times.

"He knows that I startle easily, especially around my face and around gunfire. And he just knows that I'm over-reactive to that. He says, 'I know I have to be careful of those kinds of things. You jump easily. Kurt gets mad when the Mets lose. It's just one of those things.' He knows about the multiplicity. He knows that I have integrated. And occasionally when I say he can't do something or other that he wants to do, we'll joke. He'll say, 'You promised!' and I'll say, 'No, that wasn't me. That was another me. I don't remember that!' and we'll laugh.

"As I said, my therapist has probably seen more switching than anyone. But most of my alters came out only enough to be able to listen to my therapist but not to be totally out in the room and actively participating. My therapist has never been pushy. The books tell you that you're supposed to pull out all the alters and find out where they come from and what their job is and do all of these things. But it would not have been a good thing to do with me. Actually, I wish sometimes that we had talked to them each individually because I still have gaps in my memory. But we're going to get that through hypnosis and I trust that will work.

"For me, recovering memory under hypnosis lets me reexperience events on a tolerable level of intensity. In trance, we can speed the event up a little or turn down the intensity. I can know the experience as mine but not truly have to reexperience it. Who wants to sit here and reexperience an hour-long rape? No, thank you.

"Memories are more complicated with multiplicity because — well, number one, what is being remembered, and which alter has the memory? And, two, I don't think that what I remember is necessarily the absolute, historical truth. I look more for an understanding of what it is that I remember and how it shapes how I'm feeling or doing now. I ask myself how the event made sense to me at the time it happened and whether there is a way I can understand it that will help free me up.

"Here's an example with a nontraumatic memory. I don't like things to end. I don't go to graduations. I will avoid the last time I'm getting together with somebody before they go away. Many people do that. That's not weird. But I might get weird around it. I remember as a youngster transferring from one private school to another and being picked up by my father. I told my father I wanted to say goodbye to some folks, and he said, 'There's no point in saying goodbye. Nobody here will remember you in two weeks. They will not remember that you have been here and no one will remember your name. Let's go.' Maybe that's not exactly the way the conversation was. But does remembering that make a difference, help me understand that I carry the feeling that saying goodbye means I have to confront the possibility that I haven't mattered and that they shouldn't have mattered to me? If someone can help me understand that saying goodbye is actually acknowledging how someone has mattered to me and does continue to matter to me, then that changes my experience of what goodbyes are. And it changes my experience of who I am in a relationship.

"So is this particular memory that important? On a scale of one to ten it's in there somewhere. Have I remembered it absolutely accurately? Maybe not. Does remembering it make a difference? It does make a difference when I need to finish up what I'm doing and move on in a better way than I have done.

"That was a nontraumatic memory, just one of those goofs that parents make. I think things are a little different around traumatic memories. And I think it's also different around traumatic memories having multiplicity. Because by the time I came to see this therapist I had regained many memories of abuse. But what is a memory? For most people the memory would include cognitions, smells, visual and auditory images, and emotions and physical sensations. But all of those things are not necessarily available to one of me because they are sequestered in various parts of me. So I might be able to tell something about a trauma but with essentially no sense that it's 'my' story. Because 'I' am not the one who experienced it. I'm not the one who went through the abuse. These other folks went through the various aspects of the abuse. I'm not the one who was mad. Even the one who went through the abuse wasn't the one who got mad. So what is it for a multiple like me to regain an event? I have to go back to this one and figure out what this one's experience of the event was, and then this alter's experience, and then this alter's experience, and try to bring them together—almost at the same time in the same place, so that then the event feels like it truly happened to me. Only then can *I* decide to let it go and not be tripped up by things that aren't me.

"The other thing around memory that was weird for me happened when I integrated my alters. I had trouble with simple, practical memories. Such as, a couple of the alters were male. Most of the alters were female. Some alters were right-handed. Some were left-handed. A fairly wide range in their own body concepts or the concepts of their own physical space, those kinds of things. So that when I integrated I did not have a consistent sense of how tall I was. I was always adjusting the mirrors in my car. Or I would go use the bathroom and find myself standing and unzipping my jeans, and then thinking, 'Woops, I have to sit.' Or combing my hair, and only combing the top two inches because I was combing it for a part that had short hair even though my hair was very long. And it was like that for a couple of months. To even remember that I knew how to drive. Or I would stand there baking and realize I couldn't remember whether cinnamon or sage was used in cookies. I knew there was an 'S' spice in there somewhere. Things were temporarily gone from me. Not gone. Just not as automatic. I had to relearn that I knew it. It was like recovering from a stroke. So a lot of work in therapy, for months, was just around keeping me calm, letting me know that I hadn't lost anything but that the memories had been reshuffled and I needed to allow myself to remember that I knew things. But it was very disconcerting.

"Prior to integration I hadn't had much of a problem with practical memories because my alters were not out much. But as I began to integrate I made a conscious decision to allow them to be co-conscious, in part because to integrate meant that they were going to be out all the time so they had better know about my world. The Young Adolescent wanted to know what it was to be an adult female. And so I brought her out whenever I was in the company of an adult female who I thought was a good role model so that my alter could know that there were strong women who were not easily assaulted. I'm sure anybody watching me just saw me cooking with a good friend, but what I was aware of was that the Young Adolescent was watching my friend and trying to understand what it would be like to experience the world as an increasingly competent female.

"When I was preparing to integrate, my alters began to tell me what they needed before they would integrate. The young adolescent girl said, 'I want to be sixteen before we integrate, so give me some time to get a little older.' The Little One knew some important phone numbers by sound but wanted to be able to write down phone numbers so that she would have them. I think it was just a safety thing. She wanted to know she could contact the Lady Across the River or the Man That Helps. How that came about was my watch broke and I went into a department store to buy a $14 watch. Picked out one with a leather strap. Came back out and discovered I'd bought a pink-strapped one with little balloons. Unfortunately, the date was on the watch face where the '3' should have been. So The Little One learned to do the numbers one through twelve, but she didn't learn the number three because it wasn't on the watch. I discovered this when I would get up in the morning—most of the switching and reorganizing was happening at night—and there would be this circle of numbers with no number three where she was practicing the numbers at night.

"There were some specific requests like that. One alter made it really clear that he did not want to have to come out in a female body at all.

"As I said, at first they came out mostly at night. But then I began protesting how much sleep I was losing. So they agreed to stay in at night and in the morning for several months I had to get up early to let everyone switch and resolve what they needed to resolve before I could go about my day. I would set the alarm for 5:00, go downstairs and get something to drink, sit in bed with a cup of coffee or something, allowing switch after switch after switch to happen until I felt settled down. I might go through twelve or thirteen switches in the morning. It was incredibly exhausting to just sit there and allow myself to have one or another or three of them come out and write or do a drawing, or vote on the clothes we were going to wear. I don't think I was prepared for how tiring that was going to be.

"My therapist and I are still doing this integration. Blending myself and my alters has taken well over a year. I have a continued sense that some events did not happen to 'me.' I know cognitively and intellectually that they happened to me. I could describe them. But I don't feel that they are mine yet.

"There were a couple of alters I wanted nothing to do with. So you can see how integration would be a bit of a pain in the ass because I can't get away from them now. Of course, having integrated parts of yourself you don't like is probably what non-multiples go through all the time.

"With integration, my other parts didn't go away. They are now mostly blended. But under stress—I don't actually switch alters anymore but I feel more like I'm coming from one particular alter's experience. This is probably what non-multiples do, too. An anniversary comes up and you're just kind of feeling sad about the loss of someone. Kind of in that 'place of feeling sad' despite other things that are happening. What I go through is similar to that, except it isn't a place like that, it is a part or a persona like that. So especially when under stress I feel my alters again as more discrete. But not separate anymore.

"Right now in my recovery process I'm not a whole lot different from other survivors who have lost and then regained memory in that I want to look for corroboration. So I'm trying to get my father's psychiatric records, and this summer will go back to the town I grew up in. I have a very clear sense of the building in which I had the abortion, and a reasonable sense of where it would be. If I can't find it I'll still be OK. If I can find it, it will make a lot of things easier. And I know that as more and more delayed disclosure stuff comes up legally — people sue their perpetrators or go to jail for murders after delayed memories — that I'm going to feel under increasing pressure to validate my own memories. So I think it's important to be clear about what feels like a true event and also know that my memories are from the perspective of a kid and whatever distortions and dissociations were available to that kid.

"I used to wonder if I faked my multiplicity and memories. So I tried to fake it. I tried to fake a panic reaction to a disclosure. I made up a story that I was going to pretend was true. I set my alarm for 12:00 to wake up real upset and call my friend and tell him this was happening to me. And I couldn't do it. I couldn't induce it. That doesn't necessarily mean that all the other ones are true, but that is how I tried to figure out what was true. And a few times when I got an event I tried to change it. I tried to make it happen from a different angle or I tried to make it happen in a different setting. And it was just clear: No, that wasn't right. This is what was right.

"Thank you. It's nice to be able to tell my story at no risk."

* * *

In a series of articles written throughout the 1980s, Dr. Richard Kluft, then at the Institute of Pennsylvania Hospital, described what he called the "natural history" of the relationship of the typical therapist to survivors of extreme childhood abuse. For some therapists, the psychic onslaught of listening to tales of human cruelty produces classic PTSD symptoms. Other therapists, so moved by what they hear, eventually abandon their role as therapist for that of avenger. Still other therapists crumble under the weight of horrible tales, becoming defensively skeptical of the client's story. And some therapists move directly from a phase of fascination and voyeurism into a belief that a particular survivor needs to be loved into health.

In fact, the constancy and caring post-traumatic therapists offer survivors does constitute a form of love. But a good therapist contains that love within appropriate boundaries. Some therapists, however, fail to check themselves. Acting on impulse and unrecognized arrogance, they draw the client into a romantic relationship that they believe will be healing for the client but that, because of the vulnerability of the client and the authoritative audacity of the therapist, smacks of both entrapment and incest.

A romantic or sexual relationship between any client and any therapist is almost always damaging to the client. It can be especially so for trauma survivors. At the University of California School of Medicine, psychiatrist Dr. Nannette Gartrell conducted a survey of people who had sexual relationships with their therapists. Although her survey was not limited to trauma survivors, she reports that 90% of the people who had sexual affairs with their therapists developed serious emotional problems resembling PTSD. These included difficulty trusting anyone, becoming unusually frightened of being taken advantage of in intimate relationships, and becoming severely depressed. Ten percent of the people who had affairs with their therapists needed hospitalization. One percent committed suicide. The implications that this study holds for trauma survivors are distressing, as many survivors already suffer overwhelming symptoms of post-traumatic stress.

Therapists expert at post-traumatic therapy take the findings of Drs. Kluft and Gartrell as twin cautionary tales. They know that they owe it to themselves and to their clients to take care of their own emotional needs outside of the therapy hour and in ways that free them to also provide care to their clients.

All psychodynamic therapists believe in the power of words to heal; increasingly, trauma therapists are taking advantage of the power of words to heal themselves. In therapists' support groups they talk freely and in deeply personal terms about the impact of their clients' trauma on themselves and about the rebound impact of their own vicarious traumatization on the therapy they give.

Ever since Jeffrey Masson's *Assault on Truth* exposed the circuitous route by which Freud walked away from his Seduction theory (symptoms of hysteria are the direct result of childhood sexual abuse) and arrived instead at his Oedipal theory (tales of early sexual abuse are figments of hysterical adult imaginations), Freud has taken a lot of flak. While much of that criticism is deserved, much of Freud's writings merit rescue and redemption, for they have proven to be a lodestone for trauma therapists disoriented by revulsion, fear, empathy, and doubt. Those writings include Freud's insights into the two phenomena he considered most basic to healing: transference and countertransference.

Freud understood that clients project onto their therapists attributes belonging to significant people in their own pasts. He called this tendency "transference." Initially, Freud conceived of transference as an obstacle to therapy. Eventually, however, he saw that examining transference within the therapy hour could illuminate much about how a client's experience of past relationships colors that client's experience of present relationships.

"Countertransference" Freud considered the emotional attitude of the therapist toward the client. This attitude may embody affection for the client, whom the therapist has come to know intimately. On the other hand—and especially for therapists listening to tales of trauma—countertransference may also embody resentment and contempt for the client as the messenger bearing bad tidings about personal and universal vulnerability. Freud believed that, like transference, countertransference is inevitable, even instructive, in therapy, and that it becomes a problem only when the therapist's conscious or unconscious behavior is primarily directed at satisfying his or her own needs.

Writing in the scholarly journal *Dissociation,* Dr. Richard Kluft defends Freud and his direct intellectual descendants, explaining,

"Whatever its failings and shortcomings (and there are many), psychoanalysis remains that foundation discipline in the mental health professions that has most scrupulously examined the dynamics of what should occur and what can go wrong within the therapeutic dyad and in the examination of the material that the patient brings into the crucible of therapy. No school of thought has explored resistance, transference, countertransference, the therapeutic alliance, and their vicissitudes with a comparable depth and comprehensiveness. As we struggle with issues that concern the boundaries of therapy, the management of the therapist's own feelings, the approaches to be taken to acting out and entrenched resistances, the assessment of ma-

A therapists' support group hosted by a trauma treatment center in California. At the center's request, the therapists' names have been changed.

Penny: "This is with a fireman, a male incest survivor client that I've worked with for a little under three years. He's struggling with whether I can give him what he needs and wants from our therapy. The feeling that he never gets saved, that he never gets the help he needs, is familiar to him, to the child within him. While we were talking about his struggle he used an analogy, an example from when he was working as a firefighter of a boy who couldn't be saved. A stove had been left on and an entire apartment building had caught fire. He had made it through smoke to a two-year-old boy and hauled him out. The child was fairly clearly dead, but my client was trying to revive him when the mother came upon the scene—she'd been out and had left her own mother to watch the child. Her own mother is the one who left the stove on and started the fire. The child's mother was frantic, yelling at the firefighter, trying to make him do the resuscitation just right in the hopes or with the sense that if he just did it the way 'Mom' would do it, the child would be okay. It was a very emotional story. And it was very strange, because as he was telling this story he made several references to Pasha's mother. It's an unusual name—my own son's name is Pasha. It was very powerful. It gripped me. And I know I was connecting very much with his struggle and how painful therapy is at times and how futile our relationship must feel at times, and how hard he's working, and how much he wants to figure out what he needs. And I'm wondering as I'm sitting there and my eyes are welling up with tears, 'Do I need to say something?' And I had to fight a very strong urge to tell him the personal meaning his story that day had for me. And I was back and forth a hundred times in three minutes of the session. I decided not to say anything about the personal meaning. It felt, on the one hand, like an opportunity to form another level of connection with him, which is so important for him. But on the other hand, I asked myself, 'Who I would really be serving by making the revelation?'"

Frederic: "Sometimes in moments like that it feels like the power of your bond with your client can transcend any therapeutic rationale. You're right, it's so gripping. There's such a sense of connection with the person that it's easy to just act without stopping and thinking about the real consequences to therapy."

Leila: "And when you do stop yourself you're then left alone with your feelings. And, of course, part of your wish to talk to your client about the personal impact of his story on you was so that you wouldn't have to be alone with your overpowering feelings, and that's understandable."

Penny: "During the session I was almost overwhelmed with a feeling that my telling him about the personal meaning would be good for him. In the end, I didn't convince myself. I knew that, yes, he might feel more connected, but he also might feel scared that he had scared me. And I'm also very much aware that the amount we talk here in this group about just this kind of issue allowed me to quickly think the dilemma through during that session. Because I think sometimes you can make a mistake that is fatal to therapy. I don't know that if I had told him about my own emotional connection to his story it would have been fatal to the therapy, but it just had the feeling of something that could have had a very significant impact on the therapy process. And other than him calling one weekend when he was in crisis and possibly hearing the noise of children in the background, it's never come up whether I have children or not. It's never been discussed in the therapy. So it would have clearly been a change in the therapy boundary for me all of a sudden to have not only told him something personal about myself but to have told him something intensely personal. Yet in the heat of the moment it very much felt like I wanted to share with him. . . ."

Deborah: "What did you want to share, what was the dilemma? Acknowledgment of your own . . . ."

Penny: "Yeah, of how—that's a good question. I think the name piece, how meaningful that was. But what you're asking is actually useful, because the story was already meaningful for me without the name, and that just gave it a heightened meaning. But his way of depicting that struggle of whether he is looking for something he can't get from me. And if so, how do you mourn that loss. So I guess the meaning was there already and your question makes me realize that there probably wasn't anything extra other than my own sense of wanting him not to feel like I couldn't give him what he needed."

Luis: "But in a way it was a setup for a reenactment which you very wisely didn't step into. You interpreted his story as a metaphor for how he believes the child within him can't be helped and the child within can't be saved. It sounds exactly right. And if you had said something personal from your own experience, that might have made him feel like, 'Well, you don't understand what I'm actually talking about here. You're supposed to be helping me. But you're not connecting with me, you're talking about your own experience.'"

Penny: "There's actually a vicarious traumatization piece in here that I'm just becoming aware of. Because of the work I do I sometimes play out scenarios in my head, like what would it be like if I had a child who was ever in a serious accident. My client's story really hit me, and it didn't only have to do with the name. I'm always imagining—I mean, as it went on I was thinking, you know, my mother-in-law is the kind of person that all this could very easily happen with. That's why I never leave my kids with my in-laws. So it had that personal meaning that was separate, and it was about vicarious traumatization."

Leila: "There may even be some components of your client's history that are part of why he can sort of tune in, even on an unconscious level, to what might affect you. For example, if, when you were on the phone with him that one weekend he called, at some point you said, 'Pasha, be quiet.' There can be an unconscious way in which he, in trying to find a way to be close to somebody and be taken care of, is trying to elicit your wish to jump in and give him more."

Penny: "That, by the way, isn't so far outside the realm of possibility."

Luis: "'Pasha, be quiet please'?"

Penny: "Yeah, while I was on the phone."

Frederic: "I bet it felt like smoke was coming out of your ears."

terial that often appears fantastic and difficult to comprehend, we are within the realm of ideas and concepts that have been explored most intensely and insightfully, albeit imperfectly and incompletely, in the psychoanalytic literature. We abandon this rich heritage at our peril. It remains one of the most valuable of guides through the complexity of what takes place between the therapist and the patient."

In the century since Freud and his contemporaries established the precepts of dynamic psychiatry, literally hundreds of schools of treatment have come and gone. Many have defined themselves mostly in terms of what they are not, and specifically what many are not is Freudian, a term sometimes deemed tantamount to "repressive." But Dr. Kluft's and Dr. Gartrell's separate observations about the considerable damage that can be done to both therapist and client when therapists remain in the dark about the nature and strength of their emotional responses to tales of trauma suggest that a rethinking of orthodoxy and anti-orthodoxy is in order. Therapists who toss aside all of psychotherapeutic tradition may also unwittingly and perilously toss aside its protections, forcing themselves to blaze unnecessarily chancy paths through precarious jungles.

For a therapist, listening to stories of trauma carries personal risks. The therapist must accept ambiguity. Intense feelings will be aroused, and for a while the world may seem irreversibly poisoned. Tales of trauma will force the therapist to reorder personal values and friendships and to question anew concepts like good and evil and the meaning of life. The therapist will need comfort and love — all of the supports, in fact, that survivors need.

Therapists have a duty to find the supports they need. Because constancy and conscience are the quintessential tools of their trade, trauma therapists, especially, must routinely pause and resolve where it is that their true allegiances lie. Can they believe what survivors tell them? Is believing necessary? Is it enough? Can a therapist maintain critical thinking without succumbing to critical behavior? How much of a therapist's reputation and personal security is he or she prepared to risk by believing? By acting? How can a therapist act on behalf of survivors without robbing them of the power and right to determine their own destinies? And where — to what people and to what literature — can a therapist safely turn for help when bolstering a survivor becomes too big a burden to bear alone?

These are the questions that therapists expert in post-traumatic therapy keep in mind. Trauma therapists are nontraditional in their refusal to assume that psychic troubles are always a sickness born of fantasy and self-deception. But they are avidly pro-tradition in the scrutiny to which they subject their own emotions, motivations, and behaviors. Therapists expert in post-traumatic therapy are in the business of winning the trust of people who have been grievously betrayed. They know that if they stay blind to the hidden power of the tales they hear and to their own frailties, they ask survivors to once again dance with danger.

The loyalty trauma therapists give survivors is both closely reasoned and carefully examined. As such, it is ultimately — and necessarily — incontrovertible.

Happy Endings

9

IF I HAVE LEARNED ANYTHING in the course of my research for this book, it is that hearing oral testimony is different from reading literary accounts of man's inhumanity to man. Literary accounts titrate the experience of trauma. They elide when necessary and rely on palatable devices such as analogy to portray difficult experience. This keeps the reader from closing the book in disgust. Oral testimony, on the other hand, never lets the listener off the hook. Because testifying is an act of remembering as much as it is of telling, the testifier lurches erratically between past and present. Filling with dread at the unpredictability of what she might hear, the listener longs to escape but can find no polite way to do so. She is ensnared by a tale teller who, in trying to recreate for the listener the experience of menace, occasionally and unpredictably seems menacing.

In relating the testimony of survivors, I have tried to find a happy middle between literary form and oral testimony. I hope I have avoided bowdlerizing survivors' tales, but where I believed it necessary I did interrupt testimony with small islands of commentary and safety. If I have erred at all, it is probably that I left the testimony too raw. I might have lost some readers. I imagine I depressed at least a few.

It may seem that by titling this chapter "Happy Endings" I am pandering to the needs of those readers I may have depressed to get just a taste of unabashed good news. If I were, I would be clearly contradicting myself, for it is I who have railed that our society's insistence on happy endings is insulting to survivors whose injuries defy romantic conjecture. It is I who have called into question the motives of journalists who insist on fashioning silk purses out of indisputably sowish ears.

I have titled this chapter as I have because happy endings exist. Good hardly ever publicly trounces evil. But many survivors who were once defeated eventually find that they no longer constantly carry with them the feeling that the world is not safe, that they have been reduced, destroyed. They feel stronger, better, though not all better.

Their lives never return to their antediluvian forms. The horrible memories don't evaporate. The holes in their lives are not completely filled in. But by and large, they regain a state of psychological vitality. One survivor described recovering to me as erecting from the pain of the past "a kind of wisdom in the present that might eventually be as unshakable as the hurting once was."

Therefore, in my defense, titling this chapter the way I have is not simply a last-ditch effort to titrate the experience of trauma and to keep readers from closing the book in disgust. A real optimism lies behind my choice, an optimism born not only defensively, in the heat of listening to menacing tales, but also in the course of knowing some of the survivors testifying in this book for the two years it took to write it. It comes from watching what happened to these people when they found someone (usually a trauma therapist) to trust and then discovered the trusted person to indeed be trustworthy.

Post-traumatic therapists seem to share the optimism I feel. Of course, how else could they imbue survivors with enough hope to keep them working towards recovery? And how else could they survive the work they do? How else could they remain trustworthy? Optimism for them may be as much a tool of the trade as a firecoat for the fireman.

"It takes two to speak the truth — one to speak, and another to hear," writes Henry David Thoreau. As a writer newly infatuated with the cleansing power of truth telling, I have also become enamored of optimism. A careful and fully reasoned optimism can keep people listening. Listening well can bring incalculable public and private good. I think that is important.

Maureen Terry has been in post-traumatic therapy for a little more than six months. Last April, she was stabbed repeatedly by a stranger who then stood over her, hoping to watch her die. In the aftermath of the attack, Maureen developed paralyzing phobias and a conviction that anybody and everybody might kill her. But she is functioning well again, able to go outside alone, ride the subways, go to work. In therapy she is now exploring the present-day emotional ramifications of her childhood of physical and emotional abuse.

Maureen: "This week the secretary of a friend was mugged. He asked me to call her up and try to convince her to get some therapy, because so far she's not leaving the house. When I called her, she asked me such specific questions. 'Well, what happens when you go to therapy?' She was so scared of the process. 'How does it help? Tell me specifically how it helps.'

"I told her that it's helped me immensely. She wanted to know how long I'd been in, and I told her. And she goes, 'That long?! And how often do you go?' She seemed to be very nervous about being in something that would be longer than a quick Band-Aid. She wanted, like, I go in, 1-2-3, it's all over with. And she said, 'Well, how come you've been in that long?' I said, 'I feel that I've needed it.' She goes, 'Well can you stop at any time?' And I said, 'If I wanted to stop, I would stop!' [Maureen smiles.] It sounded like she was very concerned about getting pulled into something she couldn't get out of. I just told her that I wouldn't be in it unless I felt that it has really been beneficial to me, and really has helped me. I said, 'When I look back to how I was in April, or in May, and June, and how I was even last month, when I look back and I see how far I've come, that's why I recommend it to you. Because I've come so far. My life is much better now. I don't think that I would be feeling this good or this whole had I not been going to therapy and working this out.'

"But I still got the feeling from her that she wanted a real quick fix. She's got the nightmares, she's afraid to go out, she has all this stuff I had.

"I told her, 'This therapy has worked for me, but you're a different person from me.' I didn't want to put her off. I said to her, 'For you it may be different. All I can tell you is what is working for me.' I really feel that she needs to see someone to get some kind of guidance in dealing with what happened to her. But she's afraid. I don't know what she'll do."

Dr. Mark Hall is a psychotherapist at the Traumatic Stress Institute in South Windsor, Connecticut.

"It's unrealistic to expect that you're ever going to get rid of the memories. It's unrealistic to expect that you're going to get to a point where you might have been if it had never happened. It's unrealistic to expect that you're ever going to be able to talk about it without some twinge of pain or anger or sadness or whatever. But there are other things that are realistic. It's realistic to expect that you can cope better with the memories. That in sharing it with someone you may lighten your load about it some."

Home is not always where your heart is.
Your heart may have been stolen by some disguised robber you thought was an angel.
No one ever showed you the difference.
And maybe they raped you, and after that it always hurts.
That piece of your heart is forever missing.
Then it's time to learn the difference between an angel and a black heart.
It's never too late.
We can become wise and loving mothers to ourselves!
And these wonderful mothers know safety from danger, and they can keep you and love you and patch you up when you're broken.
So let's be mothers to ourselves and to each other.
The world needs a mother.
Home is where your mother is."
Marie Wiggins/Spring, 1993

"Survival Course"
by Susan Briton

"On July 4, 1990, I went for a morning walk along a peaceful-looking country road in southern France. It was a gorgeous day and I didn't envy my husband, Tom, who had to stay inside and work on a manuscript with a French colleague. I sang to myself as I set out, stopping to pet a goat and pick some wild strawberries along the way. An hour later, I was lying near death, pleading for my life with a brutal assailant who had jumped me from behind. I hadn't heard or seen him coming. He dragged me off the road and into a deep ravine, beat me with his fist and a rock, sexually assaulted me, choked me repeatedly and, after I had passed out four times, left me for dead.

"I could describe in vivid detail the grotesque inhumanity of my attacker, the humiliation of having to obey his sadistic orders, the terror as I lost consciousness while my animal reflexes desperately fought for air, the struggle to climb out of the ravine and to run to safety with my eyes swollen shut, the dizzying pull toward oblivion battling with the galvanizing fear of dying alone. But each violent assault is gruesome in its own way, and I want to write about what I have in common with other survivors—the long, unimaginably painful process of recovery.

"In one way, my recovery has differed from that of many other victims of sexual violence in that I was assaulted by a stranger, in a "safe place," and was so visibly injured when I encountered the police and medical personnel that I was spared the insult of disbelief or blame. Still, I have found people's most common reaction to be that of denial.

"When the evidence is incontrovertible—I was hospitalized for eleven days and the assailant was caught, confessed to the attack and was indicted for rape and attempted murder—denial takes the form of attempts to explain the assault in ways that leave the observer's world unscathed. The most well-meaning individuals, caught up in the myth of their own immunity, can inadvertently add to the victim's suffering by suggesting that the attack was avoidable or somehow her fault. One court official stressed that she herself had never been a victim and told me that I would benefit from the experience by learning not to be so trusting of people and to take basic safety precautions like not going out alone late at night.

"Denial also takes the form of silence. During the first several months of my recovery, I led a spectral existence, dissociated from those around me, and my sense of unreality was reinforced by the fact that most of my relatives didn't phone, write, or even send a get-well card. These are all caring, decent people who would have sent wishes for a speedy recovery if I'd had, say, an appendectomy. Their early lack of response was so striking that I wondered whether it was a result of self-protective denial, or a reluctance to mention something so unspeakable, or a symptom of the widespread emotional illiteracy that prevents most people from conveying any feeling that can't be expressed in a Hallmark card.

"I learned later they were afraid of reminding me of what happened. Didn't they realize that I thought about the attack nearly every minute of every day and that their silence made me feel as though I had, in fact, died and no one had bothered to come to the funeral?

"For the next few months, I felt angry, scared, and helpless. I wished I could blame myself for what had happened so that I could feel more in control of my life. It would have been easier than accepting that I live in a world where I can be attacked at any time, in any place, simply because I am a woman.

"My outrage at this injustice alternated with debilitating depression. I was too terrified to direct my anger toward my assailant, so I aimed it at safer targets. Once, when Tom told me to quit moping, I wanted to choke him, just so he would know what it was like. Fortunately, Tom and my family stood by me and I learned to release my rage first by hitting pillows and then by taking a women's self-defense class. The confidence I gained from learning how to fight back effectively not only enabled me to walk down the street again. It gave me back my life.

"But it was a changed life. A paradoxical life. I began to feel stronger than ever before, and more vulnerable; more determined to fight to change the world, but in need of several naps a day. I was glad I had only myself to look after, that I didn't have a child who would grow up with the knowledge that even the protector could not be protected. But I felt an inexpressible loss when I recalled how much Tom and I had wanted a baby and how we'd hoped to conceive one on our vacation in France. I couldn't imagine getting pregnant now, because it was so hard to let even Tom near me and because it would be harder still to let a child leave my side.

"I joined a rape survivors' support group, got a great deal of therapy and started speaking out against sexual violence. I also devoted myself to getting more pleasure into my life, not so much because living well is the best revenge but because living at all had become such a challenge. We got two kittens to keep me company, and then two Dalmatian puppies. I took up tap dancing again, and each day I made a point of singing. I spent countless hours with supportive friends and survivors who brought meaning back into my world. Gradually, I was able to get back to work.

"'You will never be the same,' the facilitator told us at the first meeting of the support group. But you can be better. When your life is shattered, you're forced to pick up the pieces, and you have a chance to stop and examine them. You can say ' I don't want this one anymore' or 'I think I'll work on that one.' I have had to give up more than I ever would have chosen to. But I have gained important skills and insights, and I no longer feel tainted by my victimization. It's an honor to be a survivor, and although it's not exactly the sort of thing I can put on my résumé, it's the accomplishment of which I'm most proud.

"People ask if I'm recovered now, and I reply that it depends on what that means. Am I the way I was before the attack? No, and I never will be. I am not the person who set off, singing, on that sunny Fourth of July in the French countryside. I left her in a muddy creek bed at the bottom of a ravine. I had to in order to survive. I am changed forever, and if I insist too often that my friends and family acknowledge it, that's because I am afraid they don't know who I am.

"But if recovery means being able to incorporate this awful knowledge into my life and carry on, then yes, I'm recovered. I don't wake each day with a start, thinking: 'This can't have happened to me!' It happened. I have no guarantee it won't happen again, although my self-defense classes have given me the courage to move about in the world and to go for longer and longer walks — with my two big dogs. And I no longer cringe when I see a woman jogging alone on the country road where I live, though I may still have a slight urge to rush out and protect her, to tell her to come inside where she'll be safe. But I catch myself, like a mother learning to let go, and cheer her on, thinking, may she always be so carefree, so at home in her world. She has every right to be."

Reprinted from *The New York Times Magazine,* March 21, 1993

10

IN WRITING THIS BOOK OF UNSPEAKABLE TRUTHS I have posed a series of questions. "Survivors have stories they need to tell," I explained almost at the outset. "Unfortunately, these are the very stories that we who are their friends, family, and therapists seem to need not to hear. But if we refuse to listen to their tales, how are they to regain their lost sense of kinship with the rest of humanity? And if we do try to rally, if we could try to listen, how are we to help when the very act of listening undermines the psychological defenses we must maintain in order to live in our increasingly violent society?"

By leaving questions such as these unanswered, I may have sounded like I am rhetorically and indiscriminately assigning blame. This has not been my intent. Many people are less than careful in their attitudes towards survivors of human cruelty. But I know that many are careful, and that when they fail to be trustworthy it is in spite of their best efforts.

It is not unusual for people closest to trauma survivors to themselves be deeply shaken by the trauma. For example, researchers at the Medical University of South Carolina found that 78% of rape victims surveyed had recurrent thoughts about rape and were hypervigilant about danger. That is not a terribly surprising statistic. It is perhaps a little surprising, however, that 33% of victims' partners had recurrent thoughts about rape and that the majority (56%) became hypervigilant. Another example: A doctoral candidate interviewing partners of rape victims found that all of the partners felt powerless and vulnerable after their partners' attack. Many were plagued by their failure to protect the victim from harm. All reported difficulty with intrusive thoughts.

A growing body of psychiatric literature now recognizes the quite personal and lasting impact of a loved one's trauma on friends and family and refers to those closest to trauma survivors as co-victims. The strength of co-victims' intimate bonds with survivors means that they are likely to be called on to listen and give support. Unfortunately, the shock of their own, secondary traumatization means that, best intentions notwithstanding, co-victims may be in no real position to offer help. Researchers observing a men's group for fathers and husbands of rape victims noticed the men speaking of their own excruciating loss and of a surge of desire to protect and emotionally support their loved one. Almost uniformly, husbands acted on these loving impulses, spending more time with their wives after the rape than they had before. Significantly and sadly, however, the wives appeared to resent rather than welcome their husbands' overtures. By and large, husbands' genuine and heartfelt gestures of solidarity arose from their own unshakable needs; as such, the gestures were misjudged, inappropriate, oddly and sorrowfully off the mark.

In researching this book and listening to tales of trauma, I mostly bobbed in and out of survivors' lives. I was rarely called on to give more than a consistently empathetic look and a few words of encouragement. Friends and family of survivors are usually required to give much more. They are asked to truly share an overwhelming and seemingly endless burden of pain while somehow navigating their own way through trauma's aftershocks.

I have left my questions about how to hear unspeakable truths unanswered simply because I know that, especially for friends and family who care deeply about particular trauma survivors, there are no easy answers. Throughout this book, I have avoided taking a prescriptive tone; in fact, I hope I have been forthright about the fact that I write only with the authority of a careful observer, and not from a foundation of clinical experience. But having insisted in my writing that survivors' friends and family address certain seemingly unanswerable questions, I feel that I must at least pass on to readers some suggestions I have found that might be helpful.

One I derived from some remarks offered by Dr. Karen Saakvitne, Clinical Director of the Traumatic Stress Institute in South Windsor, Connecticut, in a speech she made about therapists' vicarious traumatization. "We therapists spend a lot of time thinking about our clients, thinking about what they bring into the office," Dr. Saakvitne explained. "We spend far too little time thinking about ourselves and what we bring into and take from the office and the relationship. It's important for us all to acknowledge to ourselves that working with survivors of trauma is difficult work, often very painful. Our clients' pain will evoke deep grief and distress in us; we need to recognize what a commitment we make when we agree to go on any journey of healing with a client. We need to take seriously the fact that we have made a commitment, and it is an intimate commitment. In fact, this commitment requires that we protect and take care of ourselves in order to support out clients in developing self-love and compassion. To do so, we must stay aware of our feelings, needs, and limits. It may be important to be able to say to our clients, 'Your need is valid. But I cannot meet it right now.' Too often, we don't give ourselves permission to protect ourselves. By not giving ourselves permission to have human feelings and foibles and to protect ourselves in ways that are quite respectful of our clients, we can end up protecting ourselves in ways that do damage to them. We say or imply to our clients something like, 'Your need is wrong. It's too much. It's bad.' Survivors don't need to hear that from us. That's what many have been hearing all their lives."

I asked Dr. Ellen Brickman, now Associate Professor in the School of Social Services at Fordham University, to suggest to me some specific ways in which Dr. Saakvitne's cautions might be useful to friends and family of survivors. "Support isn't an all or nothing proposition," she offered. "The choices aren't to be completely supportive in every way every minute to a survivor or to be of no use whatsoever. It's not realistic to expect complete support from anybody. Everyone has limitations. I think we can all work within our limitations. A rape survivor's 'significant other,' for example, might examine his own emotional capacities if he's feeling overwhelmed. Maybe not immediately post–rape, but several months down the road, he could have an honest discussion with the survivor about what he feels his limitations are. It would probably be less wounding for the survivor if the 'significant other' were eventually to say, 'I really love you and I'm really concerned about you, and I want to help you as much as I can. But I need for you to know that when you talk to me about the details of the rape I go crazy and I can't stand it. So I'm sorry that I can't be there for you in every way. I can help you in all these other areas. But this may truly be one area in which I'm not going to be able to support you in the way that I'd like to.' Hearing that might be very tough, but it still might be a lot less wounding to the survivor than sensing her boyfriend closing down emotionally with no explanation each time she brings up the rape."

A second clue I found in *Holocaust Testimonies: The Ruins of Memory*, a book-length essay by Lawrence L. Langer that is, in part, about the disinclination of many Holocaust survivors to believe their own stories, given how preposterous they sound when spoken in the context of the curiously normal present. "If somebody would tell *me* this story," Mr. Langer quotes a survivor, "I would say, 'She's lying, or he's lying.' Because this can't be true. . . . [N]obody, but nobody fully understands us. . . . I don't think you could. I don't think so."

The "seeds of anguished memory are sown in the barren belief that the very story you try to tell drives off the audience you seek to capture," explains Mr. Langer. And while he cautions that completely bridging the discontinuity between "you won't understand" and "you must understand" may be impossible, he suggests that understanding can be at least advanced when a listener is willing to engage his imagination, to imagine that what he is hearing is true until he can believe it to be so. We should not underestimate "the sympathetic power of the imagination," Mr. Langer suggests. "Perhaps it is time to grant that power the role it deserves."

"No, I can't understand," it seems a listener might admit. And then: "But I would like to try."

Inherent in questions about how to hear unspeakable truths is a deeper question: How can one live in an unlivable world? Many trauma experts agree with Dr. Ronnie Janoff-Bulman of the University of Massachusetts at Amherst, who argues that the answer is to constantly rebuild the naive assumptions about personal invulnerability that trauma shatters.

My own experience as a listener bears this out to some extent. Newfound optimism about recovery for other people aside, the after-shocks of listening are not inconsiderable. I look for ways to make my own world seem safe. Lying to myself about my invulnerability helps. But two years of listening have made the smoke screens progressively harder to erect.

How can one live in an unlivable world when one becomes too aware of universal vulnerability to fool oneself about personal peril? A clue to that narrower question comes from experts such as Dr. Bessel van der Kolk, who, in *Psychological Trauma*, suggests that the experience of helplessness is central to the experience of trauma. If Dr. van der Kolk is correct, it is possible that feeling powerful to help others, and if necessary help oneself, could remind those who listen to unspeakable truths that life may be worth living.

I suspect that this is how trauma therapists gain their optimism. They have a job to do. When they do it well, they not only "fight the good fight," they win. The world probably seems fundamentally more acceptable, at least for a while. A feeling of power put to the service of others may also be elemental to many survivors' recovery. As Dr. Judith Lewis Herman writes in *Trauma and Recovery*, "We do know from rape victims that the survivors who recover most successfully are those who discover some meaning in their experience that transcends the limits of personal tragedy. Most commonly, women find this meaning by joining with others in social action." Of course, there is only so much that one person can accomplish regardless of his or her moral authority or stamina. Feeling personally powerful may itself be one of the sanity-saving white lies upon which Dr. Janoff-Bulman suggests we all rely.

The world remains unlivable, we remain in it, and knowing the precise measure of our personal and collective vulnerability will always elude us. It is difficult to know who will be injured; it is sometimes also difficult to know what will injure. One of this book's very premises is that words can inflict a second wound. Hence, one of the anxieties I have carried with me is that, somehow, in my writing or researching, my words could hurt someone. I have feared that I would say something stupid or unwittingly unkind to an emotionally fragile survivor. I have feared that someone whose testimony I reported would be disappointed by my editing of the testimony or enraged by sloppiness in my commentary. I have even feared that someone I have never met might find the testimony provocative in a way I hadn't intended and use it as a model for further cruelty.

The more testimony I heard and recorded, the more my fears about everyone's vulnerability and unpredictability increased. At times my anxiety was so overwhelming that I became nearly obsessive about the innuendo with which each word might be loaded.

I searched to somehow soften the book's impact. I tried to give my commentary pulpier edges. If I could have enshrouded the words in cellophane, I would have.

About a week ago, feeling typically nervous, I asked a friend to review a nearly final draft. Laura Fine works in the healing professions and takes a very spiritual approach to her work. We were discussing a few sentences with which I was grappling. In Chapter One, with reference to Holocaust survivors, I had written, "These Holocaust survivors had seen human nature for what it is. It is genocidal."

I explained to my friend that although the sentence "It is genocidal" might have integrity within the context of a paragraph about the Holocaust, I felt it needed to be qualified, for we humans are certainly not all genocidal all of the time. Genocide, it seems, is not human nature *per se* but a very real and very threatening extremity of human possibility. I explained that I was concerned about the idea of extremity because assumptions we make about the periphery seem likely to reveal the hidden assumptions we make about the core. If I assume active genocide to be on the periphery of possibility, what, then, am I assuming lies at the core of human nature? Silence? Protection of stasis? The very, truly evil behaviors demonstrated by those "good" Germans who passively let genocide happen? And if those horrible characteristics lie at the core of human nature, what is my responsibility as a writer? How can I ensure that my words and the survivors' testimony I report don't ignite dormant evil?

Clearly, my nervousness about the power of words was getting beyond good reason. "Leave the sentence alone," my friend Laura said.

"Even if it's wrong, it's fairly harmless." And then she suggested something to me that quelled my anxiety and pretty well resolves my lingering doubts about how I or anyone can live in our routinely violent world. "You might consider that if genocide is an extremity of human possibility, perhaps it is only one and there are others, as well. Perhaps one of the things of which we humans are capable is being divine."

The beauty of Laura's thought reminds me of the writings of Richard Bikales, a Holocaust survivor whose work I heard two years ago when I first attended the Holocaust Writers Workshop in the Queens borough of New York City. Richard Bikales was in concentration camps during most of World War II; his parents were tortured and killed. On the cold December day that I met him, Richard read his piece, "The Faith of a Survivor."

> When we were fighting for simple, naked, raw survival, this in itself seemed to be the overwhelming purpose in life. But we did not just want to survive. We wanted to live to see the day when Hitler and his bloody empire would crumble. We believed with every fiber of our being that no matter how all-powerful and invincible our tormentors seemed, one day they would be broken, and we wanted desperately to see that day.
>
> When Hitler was defeated, we had achieved this all-consuming goal. We had survived. We had stayed alive. We had held out to see reduced to utter helplessness the men in power who had set out to destroy us and who had hunted us as their prey. We had seen the last dying wish of millions come true. So no matter what happens in this life, we have acquired a basic conviction that in the end, good wins out over evil. Not a childish, naive division of the world into good guys and bad guys, but a fundamental belief that human goodness is the norm and that the vicious, the brutal, the unconscionable, is an aberration which in the long run cannot prevail. This faith has helped us feel that life and people are worthwhile after all. It has given us the strength to live with our memories.

Richard made clear that day that he believes that good triumphs over evil. That was the very myth that I, in my writing, was hoping to clobber, for I believed (and still do believe) that imposing myths like the triumph of good over evil can inflict a second wound on survivors.

I resolved my confusion that day two years ago when I realized that Richard was not espousing a myth but speaking from personal experience. That reconciliation awaited Richard's recital of a second piece of writing, in which he told of being brutalized by SS officers and by "good" Germans, Poles, and Ukrainians, but also of being saved time and again by people fitting pretty much the same description. I learned that day from Richard that some people are genocidal, but that some people are decidedly different. Richard, I knew, had experienced the difference between good and evil incarnate, and he had witnessed good win.

I don't share my friend Laura's spirituality, but I do find her logic compelling. For I have learned from Richard Bikales and other survivors that, regardless of what is at the core of human nature, human beings are sometimes capable of, for lack of a better word, righteousness.

And while I am not quite ready to agree with Richard that "human goodness is the norm," I know that my reluctance to agree may be founded on inexperience. I haven't seen all of the heroism and rescue that Richard has.

I do find myself ready to agree with Richard that "life and people are worthwhile" and with Laura that human beings can be divine. I have put my faith in a secular sort of divinity, a trustworthiness so necessary that it must be next to godliness. Hoping we humans can find ways to nurture our individual and collective respectability will let me feel all right for a while about us, our world, and the challenges our own human nature present us.

11

I AM WELL AWARE OF THE SHORTCOMINGS of the research method I have used for this book. I met people in their therapists' offices, not in prisons or asylums or shelters for the homeless. This meant that I interviewed only the most reachable, only those who were willing and eager to talk, and probably only those who were most likely to recover.

I am also well aware that the testimony that makes up such a large part of this book casts a light on the recovery process that is perhaps too rosy. I met with people periodically but certainly not daily. I didn't hear much about, and therefore didn't write much about, the grinding work of recovery. I know that, because of this, the testimony reported should be considered no more than snapshots of survivors at distinct points in their recovery process. I assume that some of the survivors I interviewed had and will have setbacks about which I will never know.

But as problematic as my methodology may be, I find it remarkable to now number among my acquaintances quite a few survivors who have reclaimed a state of psychological vitality that they didn't have when I first met them. Although I set out to write this book with the objective of convincing readers that recovery from trauma is possible, I began with knowledge acquired only from other people's books and papers. It took two years of my own writing and listening to convince me that specialists in post-traumatic therapy were right. I have seen what they talk about happen.

Bob Howe is the Vietnam veteran whose emotional homecoming was delayed for 20 years until he marched in his state's bicentennial Fourth of July parade. Bob no longer lives in hiding. He talks to people, easily. He has finally found a motorcycle gang with which to ride. It is a Christian gang. He volunteers as a firefighter in the fire department of his small town. He and his wife are raising their four-year-old granddaughter. Bob spends a lot of time doing community service and a lot of time making sure that fighting men and women are recognized for their sacrifices. He organized a rifle salute to veterans as part of his town's Memorial Day celebration. And he was the force behind the erection of a stone memorial to all of the town's people, living and dead, who have served in this country's wars.

Sandra Donike is the architect who was sexually abused by her grandfather and who developed two personalities, one boy and one girl, as an adaptive response to the trauma. Sandra and her husband, Vinny, had very difficult times during her recovery process. Vinny grew up in an abusive family. Like his father had, Vinny insisted on his right to rule at home. It was a claim to which Sandra had always acceded until her work in therapy caused her to question some of the basic assumptions upon which her childhood had been based. This cast doubt on some of the operating assumptions of her marriage. Sandra's self-discovery created chaos for Vinny; he got angry and the steady diet of anger caused Sandra to make private plans to leave the marriage. Vinny found a notebook detailing those plans, and that threw him into an even deeper personal crisis. Eventually, Vinny, like Sandra, found a therapist expert in post-traumatic therapy. The last time I talked to Sandra and Vinny they were still a couple. They had a lot of optimism about their ability to remain one.

Dorian Davis is the ex-cop on permanent disability for work-related stress. Dorian no longer arms himself with a bevy of guns. He uses one. He has built an addition onto his home that dwarfs the original, easily defended, kitchen-sized building. And Dorian is no longer completely isolated. He substitute teaches (unarmed) in elementary schools. He is thinking of going back to college, perhaps to study early childhood education. He is looking for friends and would like a romantic relationship. He goes line dancing because it's a friendly way to meet people and talk.

Yolla Hogan is the surgery resident at a teaching hospital who was raped throughout her childhood by her father, sometimes with guns, and who developed multiple personalities to absorb the trauma. Her personalities remain integrated. She is now a practicing surgeon in New York City. Yolla specializes in pediatric injuries. Many of the children she sees have been hurt by their parents. From friends in New York who work in the city shelter system I have heard wonderful things about Yolla's manner with battered children.

Madeline Goodman is still deeply anguished by the aftershocks of the gang rape and of life dominated by her father's rage and lust. Perhaps she would have made faster emotional progress if she had stayed in therapy, but for a little over a year Madeline has been taking a break. She knows it's time now to get back to it. She will begin again in a few weeks.

I met with Madeline and her therapist a little over a week ago. The meeting was at my request. I just wanted to catch up with Madeline. As part of my effort to buffer people I interview from any serious bumblings or intrusions on my part, I usually ask to meet with them in the company of their therapists. Hence, my meeting with Madeline was a three-way meeting.

Almost, anyway. Madeline and her therapist were very moved at seeing each other again. The affection between them clearly runs deep;

to an observer it is almost palpable. They had so much to say to each other that our ostensibly three-way meeting quickly became two-way plus one, a shift that the writer in me liked because therapists generally ask better questions than I do. Madeline and her therapist talked and I mostly listened.

Listening, I learned that memories, intrusive thoughts, and self-blame still plague Madeline, and the sound of a fog horn still terrifies her. Perhaps because she wouldn't be seeing Madeline for a few weeks and Madeline was clearly upset and wanting help, her therapist gave her a rush of practical suggestions:

When you hear a fog horn, think about any boat that horn may be signaling. That boat is moving away, fast, and thoughts about the rapists can be put on the boat and carried far away, out to sea.

Madeline takes walks outdoors to calm herself, but when she walks outdoors, horrifying thoughts intrude. The therapist's suggestion: Remember that while the gang rape occurred outdoors, during the entire ordeal it was nature alone that stayed true. In fact, tree frogs chirped all night long, keeping you company and giving you something on which to focus. Remember the tree frogs and thank them.

Madeline could not save the dog from immolation that night, nor did she understand the plight of another woman who was tied up and begging to be released. Her inability to save the dog and woman still feel like failures to her. Her therapist's suggestion: Write them each a letter explaining that you were drugged against your will and would have saved them if you could have understood they needed help.

Madeline still has a lot of recovering to do. But she has also come a very long way. The woman who lay awake in bed each night with the lights on and a loaded shotgun at her side has a much calmer life. Most people seem to cry sometimes during therapy, and Madeline is no exception. But outside of therapy Madeline's manner is happy and easy. She is a lot of fun to talk to. Madeline has some friends. She has a therapist who cares about her and has made her caring emphatically evident. And Madeline now has a husband.

Two months ago, Madeline married Harry, a man I had only heard about in passing references. As our three-way meeting with her therapist ended, Madeline handed me a videotape of the wedding. She and Harry are giving them out as Christmas presents. Harry, she says, watches their copy a lot.

I held onto the tape for days before viewing it, thinking I would need to carve out enough time to sit alone for a while afterwards if the experience of watching left me shaken. It didn't. Madeline's wedding was wonderfully unremarkable as weddings go. No echoes of trauma. Just a happy time. Madeline and Harry got married on an Indian reservation. It's not unusual these days to marry outdoors. They were surrounded by friends, as most couples are when they marry. The wedding party stood on a mesa. The ceremony was Christian. There were a few giggles as, for lack of organ music, Madeline and her attendants hummed the wedding march while walking toward Harry, his best man, and the minister. The wedding party laughed a little, but these people were not clowning. Madeline is now forty-two years old. Her whole life has been dominated by violence and shame. And here she was marrying Harry, a big man, middle-aged. Physically, he reminds her of her father. Madeline thinks seriously about the implications of the similarities.

Madeline and Harry seemed the souls of hospitality as, immediately after their vows, they passed to each guest a traditional Native American wedding drink presented to them by one of their friends. Then the videotape shows more wedding stuff, all of it delightfully standard. Madeline and Harry kissed. People threw rice. Madeline threw the bouquet. Someone commented about the beautiful sky. A few people mugged for the camera.

Then, a while after the wedding ceremony, two Native American friends washed Madeline's hair in a traditional cleansing ceremony meant to symbolize that the past is over. They buried the water far away in a place where Madeline need never go. This ceremony is not on the videotape. "My friends didn't like the camera," Madeline explained to me this morning on the phone. "This needed to stay private."

I find it remarkable that Madeline chose to join her life fixedly to a man's while the aftershocks of brutality perpetrated by men continue to cloud her every day. And I find it reassuring, though in some ways almost unbelievable, that the ceremony was just about like every wedding I've ever seen.

This morning when I talked to Madeline by phone I wanted to learn from her whether there was any symbolism I had missed in the wedding ceremony that would add to my understanding of her decision to marry and her ideas about her future. I asked Madeline about her two wedding attendants and learned they were Harry's grown daughters. We laughed about how embarrassing it can be to publicly exchange vows that feel like they have more meaning when they are spoken privately. Then I told Madeline that, considering the traditional Christian vows, I had expected her to dress at least somewhat traditionally and had been surprised to see her in buckskin. Was there some symbolism in her choice of dress? Does largely unadorned buckskin have ceremonial import?

"No, nothing," Madeline said, and her voice lilted a little. It was hard to tell over the telephone, but I think that she enjoyed my question. I imagined her very broad smile as she said, "Harry had a dream that I would wear buckskin, and a few days later I had the same dream. So we just decided to go with our dreams."

POSTSCRIPT

THE DAY THAT I FIRST MET MADELINE GOODMAN she made clear to me that one of her primary motivations for telling me her story was the hope that any of the other women who had been raped along with her might read her testimony. Madeline hoped that her own memories could lend another woman validation for troubling memories she might have. She was particularly concerned about a girl she remembered as tied to the wheel hub of a car. This girl had asked for help and Madeline, in her drugged and frightened state, had failed to understand. When I first met Madeline she wanted very much to help this girl (now a woman), even if the only help she could offer would be more than two decades late in arriving.

In my last meeting with Madeline before finishing this manuscript, Madeline made it clear that she was still tormented by her inability the night of the gang rape to help either the girl or the dog that the rapists had burned alive. Madeline's therapist suggested that she might relieve some of her torment by writing letters of explanation to the girl and dog.

Shortly after I completed work on this manuscript, I received from Madeline copies of the letters that her therapist had suggested she write. In the remembering that was necessary for the writing, Madeline recalled a memory that threw much of her original motivation for telling me her story into doubt.

Madeline had wanted to help the girl she believed she had long ago failed. Clarified memory, however, suggested that it was the girl who had failed Madeline. Madeline now believes that the girl tied to the wheel hub of a car was released several hours before Madeline was left for dead. The question with which Madeline now grapples is, "Why didn't that girl go for help? Why didn't she save me?"

This book examines in depth the controversy about disinterred memory. It seems prudent to conclude from the studies reported in the body of this book that no single detail of a long interred memory should be accepted as uncontestable fact. So, granted, Madeline may be wrong about this particular newly retrieved memory. And even if Madeline is correct in surmising that the girl failed to get help for her, a compassionate interpretation of Madeline's memory leaves one wondering whether the girl was too overwhelmed by her own trauma to have even noticed what was happening to Madeline. Regardless, Madeline's newly retrieved memory is significant. To her it feels quite real, and the girl's behavior seems perhaps inexcusable. And in historical fact, Madeline's memory may be accurate and her suspicions about the girl's motivations appropriate.

I like Madeline a lot. I know her to be an extremely careful and considerate person. And her story as she understands it does not personally accuse me or anyone I love. Therefore, I am quite happy to accept her version of what transpired that night. I am glad that she has discovered another piece with which to solve her mind's puzzle. But regardless of the veracity of the memory or the motivations of the girl Madeline remembers, for me Madeline's newly retrieved memory resounds as a metaphor for a basic premise of my book: We misunderstand each other badly. We must do a better job of it. We simply must.

I report here the text of the cover letter Madeline sent to me along with excerpts from Madeline's letter to the dog and to the girl.

12/23

Rebecca,

After writing these letters I had more energy and realized that three or four of the girls that were raped and released hours before never went for help! They never helped me. I find myself angry — no wonder none of them ever try to get in touch with me.

Often [in writing] I had to stop, walk away, take a cigarette break. It was easier to write to the dog because I feel they would have set me on fire if he hadn't been there. So now I realize I have the dog, the tree frogs, and the birds that sang in the morning as allies.

It has helped me to write these two letters. . . .

Have a good holiday!
Madeline

12/22

To the dog who was burned alive,

I remember you. I remember how you wagged your tail as they saturated your fur with gasoline. So many helping hands holding you in place. . . .

It's been over twenty years. I'm still haunted by what they did to you — to us. I envy your status of death — it's over for you. God has given me this other path of travail, survival.

If the world were mine, if I had power, I would have saved you. I would have been your hero, taken everyone, male and female alike, who had hurt you . . . and dissipating them into hell. I would have carried you away to a place of peace, washed away all the pain, humiliation, and trickery. I would call you friend, love you, and help you. If the world were mine.

But I could not help you. I could not help you or myself. . . .

I know some of them went to jail, most went free, and one woman killed herself. The quality of life for me is fair on a good day.

I know what happened to us has happened before. I know it is hard to know the mind of God. The why of it all.

I would have stopped the world against such an outrage. I did nothing. I am sorry, dog. I am so sorry.

Madeline

Postscript

12/22

To the girl tied to the wheel hub of a car,

I do not know your identity but I look for you every day. I feel you know who I am. I wish you would talk to me. I want to tell you why I couldn't help you. Some things you may never know that you should know, to help you understand. You may be thinking to this day that I was one of them. I was not.
. . .

I did not take the drug voluntarily. I was expecting a party, not a gang rape. I did not know what I was doing. I do not even know what drugs they injected me with.

I can see you now begging me for help. You are tied to a wheel hub of a car. There are channel tracks in the dirt from your fruitless attempts to stand. You frightened me. In my incoherent state of mind I thought you were tied up for a reason. If I let you go free you would hurt me.

Did they rape you? Probably. I saw several girls with their hands tied being raped. Was this your first sexual experience? It was mine. . . .

Did your parents blame you? Was your father so turned on by it all that he raped you again? Were you robbed of your memories? Did your friends, classmates, giggle, smirk, and shove you in school? This is my legacy.

You were released hours before I was left in the field. Why didn't you go for help? Surely you must still hear my screams.

Madeline

NOTES

PART 1

Page 2. "The United States Department of Justice says that as many as 850,000 rapes, robberies, and assaults with firearms are committed each year in the United States." Statistics are published in a U.S. Department of Justice press release dated February 26, 1994. They cover the years 1987-1992.

Page 2. The National Institute of Justice's prediction that 80% of Americans will be victimized by a serious crime was quoted in the national edition of the *New York Times* of May 3, 1990, p. B7.

Page 2. "The Bureau of Justice Statistics says that criminals are increasingly likely to be armed and dangerous." A U.S. Department of Justice press release dated February 26, 1994 says, "Violent offenders are increasingly likely to be armed, the Bureau of Justice Statistics (BJS) said today. . . . [T]he rate of offenses committed with pistols and revolvers rose from 9.2 percent in 1979 to 12.7 percent in 1992."

Page 2. "Recent survey data gathered under the auspices of the National Institutes of Mental Health from 6,159 female students at thirty-two colleges indicated that 15% of college women have experienced rape since their fourteenth birthday." This survey was conducted by the *Ms.* Magazine Campus Project on Sexual Assault, funded by the National Institutes of Mental Health, and reported to the Judiciary Committee hearings in 1990. The survey was structured to rely on a legal definition of the term *rape*. Data from this study are published in M. P. Koss, C. A. Gidycz, and N. Wisniewski, "The Scope of Rape: Incidence and Prevalence of Sexual Aggression and Victimization in a National Sample of Higher Education Students," *Journal of Consulting and Clinical Psychology* 55: 162-170 (1987).

Page 2. "According to Dr. Dean G. Kilpatrick, Director of the National Crime Victims Research and Treatment Center of the Medical University of South Carolina, victims of crime are about ten times more likely than the general population to become depressed. One in every five women who has been raped attempts suicide. Over 40% of rape victims have suicidal thoughts." Dr. Kilpatrick based his conclusions about the emotional aftershocks of crime and rape on the results of a random sampling of 2,009 women around the country. In the May 3, 1990 article of the *New York Times* cited above, Dr. Kilpatrick is referred to as saying that other studies conducted by him have found that men as well as women are ten times more likely than the general population to be depressed even a decade or more after being victimized by crime.

Notes

Page 3. Statistics about the Holocaust and the description of liberation derived are from H. Epstein, *Children of the Holocaust* (Viking, 1988). See especially pp. 11-12 and 67-68.

Page 3. Dr. Paul Friedman published articles about the institutional neglect of Holocaust survivors' psychological problems in at least two sources: P. Friedman, "The Road Back for the D. P.'s: Healing the Psychological Scars of Nazism," *Commentary* 6(6): 502-510 (1948) and *Journal of the Hillside Hospital* 10: 233-247 (1961). The quote about the assumption of physical and psychological superiority is from the second of these two sources.

Page 4. Drawing on her formal research with Holocaust survivors, their children, and their therapists as well as on her informal, clinical observations, Dr. Yael Danieli has published widely on issues such as society's and psychotherapists' refusal to hear or believe the stories of Holocaust survivors. Her most recent book is Yael Danieli, et al., eds., *International Responses to Traumatic Stress: Humanitarian, Human Rights, Justice, Peace, and Development Contributions, Collaborative Actions, and Future Initiatives* (Baywood, 1996). The quote about going like sheep to the slaughter is taken from Y. Danieli, "The Treatment and Prevention of Long-term Effects and Intergenerational Transmission of Victimization: A Lesson from Holocaust Survivors and Their Children," *Trauma and its Wake*, edited by C. R. Figley (Brunner/Mazel, 1985), p. 298. Her observations on therapists' reactions to Holocaust stories are in Y. Danieli, "Confronting the Unimaginable: Psychotherapists' Reactions to Victims of the Nazi Holocaust," *Human Adaptation to Extreme Stress: From the Holocaust to Viet Nam*, edited by J. P. Wilson, Z. Harel, and B. Kahana (Plenum, 1988), pp. 224-225. Readers are also referred to Y. Danieli, *Therapists' Difficulties in Treating Survivors of the Nazi Holocaust and their Children* (Ph.D. diss., New York University), University Microfilms International, #949-904.

Page 4. Dr. Lucy Friedman's quotes are excerpted from an unpublished address on the topic of stigmatized death, which she gave at Yeshiva University in New York City on October 18, 1988.

Page 11. *Massive Psychic Trauma*, edited by Henry Krystal, M.D., was published in 1968 by International Universities Press.

PART 2

Page 29. "But the specific problems Madeline had been suffering — anxiety, depression, suicidal thoughts, hypervigilance, sleep disturbances, concentration difficulties, self-loathing, nightmares, flashbacks, and problems with intimacy and addiction — are some of the common emotional aftershocks suffered by victims of violence." The typical symptoms of post-traumatic stress are listed in *Diagnostic and Statistical Manual of Mental Disorders* (4th ed.) (American Psychiatric Press, 1994).

Page 30. The ease with which the symptoms of post-traumatic stress are confused with those of other psychiatric problems has been raised in a variety of articles and text-books. Two of the most prominent are B. A. van der Kolk, A. C. McFarlane, and L. Weisaeth, eds., *Traumatic Stress: The Effects of Overwhelming Experience on Mind, Body, and Society* (Guilford, 1996), pp. 47–76 and M. J. Horowitz, *Stress Response Syndromes* (Jason Aronson, 1986), pp. 22–34.

Page 30. "Since the dawn of modern psychiatry, psychotherapists have noticed that traumatic memories are sometimes unavailable to a survivor's conscious memory. "Survivors' propensity to repress traumatic memories has been widely discussed in the psychiatric literature since Freud's time. Excellent recent books on the topic include Susan L. Reviere, *Memory of Childhood Trauma: A Clinician's Guide to the Literature* (Guilford, 1996); Kenneth S. Pope and Laura S. Brown's *Recovered Memories of Abuse: Assessment, Therapy, Forensics* (American Psychological Association, 1996), Charles L. Whitfield's *Memory and Abuse: Remembering and Healing the Effects of Trauma* (Health Communications, 1995), Jennifer J. Freyd's *Betrayal Trauma: The Logic of Forgetting Childhood Abuse* (Harvard University Press, 1996), and Daniel L. Schacter's *Searching for Memory: The Brain, the Mind, and The Past* (Basic, 1996). Readers are also directed to the "Memory: Mechanisms and Processes" section on pages 279–330 of *Traumatic Stress: The Effects of Overwhelming Experience on Mind, Body, and Society.*

Page 30–31. Dr. Mark Hall's and Dr. Karen Saakvitne's observations about repressed memories are quoted from an interview conducted at the Traumatic Stress Institute on March 30, 1992.

Page 31. "Clinical observations of discrete populations such as war veterans, crime victims, incest survivors, and war refugees have amply shown that, regardless of whether trauma survivors have repressed their traumatic memories, there may be a span of years or even decades between the actual traumatic event and the onset of stress symptoms." The phenomenon of delayed onset of symptoms of post-traumatic stress is discussed in *Diagnostic and Statistical Manual of Mental Disorders* (4th ed.).

Page 32. *Studies in Hysteria*, originally published in 1895, has been reprinted by Pelican. J. Breuer and S. Freud, *Studies in Hysteria* (Pelican, 1986).

Page 32. Freud's "The Aetiology of Hysteria" (1896) is published in *The Standard Edition of the Complete Psychological Works of Sigmund Freud*, vol. 3, trans. J. Strachey (Hogarth, 1962). The reader is referred specifically to p. 203.

Page 32–33. Freud's acknowledgment of the hostile response of Viennese society to "The Aetiology of Hysteria" and the reasons for his abandonment of the seduction theory he expounded in "The Aetiology of Hysteria" are mentioned by Freud in correspondence to William Fleiss. See Freud, Sigmund, *The Complete Letters of Sigmund Freud to Wilhelm Fleiss, 1877-1904,* translated by Jeffrey Moussaieff Masson, Belknap Press of Harvard University Press, 1985.

Notes

It is odd that Freud eventually expressed embarrassment about his "credulity" in having believed his patients' accounts of sexual abuse, for he had published several case studies in which the survivor's account of sexual abuse was corroborated by either the abuser, a co-victim, or a witness. See M. Balmary, *Psychoanalyzing Psychoanalysis* (Johns Hopkins University Press, 1982).

Page 33. Dr. Finkelhor's analysis of the nineteen surveys was reported by Gannett News Service in a news wire dated April 16, 1996. The results of the surveys were occasionally at odds with one another, a fact that Dr. Finkelhor apparently attributes to the methodological difficulty with which such sensitive and retrospective data are gathered. Dr. Finkelhor is quoted by Gannett as complaining, "It's a mess, and I find that inexcusable. You can find how many people were injured by farm machinery with far more precision than how many children are abused."

Page 33. The chronology of Freud's early thoughts on what he eventually called his Oedipal theory can be found in his letters to Wilhelm Fleiss. See Freud, Sigmund, *The Complete Letters of Sigmund Freud to Wilhelm Fleiss, 1877-1904,* translated and edited by Jeffrey Moussaieff Masson. For synopses of discussions of the Oedipal theory by the Vienna Psychoanalytic Society, of which Freud was an active member, see H. Nunberg and E. Federn, eds. *Minutes of the Vienna Psychoanalytic Society,* translated by M. Nunberg (International Universities Press, 1962-1975), Vol. 4: 1912-1918.

Page 33. "In a 1986 study of the sexual assault histories of 930 women in San Francisco, sociologist Dr. Diana Russell, then a Professor at Mills College in Oakland, California, discovered that two-thirds of those women who were sexually assaulted as children were victimized again as adults by rape or attempted rape. . . ." Dr. Russell's landmark study was reported in D. E. H. Russell, *Sexual Exploitation: Rape, Child Sexual Abuse, and Sexual Harassment* (Sage, 1984), p. 35. The studies corroborating the phenomenon of revictimization include M. P. Koss and T. E. Dindero, "Discriminant Analysis of Risk Factors for Sexual Victimization among a National Sample of College Women," *Journal of Consulting and Clinical Psychology* 57: 242-250 (1989); B. M. Atkeson, K. S. Calhoun, and K. T. Morris, "Victim Resistance to Rape: The Relationship of Previous Victimization, Demographics, and Situational Factors," *Archives of Sexual Behavior* 18: 497-507 (1989); R. P. Kluft, "Incest and Subsequent Revictimization: The Case of Therapist-Patient Sexual Exploitation, with a Description of the Sitting Duck Syndrome," R. P. Kluft, ed., *Incest-Related Syndromes of Adult Psychopathology* (American Psychiatric Press, 1990), pp. 263-287; G. E. Wyatt, D. Guthrie, and C. M. Notgrass, "Differential Effects of Women's Child Sexual Abuse and Subsequent Sexual Revictimization," *Journal of Consulting and Clinical Psychology* 60: 167-173 (1992).

Page 34. The phenomenon of self-imposed repetitions of traumatic experiences is addressed in a variety of sources. Excellent discussions are to be found in Bessel A. van der Kolk, "The Complexity of Adaptation to Trauma: Self-Regulation, Stimulus Discrimination, and Characterological Development" in *Traumatic Stress: The Effects of Overwhelming Experience on Mind, Body, and Society* (Guilford, 1996), pp. 199-201; Steven Krugman, "Trauma in the Family: Perspectives on the Intergenerational Transmission of Violence," in B. A. van der Kolk, ed., *Psychological Trauma*, pp. 134-135, and Herman, *Trauma and Recovery*, pp. 15-16 and 39-42.

The example of combat veterans reenacting their traumatic experiences through police work was derived from a telephone interview of October 3, 1991 with Dr. Christine Dunning, of the Governmental Affairs Department of the University of Wisconsin in Milwaukee. In that interview, Dr. Dunning pointed out that "a significant majority— 80-90%— of police officers are combat vets."

Throughout her book, *The Healing Power of Play* (Guilford, 1991), child psychologist Eliana Gil discusses ways in which children's trauma becomes manifest in their play. Readers are referred especially to p. 24.

Page 34. Dr. Laurie Anne Pearlman's quote about the inability of some trauma survivors to adequately assess danger is from an interview conducted at the Traumatic Stress Institute on March 30, 1992.

Page 45. "Historically, soldiers traumatized by the horrors of war have been diagnosed as morally deficient or constitutionally cowardly." Dr. Judith Lewis Herman examines the stigmatized diagnoses applied to combat veterans in *Trauma and Recovery*, p. 21. The many shades of misunderstanding of the effects of combat stress are also addressed in M. R. Trimble, "Post-Traumatic Stress Disorder: History of a Concept" in C. R. Figley, ed., *Trauma and Its Wake: The Study and Treatment of Post-Traumatic Stress Disorder.* (Brunner/Mazel, 1985), pp. 5-14.

Page 45. "Wives terrorized by violent husbands have long been diagnosed as overemotional, masochistic, and passive-aggressive." J. E. Snell, R. J. Rosenwald, and A. Robey, "The Wife-Beater's Wife," *Archives of General Psychiatry* 11: 107-112 (1964), is a remarkable example of the historical blindness of the psychotherapeutic profession to the plight of battered women. In that paper, the authors purport to illustrate how the personalities and needs of battered wives drive husbands to battering. Less prejudiced discussions of battering and of the complex interactions often found in violent marriages have abounded over the past decade. Good examples include: E. Stark and A. Flitcraft, "Personal Power and Institutional Victimization: Treating the Dual Trauma of Woman Battering," in F. Ochberg, ed., *Post-Traumatic Therapy and Victims of Violence* (Brunner/Mazel, 1988); L. E. Walker, *The Battered Woman Syndrome* (Springer, 1984); D. D. Stout and P. Brown, "Legal and Social Differences Between Men and Women Who Kill Intimate Partner," *Affilia* 10: 194 (1995); and M. T. Loring and R. W. Smith, "Health Care Barriers and Interventions for Battered Women," Public Health Reports, Vol. 109, U.S. Department of Health and Human Services, p. 328 (1994).

Notes

Page 45. In *Trauma and Recovery*, Dr. Herman gives an excellent overview of the contributions made by anti-war Vietnam veterans and by the women's movement to the evolution of a humanistic and realistic concept of the effect of trauma on the human psyche. See the chapter titled "A Forgotten History," pp. 7-32.

Page 46. Dr. Herman discusses the concept of internalized trauma in *Trauma and Recovery* in a chapter titled "Captivity," pp. 51-73.

In the late 1980s and early 1990s the role of trauma in the histories of people diagnosed with personality disorders became a lively area of investigation. Too many excellent reviews and original studies have been published to name here. Readers are referred especially to B. A. van der Kolk, J. C. Perry, and J. L. Herman, "Childhood Origins of Self-Destructive Behavior," *American Journal of Psychiatry* 148(12): pp. 1665-1671 (1991); J. L. Herman, J. C. Perry, and B. A. van der Kolk, "Childhood Trauma in Borderline Personality Disorder," *American Journal of Psychiatry* 146(4): pp. 490-495 (April 1989); and J. C. Perry, J. L. Herman, B. A. van der Kolk, and L. A. Hoke, "Psychotherapy and Psychological Trauma in Borderline Personality Disorder," *Psychiatric Annals* 20(1): 33-43 (January 1990). Dr. Herman gives a superb overview of the controversy in *Trauma and Recovery*, pp. 74-95. Dr. van der Kolk's equally astute overview can be found in *Traumatic Stress: The Effects of Overwhelming Experience on Mind, Body, and Society*, 201-205.

Page 49. That the diagnosis of PTSD "tacitly recognizes that the world can drive a normal person crazy" is quoted from J. Jay, "Terrible Knowledge," *Networker*, p. 21 (November/December 1991).

Page 49. The 29% PTSD rate among high school juniors was reported in "Exposure to Violence and Post-Traumatic Stress Disorder in Urban Adolescents" (1996) Libra Publishers, Inc. Five years earlier, a PTSD prevalence among young urban adults of 9% was reported. See N. Breslau, G. C. Davis, P. Andreski et al., "Traumatic Events and Posttraumatic Stress Disorder in an Urban Population of Young Adults," *Archives of General Psychiatry* 48: 216-22 (1991).

Page 49. The estimate of the prevalence of PTSD among Holocaust survivors was reported in *Science News* 141(1): 173 (March 14, 1992).

Page 49. The results of the congressionally mandated Vietnam Veteran Readjustment Study were published in R. A. Kulka, W. E. Schlenger, J. A. Fairbank et al., *National Vietnam Veteran Readjustment Study (NVVRS): Executive Summary* (Research Triangle Institute, 1988). The more recent data — a Department of Veterans Affairs report that 31% of Vietnam era veterans had been treated for psychiatric and neurologic disorders — were reported in the *Los Angeles Times* of April 27, 1995.

Page 49. The estimate of the prevalence of PTSD among American women was reported in *Science News* 140: 141 (Aug. 31, 1991).

Page 50. The laundry list of traumatic stressors is to be found on page 424 of *Diagnostic and Statistical Manual of Mental Disorders* (4th ed.).

Page 50-51. "For example, the results of a 1979 survey conducted by Dr. Diana Russell of the sexual assault histories of women in San Francisco suggest that one in four, or 25%, has been or will be raped (with rape being defined as completed intercourse obtained by force or by threat of force or when the woman was drugged, unconscious, asleep, or otherwise totally helpless and therefore unable to consent)." See D. E. H. Russell, *Sexual Exploitation: Rape, Child Sexual Abuse, and Sexual Harassment* (Sage, 1984), p. 35.

Page 51. "Considering more recent survey data—of 6,159 female students interviewed at thirty-two colleges, 15% had been raped since their fourteenth birthday—the prediction seems tame if anything." See M. P. Koss, C. A. Gidycz, and N. Wisniewski, "The Scope of Rape: Incidence and Prevalence of Sexual Aggression and Victimization in a National Sample of Higher Education Students," *Journal of Consulting and Clinical Psychology* 55: 455-457 (1987).

Page 51. The effect of coping skills and self-esteem on one's resilience to PTSD is discussed quite thoroughly in several sections of *Traumatic Stress: The Overwhelming Experience on Mind, Body, and Society*. The authors of those discussions drew heavily upon the research and insight of many who came before them, including: B. L. Green, J. P. Wilson, and J. D. Lindy, "Conceptualizing Post-Traumatic Stress Disorder: A Psychosocial Framework" in C. R. Figley, ed. *Trauma and its Wake: The Study and Treatment of Post-Traumatic Stress Disorder* (Brunner/Mazel, 1985); H. Hendin and A. P. Haas, "Combat Adaptations of Vietnam Veterans Without Posttraumatic Stress Disorder," *American Journal of Psychiatry* 141: 956-960 (1984); H. Hendin and A. P. Haas, *Wounds of War: The Psychological Aftermath of Combat in Vietnam* (Basic, 1984), p. 214; S. B. Kleinman, "Terror at Sea: Vietnamese Victims of Piracy," *American Journal of Psychoanalysis* 50(4): 351-362 (December 1990); S. B. Kleinman, "A Terrorist Hijacking: Victims' Experiences Initially and Nine Years Later," *Journal of Traumatic Stress* 2(1): 49-58 (January 1989); E. R. Worthington, "The Vietnam Era Veteran Anomie and Adjustment," *Military Medicine* 141(3): 169-170 (March 1976); and R. J. Ursano, R. Wheatley, W. Sledge, A. Rahe, et al., "Coping and Recovery Styles in the Vietnam Era Prisoner of War," *Journal of Nervous & Mental Disease* 174(12): 707-714 (1986).

Page 51-52. Dr. Lenore Terr's insights about resilience or lack thereof in children four years post-trauma are written up as L. C. Terr, "Chowchilla Revisited: The Effects of Psychic Trauma Four Years After a School-Bus Kidnapping," *American Journal of Psychiatry* 140(12): 1543-1550 (1983) and L. Terr, *Too Scared to Cry* (HarperCollins, 1990), pp. 22-24.

Page 52. The Traumatic Stress Study Center of the University of Cincinnati College of Medicine's study of resilience to war stress is written up as B. L. Green, M. C.

Notes

Grace, J. D. Lindy, et al., "Risk Factors for PTSD and Other Diagnoses in a General Sample of Vietnam Veterans," *American Journal of Psychiatry* 174: 729-733 (1990).

Other research conducted with Vietnam veterans and supporting the hypothesis of a simple linear correlation between the strength of the stressor and the intensity of the distress include two studies conducted by investigators at the Uniformed Services University of the Health Sciences in Bethesda, Maryland. In the first study, data gathered from 253 former prisoners of war indicated that psychiatric problems were greater among prisoners who had been captured before 1969, and had therefore suffered longer and harsher captivities. (See J. Ursano, J. A. Boydstun, and R. D. Wheatley, "Psychiatric Illness in U.S. Air Force Viet Nam Prisoners of War: A Five-year Follow-up," *American Journal of Psychiatry* 138[3]: 310-314 [March 1981]). In the second study, data gathered from 294 former prisoners of war indicated that POWs captured before 1969 showed greater repression, denial, suspicion, and distrust than their post-1969 peers. See R. D. Wheatley and R. J. Ursano, "Serial Personality Evaluations of Repatriated U.S. Air Force Southeast Asia POWs," *Aviation, Space, & Environmental Medicine* 53(3): 251-257 (March 1982).

Page 52. "Extreme negative events that induce trauma are unique in that they force victims to come face to face with their vulnerability, with their essential fragility" is quoted from R. Janoff-Bulman, *Shattered Assumptions* (Free Press, 1992), pp. 59 and 62.

Page 52. "Trauma occurs when one loses the sense of having a safe place to retreat within or outside oneself to deal with frightening emotions or experiences. This results in a state of helplessness, a feeling that one's actions have no bearing on the outcome of one's life" is quoted from B. A. van der Kolk, *Psychological Trauma*, p. 31.

Page 52-53. Over the course of a year, Drs. Ann Wolbert Burgess and Lynda Lyttle Holmstrom asked a series of open-ended questions of ninety-two women who were treated in the Boston City Hospital Emergency Department after having been raped. Their objective was to determine how the victims felt and reacted to rape immediately before, during, and after the attack. They noted that during the rape, most victims used cognitive strategies to make the rape in some way more tolerable. These strategies included mentally focussing their attention away from the reality of the event, memorizing details that might later prove useful in court, recalling advice people had given about rape, recalling their own successful coping strategies during previous encounters with violence, concentrating on the assailant's possible motives, and praying. See A. W. Burgess and L. L. Holmstrom, "Coping Behavior of the Rape Victim," *American Journal of Psychiatry* 133(4): 413-418 (1976). See especially p. 415.

Burgess and Holmstrom's work ignited a stream of research into rape victims' coping strategies. Interestingly, however, researchers tended to focus not on the effects of cognitive strategies on psychological survival but on the question of whether physical resistance helps stave off rape. Readers interested in that line of inquiry are directed to: S. E. Ullman and R. A. Knight, "Women's Resistance Strategies to Different Rapist Types," *Criminal Justice & Behavior* 22: 263 (1995), which presents recent findings and an overview of the twenty years of literature.

Page 53. Dr. Ronnie Janoff-Bulman thoroughly examines the functions and mechanisms of self-blame. See R. Janoff-Bulman, *Shattered Assumptions*, pp. 125-130.

Page 53. "Ever since World War II, military psychiatrists have assumed that soldiers fighting in small combat groups characterized by mutual encouragement and support sometimes derive feelings of self-worth and safety that protect than them from trauma's aftershocks." During and after World War II, Dr. Roy R. Grinker, Sr. of Michael Reese Hospital Medical Center in Chicago and Dr. John P. Spiegel of Harvard Medical School worked with thousands of trauma-wounded soldiers both in Europe and in the United States. Doctors Grinker and Spiegel observed that bonds of friendship between men in combat groups provide enormous protection from the psychic wounds of war. See R. R. Grinker and J. Spiegel's *Men Under Stress* (Blakeston, 1945). See especially p. 22.

Page 53-54. The finding that rape victims enjoying stable relationships with men recovered faster than those not in stable relationships was derived from a followup study of eighty-one rape victims. See A. Burgess and L. Holmstrom, "Adaptive Strategies and Recovery from Rape," *American Journal of Psychiatry* 136: 1278-1282 (1979).

Page 54. The quote by Dr. Lucy Friedman concerning the social exile of the families of homicide victims is taken from her lecture on stigmatized death given at Yeshiva University on October 18, 1988.

Page 54. Dr. Ellen Brickman's quote is from an interview of August 7, 1992.

Page 54. Dr. Ronnie Janoff-Bulman's quote about trauma victims' plights shattering society's sacred illusions and resulting in society's hostile rejection of the victim is from *Shattered Assumptions*, p. 148. That quote is in the midst of a lengthy and lucid discussion of society's fear and loathing of victims.

Page 54. Dr. Bessel van der Kolk gives a rather eloquent description of the progressive isolation of trauma survivors on pp. 154 and 155 of *Psychological Trauma*. His quote about vulnerability and the loss of faith in human relationships is from p. 154.

Page 65. Dr. van der Kolk's quote about the communal blaming of Vietnam veterans for the nation's war trauma is from p. 154 of *Psychological Trauma*.
An excellent discussion of the tendency of communities to search for a scapegoat post-trauma can be found in J. D. Lindy and M. Grace, "The Recovery Environment: Continuing Stressor Versus a Healing Psychosocial Space," *Disasters and Mental Health*, edited by B. J. Sowder (Center for Mental Health Studies of Emergencies, U.S. Department of Health and Human Services Publication No. 85-1421, 1985), pp. 137-149. See especially pp. 142-144.

Page 68. "Studies with veterans have shown that one of the attributes that can protect someone from the psychological aftershocks of trauma is emotional (and chronological) maturity." Combining an analysis of clinical evaluations of ten Vietnam combat veterans who did not appear to be suffering from PTSD with data on approximately one hundred veterans with PTSD, Drs. Herbert Hendin and Ann Pollinger Haas surmised that combat veterans who have the firm sense of identity characteristic of emotional maturity are better defended against the development of PTSD than others. See H. Hendin and A. P. Haas, "Combat Adaptations of Vietnam Veterans without Posttraumatic Stress Disorder," *American Journal of Psychiatry* 141(8): 956–960 (1984).

Page 68. Dr. Herman's quote concerning the need of war veterans for public recognition of their sacrifice is found in *Trauma and Recovery*, p. 70.

Page 69. Dr. Jeffrey Jay's quote about society's intolerance for trauma survivors' extreme emotions is from p. 24 of J. Jay, "Terrible Knowledge," cited above.

Page 76. Dr. Laurie Anne Pearlman's observation that people's personalities are shaped by their environment is quoted from an interview conducted at the Traumatic Stress Institute on March 30, 1992.

Page 76. The original understanding of borderline personality disorder is spelled out in a series of scholarly articles by Dr. Otto F. Kernberg: O. F. Kernberg, "Prognostic Considerations Regarding Borderline Personality Organization," *Journal of American Psychoanalytic Association* 19(4): 595–635 (1971); O. F. Kernberg, "A Psychoanalytic Classification of Character Pathology," *Journal of the American Psychoanalytic Association* 18(4): 800–822 (1970); and O. F. Kernberg, "Two Reviews of the Literature on Borderlines: An Assessment," *Schizophrenia Bulletin* 5(1): 53–58 (1979).

Page 77. The 1984 analysis of the results achieved by eleven therapists highly experienced in treating BPD were published in R. J. Waldinger and J. G. Gunderson, "Completed Psychotherapies with Borderline Patients," *American Journal of Psychotherapy* 38: 190–201 (1984).

Page 77. The results of the study indicating that 81% of BPD patients have profoundly traumatic childhood histories were published in J. L. Herman, J. C. Perry and B. A. van der Kolk, "Childhood Trauma in Borderline Personality Disorder," *American Journal of Psychiatry* 146(4): 490–495 (1989).

Page 78. Dr. Herman's distillation of the research concerning the effects of long-term trauma on survivors is to be found in *Trauma and Recovery*, pp. 74–114. Readers are also directed to R. Langer, "Post-Traumatic Stress Disorder in Former POWs" in T. Williams, ed., *Post-Traumatic Stress Disorder: A Clinician's Handbook*, pp. 35–49; L. E. Walker, *The Battered Woman* (Harper & Row, 1979); and L. E. Walker, *Final Report: The Battered Woman Syndrome* (NIMH Grant #R01MH30147, 1981).

Page 79. "'The clinical picture of a person who has been reduced to elemental concerns of survival is still frequently mistaken for a portrait of the victim's underlying character. Concepts of personality organization developed under ordinary circumstances are applied to victims, without any understanding of the corrosion of personality that occurs under condition of prolonged terror.'" Dr. Herman's observations about the inadequacy of current diagnostic categories for helping clinicians understand the complexities of survivors' emotional problems are quoted from *Trauma and Recovery*, p. 117.

Page 79. "Raising the issue of personality disorders and of antisocial, violent behavior necessarily raises the uncomfortable issue of evil and the question of whether evil is inborn. No data exist to prove that it is. Plenty exist to indicate that evil frequently breeds evil." A 1995 study demonstrated that victims of childhood sexual abuse were nearly five times more likely than a control group of nonvictims to be arrested as adults for sex crimes. See C. S. Widom, "Victims of Childhood Sexual Abuse: Later Criminal Consequences" (National Institute of Justice, 1995). Earlier studies supported the idea that children who had been abused by parents became delinquent as juveniles. See P. Strasburg, "Violent Delinquents: A Report to the Ford Foundation" (Monarch Press, 1978) and J. Fagen, D. V. Hansen, and M. Jang, "Profiles of Chronically Violent Delinquents: Empirical Test of an Integrated Theory" in J. Kleugel, ed., *Evaluating Juvenile Justice* (Sage, 1983).

Page 79. "The vast majority of adult survivors of child abuse can become loving parents; a disproportionate number, however, abuse their own children or allow their spouses to do so." Many researchers have described a relationship between growing up in a violent home and acting violently as an adult. For example:

In extensive interviews conducted with 403 battered women, Dr. Lenore Walker and other investigators at the Battered Women Research Center at Colorado Women's College were unable to identify a victim-prone personality in women. The investigators did conclude, however, that certain personal experiences may contribute to the formation of a violence-prone personality in men. They found that, as children, 81% of the men who had battered women in their study had witnessed or been subject to violent acts in their homes. See L. E. Walker, "Violence Against Wives" in D. Finkelhor, R. Gelles, G. T. Hotaling, and M. A. Straus, eds., *The Dark Side of Families: Current Family Violence Research* (Sage, 1983), pp. 29-48. See especially pp. 37-38.

Investigators at Lehigh University conducted extensive interviews with both abusive and non-abusive parents in families in which abuse had been reported. The questions concerned the nature of the parents' experiences as children and the type and severity of discipline practices the parents used with their own children. The investigators found that, of the 206 parents who claimed to have had nonabusive caretakers, only eighty-eight used abusive discipline techniques with their own children. Of the 124 who claimed to have had abusive caretakers as children, 111 used abusive discipline techniques with their own children. See E. C. Herrenkohl, R. C. Herrenkohl, and L. J. Toedter, "Perspectives on the Intergenerational Effects of Abuse," in *The Dark Side of Families: Current Family Violence Research*, pp. 308-316. See especially p. 310.

In 1969, at the Eastern District Hospital in Glasgow, Scotland, investigators found that of ten psychiatric clients who had assaulted their children, all had personality disorders characterized by inadequacy and impulsive behavior. See E. Bennie and A. Sclare,

Notes

"The Battered Child Syndrome," *American Journal of Psychiatry* 125(7): 975-979 (1969). Other, more recent investigations of the cycle of violence in families include J. Kaufman and E. Zigler, "Do Abused Children Become Abusive Parents?" *American Journal of Orthopsychiatry* 57: 186-192 (1987).

Page 82. Madeline Goodman quotes Jennierose Lavender's words from Ellen Bass and Laura Davis, *The Courage to Heal* (Harper & Row, 1988), p. 33.

PART 3

Page 85. "Most trauma victims benefit initially from individual therapy," writes Dr. Bessel A. van der Kolk on p. 162 of *Psychological Trauma* (American Psychological Association, 1987). "It allows disclosure of the trauma, the safe expression of related feelings, and the reestablishment of a trusting relationship with at least one person. Patients can explore and validate perceptions and emotions and experience consistent and undivided attention from one other individual. Provided that a degree of safety can be established in the individual therapy relationship, a trauma victim can begin dealing with both the sense of shame and the vulnerability."

Page 85. An excellent overview of trauma therapy is John Briere, ed., *Assessing and Treating Victims of Violence* (Jossey-Bass, 1994).

Page 85. Dr. van der Kolk's comments beginning with, "Pay more attention to the therapist's intellectual and emotional equipment . . ." are from a telephone interview conducted in October of 1992.

Page 85-86. Dr. Judith Lewis Herman's quote describing psychological trauma as disempowerment and disconnection and post-traumatic therapy as empowerment and reconnection is from *Trauma and Recovery*, p. 133.

Page 108. "Strikeouts and Psych-outs" appeared in the *New York Times Magazine*, July 7, 1991.

Page 109. On p. 181 of *Psychological Trauma*, Dr. van der Kolk writes, "In posttraumatic stress disorder the warding off of the return of unresolved psychological trauma becomes a central focus in people's lives. For over a hundred years psychiatrists have recognized the price that people pay for this walling off the memories of the trauma." On p. 3 he explains that isolation "can be understood as a way of warding off recurrent intrusive recollections of the trauma. Traumatized individuals may gain some sense of subjective control by shunning all situations or emotions related to the trauma. Often they avoid intimate relationships, apparently out of fear of a renewed violation of the attachment bond. Avoiding emotional involvement further diminishes the significance of life after the trauma, and thus perpetuates the central role of the trauma."

Page 109. Dr. Raymond Scurfield writes of the pain of the recovery process in "Post-trauma Stress Assessment and Treatment," *Trauma and its Wake,* Charles Figley, ed., (Brunner/Mazel, 1985), p. 242.

Page 109-112. Dr. Herman describes the dangers of cathartic cures on p. 172 of *Trauma and Recovery* and, on p. 174, discusses the value of delaying memory exploration until the survivor has built a significant measure of emotional mastery.

Page 112-113. Dr. Laurie Anne Pearlman's comments throughout this chapter are from two sources: a telephone interview conducted on August 21, 1991 and an interview conducted at the Traumatic Stress Institute on March 30, 1992.

Page 113. Dr. van der Kolk's quote, "Once a patient can start remembering the trauma and is able to understand the connections between events and subsequent emotional experiences, there is a gradual reduction in the intensity and frequency of the intrusive nightmares, reenactments, or anxiety and panic attacks," can be found on p. 118 of *Psychological Trauma.*

Page 114. Dr. George Ganaway writes of the bizarre and exotic quality of many disinterred memories in "Historical Versus Narrative Truth: Clarifying the Role of Exogenous Trauma in the Etiology of MPD and its Variants," *Dissociation* 2(4): 207 (December 1989).

The journal *Dissociation* has been a rich resource for my own research into the role of remembering in post-traumatic therapy. The journal has vigorously and rationally discussed both the ethical and practical ramifications of memory distortions. In addition to the already referenced Ganaway article, readers are particularly directed to the following articles: R. Kluft, "Editorial: Reflections on Allegations of Ritual Abuse," 2(4): 191-193 (December 1989); S. Van Benschoten, "Multiple Personality Disorder and Satanic Ritual Abuse: The Issue of Credibility," 3(1): 22-29 (March 1990); R. Kluft, "Editorial: Living with Uncertainty," 4(4): 178-179 (December 1991).

Recently several excellent full-length books on the vagaries of traumatic memory have been published. They were mentioned in the notes for Chapter 2 but I repeat them here to draw them to the attention of people intrigued by the recovered memory debate. The books include: Susan L. Reviere's *Memory of Childhood Trauma: A Clinician's Guide to the Literature* (Guilford, 1996); Kenneth S. Pope and Laura S. Brown's *Recovered Memories of Abuse: Assessment, Therapy, Forensics* (American Psychological Association, 1996), Charles L. Whitfield's *Memory and Abuse: Remembering and Healing the Effects of Trauma* (Health Communications, 1995), Jennifer J. Freyd's *Betrayal Trauma: The Logic of Forgetting Childhood Abuse* (Harvard University Press, 1996), and Daniel L. Schacter's *Searching for Memory: The Brain, the Mind, and The Past* (Basic, 1996). Readers are also directed to the "Memory: Mechanisms and Processes" section on pp. 279-330 of B. A. van der Kolk, A. C. McFarlane, and L. Weisaeth, eds., *Traumatic Stress: The Effects of Overwhelming Experience on Mind, Body, and Society* (Guilford, 1996).

Notes

Page 115. My description of memory encoding is distilled from three sources. The primary source is B. A. van der Kolk, "Biological Considerations about Emotions, Trauma, Memory, and the Brain" in S. L. Ablon, D. Brown, E. J. Khantzian and J. E. Mack, eds., *Human Feelings* (Analytic, 1993). The other two sources are chapters in Helen M. Pettinati, ed., *Hypnosis and Memory* (Guilford, 1988). Those chapters are K. S. Bowers and E. R. Hilgard, "Some Complexities in Understanding Memory" and F. H. Frankel, "The Clinical Use of Hypnosis in Aiding Recall."

Page 115-116. Dr. Richard P. Kluft's quote beginning "Traumatized persons must come to terms with their pasts" is from "Editorial: Reflections on Allegations of Ritual Abuse," *Dissociation* 2(4): 191-193 (December 1989).

Page 118. An impassioned overview of a large body of experimental data casting doubt on the reliability of eyewitness testimony is Dr. Elizabeth Loftus's *Eyewitness Testimony* (Harvard University Press, 1979).

Page 118-119. Two admirable and objective overviews of research on memory and hypnosis are Alan W. Scheflin and Jerrold Lee Shapiro's *Trance on Trial* (Guilford, 1989) and Helen M. Pettinati, ed., *Hypnosis and Memory* (Guilford, 1988).

Page 119. Dr. Loftus's experiment with hypnosis and memory was reported in the *New York Times*. "A pertinent experiment on the malleability of human memory will be presented next month at the annual meeting of the American Psychological Association by Dr. Elizabeth F. Loftus, a psychologist at the University of Washington who is a specialist in eyewitness testimony. In a preliminary study, Dr. Loftus was able by suggestion to persuade people to remember details of an imaginary incident when they were supposedly lost at age five, while their family was shopping.

"With James Coan, a graduate student, Dr. Loftus had a close relative of her experimental subjects describe three events from the subject's childhood, and offer specifics for the setting of a fictitious fourth event, the time the person supposedly got lost. 'We told the subjects we were studying childhood memories, and asked them to write everything they could remember about each of these incidents,' said Dr. Loftus.

"In the pilot study, the subjects, two children and three adults, proceeded to supply details of the fictitious incident, apparently not realizing it was not true." (*New York Times*, July 21, 1992, page C5.)

Page 119. The late Dr. Nicholas P. Spanos's discourse on hypnotically-introduced past lives is found in "Past-Life Hypnotic Regression: A Critical Review," *Skeptical Inquirer* 12: 174-180 (Winter 1987-88). In a previous study (N. P. Spanos and J. McLean, "Hypnotically Created Pseudomemories: Memory Distortions or Reporting Biases?" *British Journal of Experimental and Clinical Hypnosis* 3[3]: 155-159 [1985-86]), Dr. Spanos and collaborator Dr. Joanne McLean introduced the intriguing hypothesis that hypnosis does not necessarily distort memory retrieval. Instead, most hypnotized people may simply be so "strongly invested in sustaining a self-presentation as 'deeply hypnotised' . . .

[that they] incorporate information provided by suggestions into a convincing hypnotic performance."

To test this hypothesis, the investigators hypnotized eleven experimental subjects and, during hypnosis, "implanted" a pseudomemory: they had heard loud noises during the middle of the night. Post-hypnotically, most of the experiment's subjects stated that they heard the suggested noises. Those who did were re-hypnotized and, during hypnosis, told:

"During deep hypnosis people often confuse reality with things that were only imagined. The hypnotized part of a person's mind accepts suggestions so completely that what was suggested actually seems to have been happening. . . . Yet at the same time that you are experiencing suggestions, there is some other part of your mind, a hidden part, that knows what is really going on. . . . The hidden part can always distinguish what was suggested from what really happened. . . ."

After receiving that information in the hypnotized state and being specifically told to access the knowledge held by the "hidden part" of their mind, almost all subjects changed their initial report about noises in the night and ascertained that the noises they had once reported as real had only been imagined.

Dr. Spanos's ideas about hypnosis, multiple personalities, and memory function are detailed in a posthumously published book, *Multiple Identities and False Memories* (American Psychological Association, 1996).

Page 120. Dr. Ganaway writes about the importance to a survivor of the therapist's ability to stay grounded in reality on p. 216 of "Historical Versus Narrative Truth," referenced above.

Page 120-121. Dr. George P. Ganaway's suggestion that dissociative survivors spontaneously move in and out of trance is on p. 205 of "Historical Truth Versus Narrative Truth."

An excellent paper giving an overview of literature describing spontaneous hypnoid states in psychotherapy clients believed to have survived early childhood trauma is F. Putnam, "Dissociation as a Response to Extreme Childhood Trauma," R. Kluft, ed., *Childhood Antecedents of Multiple Personality* (American Psychiatric Press, 1985).

Page 121. Dr. Ganaway's suggestion that dissociative people be considered at high risk for contamination by a therapist's questions is on pp. 208-209 of "Historical Versus Narrative Truth."

Page 122. Dr. Ganaway's comments that outlandish memories can "represent dissociatively mediated distortions and fantasies created in an effort to achieve mastery and psychic restitution in the wake of genuine and factual trauma of a more prosaic (but not necessarily less heinous) nature" were presented in 1989 in Akron, Ohio at the Fourth Regional Conference on Multiple Personality and Dissociative States in a paper titled "Exploring the Credibility Issue in Multiple Personality Disorder."

Notes

Page 129-136. My summary of the early history of studies on dissociation and hypnosis is distilled from Henri F. Ellenberger's *The Discovery of the Unconscious: The History and Evolution of Dynamic Psychiatry* (Basic, 1970), Ernest Jones's *The Life and Work of Sigmund Freud* (Basic, 1961), Jeffrey Moussaieff Masson's *The Assault on Truth: Freud's Suppression of the Seduction Theory* (Farrar, Straus & Giroux, 1984) and from entries on Mesmer, Charcot, Janet, Freud, and Breuer in *Encyclopedia Britannica Micropaedia*, 15th ed., 1982. Much of what I write here about Freud is derived from Jeffrey Masson's *The Assault on Truth*, the landmark book that brought into question Freud's motives and ethics in his abandonment of the theories he set out in "The Aetiology of Hysteria." In the preface to the Harper Perennial edition of *The Assault on Truth*, Jeffrey Masson writes, "I would like to take this opportunity to clarify a misunderstanding about my attitude toward Freud. I found a large number of previously unpublished documents that clarified the question of Freud's abandonment of the seduction hypothesis. But these documents, while permitting a much fuller explanation of the historical circumstances surrounding this crucial event in Freud's intellectual life, do not permit anybody to claim with certainty that he or she now understands Freud's motivation. I certainly speculate in this book what that motivation might be: a fear of losing his friendship with Fliess; a fear of standing up for the least advantaged in society; a desire to distance himself from any responsibility in the failed operation on a favorite patient; a fear of the wrath of the more powerful men — men of the middle class elite whom Freud's patients were accusing of sexual abuse, and a desire to remain in the good graces of these men so that he could continue to practice his profession. However, I must emphasize that these are mere speculations. I do not know for certain what Freud's motivation was, and I cannot imagine that any document as yet undiscovered will eventually disclose it. I may disapprove of what I call Freud's loss of moral courage, but I cannot claim that I understand it." (*Assault on Truth*, pp. xxi-xxii.)

Page 134. Josef Breuer's quote, "sexuality is one of the great components of hysteria," is from the "Theory" chapter of *Studies on Hysteria*.

Page 135. Freud's "The Aetiology of Hysteria" (1896) is published in *The Standard Edition of the Complete Psychological Works of Sigmund Freud*, vol. 3, trans. J. Strachey (Hogarth, 1962). The reader is referred specifically to p. 203.

Page 135. The "scientific fairy tale" comment is reported by Freud to his friend Wilhelm Fliess in a letter of April 26, 1986. See Freud, Sigmund, *The Complete Letters of Sigmund Freud to Wilhelm Fliess, 1877-1904,* translated and edited by Jeffrey Moussaieff Masson, Belknap Press of Harvard University Press, 1985.

Page 135. Evidence of Freud's waffling on the evident veracity of patients' accounts of rape is evident in his letters to Wilhelm Fleiss. See Freud, Sigmund, *The Complete Letters of Sigmund Freud to Wilhelm Fleiss, 1877-1904,* translated and edited by Jeffrey Moussaieff Masson.

Page 135-136. *Three Essays on the Theory of Sexuality* was originally published as *Drei Abhandlungen zur Sexualtheorie*. A James Strachey translation is in Volume 7, pp. 125-245 of *The Standard Edition of the Complete Psychological Works of Sigmund Freud*.

Page 136-140. My overview of multiple personality disorder is derived primarily from four sources: C. Ross, *Dissociative Identity Disorder: Diagnosis, Clinical Features, and Treatment of Multiple Personality* (Wiley, 1997) and the earlier edition of the same book, *Multiple Personality Disorder, Diagnosis, Clinical Features, and Treatment* (Wiley, 1989); F. W. Putnam, *Diagnosis and Treatment of Multiple Personality Disorder* (Guilford, 1989); C. Ross, ed., *The Psychiatric Clinics of North America: Multiple Personality Disorder* 14(3): (September 1991); and R. P. Kluft and C. G. Fine, *Clinical Perspectives on Multiple Personality Disorder* (American Psychiatric Press, 1993).

Page 137. "Sadly, even though MPD appears to be highly treatable, many therapists fail to diagnose MPD, even in clients showing clear diagnostic clues." According to Dr. Colin Ross, after the year 1910, people with MPD were most often diagnosed as schizophrenic. See *Multiple Personality Disorder: Diagnosis, Clinical Features and Treatment* (Wiley, 1989), pp. 38-39. More recently, the most common diagnoses given to people with MPD are, in descending order of frequency, affective disorder, personality disorder, anxiety disorder, schizophrenia, substance abuse, adjustment disorder, multiple personality disorder, somatization disorder, eating disorder, and organic mental disorder. (So indicate data collected in a survey of 236 survivors with MPD and reported by Ross, Norton, and Wozney in the *Canadian Journal of Psychiatry*, 34[5]: 413-418 [1989]. These data are reprinted on p. 96 of *Multiple Personality Disorder: Diagnosis, Clinical Features, and Treatment*.)

Page 137. The NIMH study finding that ninety-seven of one hundred MPD patients report histories of severe childhood abuse is F. W. Putnam, J. J. Guroff, E. K. Silberman, L. Barban, and R. M. Post, "The Clinical Phenomenology of Multiple Personality Disorder: A Review of 100 Recent Cases," *Journal of Clinical Psychiatry*, 47: 285-293 (1986).

Page 137. On pp. 503-616 of *The Psychiatric Clinics of North America: Multiple Personality Disorder*, Dr. Ross and colleagues at the University of Manitoba report the results of a survey of a sample of 1055 members of the general adult population (age 18 and older) in the city of Winnipeg, Manitoba. Generalizing from the data, the investigators suggest that about 1% of adults in North America have multiple personality disorder related to childhood abuse and about 10% of the adult population have a dissociative disorder of some kind. Dissociative disorders, the investigators conclude, are about as common as anxiety, mood, and substance abuse disorders.

Page 137. The *Diagnostic and Statistical Manual of Mental Disorders* (4th ed.) lists self-mutilation, suicide attempts, and externally directed violence (including child abuse, assault, or rape) as complications of MPD. See p. 485.

Page 137. "Contrary to popular belief, most people with multiple personalities are not Dr. Jekyll/Mr. Hydes. . . ." The clinical presentation of people with MPD is well described throughout Colin Ross's *Dissociative Identity Disorder: Diagnosis, Clinical Features, and Treatment*, by Dr. Richard P. Kluft in "Clinical Presentations of Multiple Personality Disorder," in *Psychiatric Clinics of North America: Multiple Personality Disorder*, pp. 605-630, and by Dr. Frank Putnam on pp. 45-70 of *Diagnosis and Treatment of Multiple Personality Disorder*.

Page 140. Dr. Ross's description of MPD as a little girl imagining the abuse happening to someone else is on p. 55 of *Multiple Personality Disorder: Diagnosis, Clinical Features, and Treatment*.

Page 140. Regarding the theoretical construct for therapy for survivors with MPD, on p. 216 of *Multiple Personality Disorder: Diagnosis, Clinical Features, and Treatment*, Dr. Ross writes, "As a brief general outline of therapy, I think that the patient needs to recover her abuse memories, come to terms with them, integrate into one person, and learn how to live effectively without pathological dissociation. I don't think there is any need to get into hairsplitting arguments about how integrated a 'normal' person is. Most people feel as if they are one person most of the time, and so do integrated MPD patients."

Page 140. The late Dr. Nicholas P. Spanos of Ottawa's Carleton University was one of the chief detractors of the concept of MPD as a clinical entity rooted in childhood trauma. His and his colleagues' objections are spelled out in N. P. Spanos, J. R. Weekes, E. Menary, and L. D. Bertrand, "Hypnotic Interview and Age Regression Procedures in the Elicitation of Multiple Personality Symptoms: A Simulation Study," *Psychiatry* 49: 298-311 (November 1986) and in D. Spanos, *Multiple Identities and False Memories: A Sociocognitive Perspective* (American Psychological Association, 1996).

Page 140. The outcomes for various treatments of MPD (conventional talk therapy vs. anti-psychotic medications vs. post-traumatic therapy) are discussed by Dr. Ross on pp. 38 and 100 of *Multiple Personality Disorder: Diagnosis, Clinical Features, and Treatment*.

Page 140-141. Dr. Kluft's outcome data for treatment of 123 cases of MPD are reported in R. P. Kluft (1984), "Treatment of Multiple Personality Disorder," *Psychiatric Clinics of North America* 7: 121-134.

Page 141. The 1986 NIMH survey of 100 MPD patients, reported by Dr. Frank Putnam and colleagues in "The Clinical Phenomenology of Multiple Personality Disorder: A Review of 100 Recent Cases," determined that MPD patients spend an average of 6.8 years in the mental health system and in that time experienced an average of 3.6 misdiagnoses. This same study found a female-to-male ratio of MPD of 5:1. The Winnipeg survey of 236 patients (Ross, Norton, and Wozney, reported in the *Canadian Journal of Psychiatry* 34(5): 413-418 [1989]) found a female-to-male ratio of 9:1. The study's data are tabulated on p. 96 of *Multiple Personality Disorder: Diagnosis, Clinical Features, and Treatment*.

Page 142. Speculation that many of the men with MPD are in prison is widespread. It seems to have originated with Myron Boor, "The Multiple Personality Epidemic: Additional Cases and Inferences Regarding Diagnosis, Etiology, Dynamics, and Treatment," *Journal of Nervous and Mental Disease* 173: 533–534 (1985).

Page 157–158. Dr. Kluft's series of articles on the natural history of a therapist's emotional response to therapy with a trauma survivor include "Aspects of the Treatment of Multiple Personality Disorder," *Psychiatric Annals* 14: 51–55 (1984); "On Giving Consultations to Therapists Treating Multiple Personality Disorder: Fifteen Years' Experience—Parts I and II," *Dissociation* 1(3): 23–25 (1988); "On Optimism in the Treatment of MPD: A Status Report by a Participant Observer," *Trauma and Recovery Newsletter* 2(1): 2–5 (1989); and C. B. Wilbur and R. P. Kluft, "Multiple Personality Disorder," in T. B. Karasu, ed., *Treatment of Mental Disorders* (American Psychiatric Press, 1989).

Page 158. The statistics about the troubling effects on therapy clients of sexual relationships with their therapists were reported by the *New York Times* on December 20, 1990 (p. B21). In that article, Dr. Nannette Gartrell is quoted as saying, "These patients end up with the same emotional problems you see in incest victims. They have trouble trusting anyone, they're frightened of being taken advantage of in intimate relationships, and they are severely depressed."

Page 159. Throughout his career, Freud refined his ideas on transference and countertransference. He first considered the idea of transference in *Studies on Hysteria*, which he published in 1895 with Josef Breuer. Countertransference was first addressed in 1910 in a pamphlet titled "Wild Analysis."

Page 159. Dr. Richard Kluft expounds on the values of the psychoanalytic literature in "Editorial: Collage with Red Thread," *Dissociation* 3(4): 175 (December 1989). Recently three books of particular merit have been published that can help guide therapists through the difficult task of managing their own emotions so that they can provide excellent care to traumatized patients. These are: Laurie Anne Pearlman and Karen W. Saakvitne, *Trauma and the Therapist: Countertransference and Vicarious Traumatization in Psychotherapy with Incest Survivors* (Norton, 1995); Karen W. Saakvitne and Laurie Anne Pearlman, *Transforming the Pain: A Workbook on Vicarious Traumatization* (Norton, 1996) and B. Hudnall Stamm, *Secondary Traumatic Stress: Self-Care Issues for Clinicians, Researchers, and Educators* (Sidran, 1995).

PART 4

Page 167. Thoreau's "It takes two to speak the truth—one to speak, and another to hear" is from "Wednesday" of *A Week on the Concord and Merrimack Rivers* (Viking 1985).

Page 173. The study conducted at the Medical University of South Carolina, in which symptoms of PTSD were assessed in partners of rape victims, was presented by

H. S. Resnick, L. J. Veronen, and B. E. Saunders as a speech entitled "Symptoms of Post-traumatic Stress Disorder in Rape Victims and Their Partners: A Behavioral Formulation" at the Fourth Annual Meeting of the Society for Traumatic Stress Studies, October 23-26, 1988, Dallas, Texas.

Page 173. The doctoral dissertation reporting interviews with partners of rape victims is K. Stone, *The Second Victims: Altruism and the Affective Reactions of Affiliated Males to their Partner's Rape* (University Microfilms International, 1983).

Page 173-174. The reactions of members of a men's support group to their partners' rapes are reported in L. I. Rodkin, E. J. Hunt, and S. D. Cowan, "A Men's Group for Significant Others of Rape Victims," *Journal of Marital and Family Therapy* 8(1): 91-97 (1982).

Page 174-175. Dr. Karen Saakvitne's remarks are edited from a speech entitled "Countertransference and Vicarious Traumatization: Therapist Issues in Psychotherapy with Trauma Survivors" given on April 3, 1992 as part of a Psychiatric Grand Rounds series at Holyoke Hospital in Holyoke, Massachusetts.

Page 175. Dr. Ellen Brickman's remarks are quoted from an interview conducted on August 7, 1992.

Page 175-176. Lawrence L. Langer's *Holocaust Testimonies* was published in New Haven by Yale University Press, 1991.

Page 176. Dr. Herman's quote about social action and rape survivors is from p. 73 of *Trauma and Recovery*.

RESOURCE GUIDE

PSYCHTRAUMA RESOURCE AND INFORMATION SERVICE

The Sidran Foundation is continually compiling an extensive database of information about the psychological impact of trauma and is able to provide resource material about psychological trauma and dissociation to survivors, supporters, and professionals at no charge. All inquiries are kept strictly confidential. The information includes listings of organizations; trauma and dissociative disorder treatment programs; survivor newsletters and professional journals; and information on how to locate therapists who have an interest in treating trauma and dissociative disorders. Resource information is also organized into categories by state including local or regional organizations, professional training workshops and study groups, support groups, treatment centers, therapists, and conferences. Information on resources outside the United States is also included in the database but is limited.

The Sidran Foundation is not responsible for the quality of services provided by any resource. It recommends that individuals verify the appropriateness of each resource.

There are three ways to request information or to contribute to the database:

- Write to the Resource Specialist, The Sidran Foundation, 2328 W. Joppa Rd., Suite 15, Lutherville, MD 21093.
- Call between 10:00 a.m. and 3:00 p.m., Eastern Time (410) 825-8888.
- Send e-mail to <sidran@access.digex.net> and put "Attention resource specialist" in the subject line. Please include your postal mailing address in your e-mail message.

BIBLIOGRAPHY

BOOKS

Many of these books are written for a readership of therapy professionals. However, even those may have significant value for readers who are survivors or survivors' friends and family.

The following list of books is annotated only when its title seems to inadequately describe its content.

While many of the books listed below are out of print, they can still be found in libraries. Many of the current books are available for purchase from the Sidran Foundation Bookshelf catalog.

Allies in Healing: When the Person You Love Was Sexually Abused as a Child. Davis, Laura. HarperPerennial, 1991.

Assessing and Treating Victims of Violence. Briere, John (Ed.). Jossey-Bass, 1994.

Against All Odds: Holocaust Survivors and the Successful Lives They Made in America. Helmreich, William B. Simon and Schuster, 1992.

American Daughter Gone to War: On the Front Lines with an Army Nurse in Vietnam. Smith, Winnie. William Morrow, 1992.

The Battered Woman. Walker, Lenore. Harper & Row, 1979. Includes an overview of how battering comes to be and how to get out of the destructive situation. The book evolved from the NIMH-funded federal report cited below.

The Best Kept Secret: Sexual Abuse of Children. Rush, Florence. Prentice Hall, 1980.

Betrayal. Freeman, L., and J. Roy. Stein & Day, 1976. The true story of the first woman to successfully sue her psychiatrist for obtaining sex in the guise of therapy.

Betrayal Trauma: The Logic of Forgetting Childhood Abuse. Freyd, Jennifer J. Harvard University Press, 1996.

Bloods: An Oral History of the Viet Nam War by Black Veterans. Terry, W. Ballantine, 1985.

Casualties: Death in Viet Nam, Anguish and Survival in America. Brandon, Heather. St. Martin's, 1984. The testimony of thirty-seven relatives of people killed in Vietnam, talking of the toll that the war took on them.

Child Abuse Trauma: Theory and Treatment of the Lasting Effects. Briere, John N. Sage, 1992.

Child Sexual Abuse: New Theory & Research. Finkelhor, David. Free Press, 1984.

Childhood Antecedents of Multiple Personality. Kluft, Richard P. American Psychiatric Press, 1985.

Children of the Holocaust. Epstein, Helen. Viking, 1988. Written by a child of Holocaust survivors.

Clinical Perspectives on Multiple Personality Disorder. Kluft, Richard P. and Catherine G. Fine. American Psychiatric Press, 1993.

Compassion Fatigue: Coping with Secondary Traumatic Stress Disorder in Those Who Treat the Traumatized. Figley, C. Brunner/Mazel, 1995.

Coping with Family Violence: Research and Policy Perspectives. Hotaling, Gerald T., David Finkelhor, John T. Kirkpatrick, and Murray A. Straus, eds. Sage, 1988.

Coping with Trauma: Theory, Prevention, and Treatment. Kleber, Rolf, and Danny Brom. Swets & Zeitlinger, 1992.

The Courage to Heal. Bass, Ellen, and Laura Davis. Harper & Row, 1988. An immensely popular book for adult survivors of childhood sexual abuse.

Critical Incidents in Policing. Reese, James T., James M. Horn, and Christine Dunning, eds. U.S. Dept. of Justice and FBI, 1990. Includes a workbook for police officers who have undergone a critical incident. "Critical incident" generally means a shooting or some other violent incident on the job.

The Dark Side of Families: Current Family Violence Research. Finkelhor, David, Richard J. Gelles, Gerald T. Hotaling, and Murray A. Straus, eds. Sage, 1983.

Diagnosis and Treatment of Multiple Personality Disorder. Putnam, Frank W. Guilford, 1989.

Disasters and Mental Health. Sowder, B. J. Center for Mental Health Studies of Emergencies, U.S. Department of Health and Human Services Publication No. 85-1421, 1985.

Dissociative Disorders: A Clinical Review. Spiegel, David. Sidran, 1993.

Dissociative Identity Disorder: Diagnosis, Clinical Features, and Treatment of Multiple Personaliy (2nd ed.). Ross, Colin. John Wiley & Sons, 1997.

Family Abuse and its Consequences: New Directions and Research. Hotaling, Gerald T., David Finkelhor, John T. Kirkpatrick, and Murray A. Straus, eds. Sage, 1988.

Father-Daughter Incest. Herman, Judith Lewis. Harvard University Press, 1981.

Final Report: The Battered Woman Syndrome. Walker, Lenore E. NIMH Grant number R01MH30147, 1981.

Generations of the Holocaust. Bergmann, M., and M. Gucovy. Basic, 1982. Presents ways in which children of Holocaust survivors reenact the sufferings of their parents.

Getting Free: A Handbook for Women in Abusive Relationships. NiCarthy, Ginny. Seal, 1986.

Group Treatment for Sexually Abused Children. Mandell, J. G., L. Damon., P. Castaldo, E. Tauber, L. Monise, and N. Larsen, eds. Guilford, 1990.

Healing the Incest Wound: Adult Survivors in Therapy. Courtois, Christine. Norton, 1988. A guidebook for therapists.

Holocaust Testimonies: The Ruins of Memory. Langer, Lawrence L. Yale University Press, 1991. A remarkable book about the vagaries of intolerable memories.

Human Adaptation to Extreme Stress: From the Holocaust to Viet Nam. Wilson, John P., Zev Harel, and Boaz Kahana. Plenum, 1988.

Human Feelings. Ablon, S. L., D. Brown, E. J. Khantzian, and J. E. Mack, eds. Analytic, 1993.

I Can't Get Over It: A Handbook for Trauma Survivors. Matsakis, Aphrodite. New Harbinger, 1992.

International Responses to Traumatic Stress: Humanitarian, Human Rights, Justice, Peace and Development Contributions, Collaborative Actions, and Future Initiatives. Danieli, Yael, et al., eds. Baywood, 1996.

It's Never OK: A Handbook for Professionals on Sexual Exploitation by Counselors and Therapists. Sanderson, B., ed. Minnesota Department of Corrections, 1989.

A Killing Cure. Walker, E., and P. Young. Holt, 1986. About a lawsuit resulting from sexual abuse in therapy.

License to Rape: Sexual Abuse of Wives. Finkelhor, David, and Kersti Yllo. Holt, 1985.

Managing Traumatic Stress Through Art: Drawing From the Center. Cohen, Barry M., Mary-Michola Barnes, and Anita B. Rankin. Sidran, 1995.

Massive Psychic Trauma. Krystal, Henry. International Universities Press, 1968. The findings and recommendations of a conference regarding the trauma of the Holocaust and the bombs dropped on Hiroshima and Nagasaki.

Memory and Abuse: Remembering and Healing the Effects of Trauma. Whitfield, Charles L. Health Communications, Inc., 1995.

Memory of Childhood Trauma: A Clinician's Guide to the Literature. Reviere, Susan L. Guilford, 1996.

The Mother's Book: How to Survive the Incest of Your Child. Byerly, Carolyn. Kendall/Hunt, 1985.

Multiple Identities & False Memories. Spanos, Nicholas P. American Psychological Association, 1996.

Multiple Personality and Dissociation, 1791–1992: A Complete Bibliography, 2nd ed. Goettman, Carole, George B. Greaves, and Philip M. Coons. Sidran, 1994.

Multiple Personality Disorder from the Inside Out. Cohen, Barry, Esther Giller, and Lynne W. Sidran, 1991.

My Mom Is Different. Sessions, Sidran, 1994. Illustrated book, for children, written from the point of view of a child of a parent with multiple personality disorder.

Native American Post-Colonial Psychology. Duran, Eduardo, and Bonnie Duran. State University of New York Press, 1995. Has an extensive section on inter-generational PTSD as experienced by American Indians.

Nursery Crimes: Sexual Abuse in Day Care. Finkelhor, David, Linda M. Williams, and Nanci Burns, eds. Sage, 1988.

Outgrowing the Pain: For and about Adults Abused as Children. Gil, Eliana. Launch, 1983.

Perspectives on Disaster Recovery. Laube, Jeri, ed. Prentice-Hall, 1985.

Post-Traumatic Stress Disorder: A Clinical Review. Pynoos, Robert S., ed. Sidran, 1993.

Post-Traumatic Stress Disorders: A Handbook for Clinicians. Williams, Tom, ed. Disabled American Veterans, 1987.

Psychological Trauma. van der Kolk, Bessel, ed. American Psychiatric Press, 1987.

Psychological Trauma and the Adult Survivor: Theory, Therapy, and Transformation. McCann, I. Lisa, and Laurie Anne Pearlman. Brunner/Mazel, 1990. By "Adult Survivor" the authors mean "adult survivor of incest." This book is written for professionals.

Recovered Memories of Abuse: Assessment, Therapy, Forensics. Pope, Kenneth S., and Laura S. Brown. American Psychological Association, 1996.

Recovering From Rape. Ledray, Linda E. Holt, 1986. Very useful emotional support and practical guidance, especially in dealing with the immediate aftermath of being raped. Has (dated) listings of resources in each state.

Recovering from the War: A Woman's Guide to Helping Your Vietnam Vet, Your Family, and Yourself. Mason, Patience. Penguin, 1990.

Searching for Memory: The Brain, the Mind, and the Past. Schacter, Daniel L. Basic, 1996.

Secondary Traumatic Stress: Self-Care Issues for Clinicians, Researchers, and Educators. Stamm, B. Hudnall, ed. Sidran, 1995.

The Secret Trauma: Incest in the Lives of Girls and Women. Russell, Diana E. Basic, 1986.

Sexual Exploitation: Rape, Child Sexual Abuse, and Sexual Harassment. Russell, Diana E. Sage, 1984.

Sexually Victimized Children. Finkelhor, David. Free Press, 1981.

Shattered Assumptions. Janoff-Bulman, Ronnie. Free Press, 1992.

Soldier's Heart: Survivors' Views of Combat Trauma. Hansel, Sarah, Ann Steidle, Grace Zaczek, and Ron Zaczek. Sidran, 1994.

Stress Response Syndrome. Horowitz, M. J. Jason Aronson, 1986.

Strong at the Broken Places: Overcoming the Trauma of Childhood Abuse. Sanford, Linda T. Random House, 1990. Sets out to debunk the myth of once a victim, always damaged.

Therapists' Difficulties in Treating Survivors of the Nazi Holocaust and their Children. Danieli, Yael. Ph.D. diss., New York University, University Microfilms International, number 949-904.

Too Scared To Cry: Psychic Trauma in Childhood. Terr, Lenore. Harper & Row, 1990.

Transforming the Pain: A Workbook on Vicarious Traumatization. Saakvitne, Karen W,. and Laurie Anne Pearlman. Norton, 1996.

Trauma and its Wake. Vol. I and II. Figley, Charles R. Brunner/Mazel, 1985 and 1986, respectively.

Trauma and Recovery: The Aftermath of Violence, from Domestic Abuse to Political Terror. Herman, Judith Lewis. Basic, 1992.

Trauma and the Therapist: Countertransference and Vicarious Traumatization in Psychotherapy with Incest Survivors. Pearlman, L. A., and Saakvitne, K. W. Norton, 1995.

The Trauma of War: Stress and Recovery in Viet Nam Veterans. Sonnenberg, S. American Psychiatric Press, 1985.

Trauma Research Methodology. Carlson, Eve Bernstein, ed. Sidran, 1996.

Traumatic Stress: The Effects of Overwhelming Experience on Mind, Body, and Society. van der Kolk, Bessel A., Alexander C. McFarlane, and Lars Weisaeth, eds. Guilford, 1996.

Treating Traumatized Children: New Insights and Creative Interventions. James, Beverly. Lexington, 1989.

Unchained Memories: True Stories of Traumatic Memories Lost and Found.
Terr, Lenore. Basic, 1994.

*Victims No Longer: Men Recovering from Incest and Other Sexual Child
Abuse.* Lew, Mike. Harper & Row, 1990.

*Vietnam Wives: Facing the Challenges of Life with Veterans Suffering Post-
Traumatic Stress.* Matsakis, Aphrodite. Sidran, 1996.

The Way of the Journal: A Journal Therapy Workbook for Healing. Adams,
Kathleen. Sidran, 1993.

Wounds of War: The Psychological Aftermath of Combat in Vietnam.
Hendin, H., and A. P. Haas. Basic, 1984.

BROCHURES

The following two brochures are intended for survivors of severe
trauma, their families, and members of the lay public.

Dissociative Identity Disorder. Sidran, 1993.

Traumatic Memories. Sidran, 1994.

PROFESSIONAL JOURNALS

Dissociation: Progress in the Dissociative Disorders. Ridgeview Institute
& ISSD. The official journal of the International Society for the
Study of Dissociation.

Journal of Interpersonal Violence. Sage.

Journal of Personal and Interpersonal Loss. Taylor & Francis.

Journal of Traumatic Stress. Plenum. The official journal of the International Society for Traumatic Stress Studies.

PTSD Clinical Quarterly and *PTSD Research Quarterly.* Published by the
National Center for Post-Traumatic Stress Disorder, White River
Junction, VT 05009.

INTERNET RESOURCES

The Sidran Foundation maintains a page on the World Wide Web that
provides links to many trauma-related Internet resources. On the Internet the Sidran Foundation can be found at http://www.sidran.org.

INDEX

Ablon, S. L., 202
"Adaptive Strategies and Recovery from Rape" (Burgess and Holmstrom), 197
"Aetiology of Hysteria, The" (Freud), 32, 135, 191, 204
Alter personality, 137, 140–141, 142
Andreski, P., 194
Anna O., treatment by Breuer, 133–143
"Aspects of the Treatment of Multiple Personality Disorder" (Kluft), 207
Assault on Truth, The: Freud's Suppression of the Seduction Theory (Masson), 159, 191
Assessing and Treating Victims of Violence (Briere), 202
Atkeson, B. M., 192

Barban, L., 137
Bass, Ellen, 200
"Battered Child Syndrome, The" (Bennie and Sclare), 199–200
Battered Woman Syndrome, The (Walker), 193
Battered Woman, The (Walker), 198
Battered Women Research Center (Colorado Women's College), 199
Battered women, blindness of psychotherapeutic profession to, 193
Behavior modification, 85
Bennie, E., 199–200
Benschoten, S. Van, 201
Berry, Patricia (testimony of, on murder of a child), 7
Berton, Margaret Wright, 47
Bertrand, L. D., 206
Betrayal Trauma: The Logic of Forgetting Childhood Abuse (Freyd), 191, 201
Bikales, Richard (testimony of, on Holocaust), 5, 15–18, 178–179

"Biological Considerations about Emotions, Trauma, Memory, and the Brain" (van der Kolk), 202
Blaming the victim, 34, 53, 65, 69; by partners of rape victims, 54, and Vietnam War veterans, 65, 68, 197
Boor, Myron, 206–207
Borderline personality disorder (BPD), 76, 77, 78, 79, 198, 218
Bosnia, 123
Bowers, K. S., 202
Boydstun, J. A., 196
Breslau, N., 194
Breuer, Josef, 32; 136, 141, 191, 204, 207; and Freud, 133–134, 135; and *Studies on Hysteria*, 32; and treatment of Anna O., 133–134, 135
Brickman, Ellen, 54, 55, 175, 197, 208
Briere, John, 202
Briton, Susan (testimony of, on rape and attempted murder by a stranger), 170–172
Brown, D., 202
Brown, Laura S., 191, 201
Brown, P., 193
Bureau of Justice Statistics, The, 2, 189
Burgess, Ann Wolbert, 53–54, 196, 197

Calhoun, K. S., 192
Center for Post-Traumatic Stress Studies (Washington, DC), 47, 69
Charcot, Jean-Martin, x, 131–133, and Freud, 133, 134; and hypnosis, 131; and Janet, 133; and study of traumatic paralysis ("railway spine" and "railway brain"), 131–133
Child abuse, 77, 78, 79, 199, 205. *See also* Testimonies of Christine Dodge, Sandra Donike, Yolla Hogan, Amy Okeefe

Index

Index

Index

THE SIDRAN FOUNDATION is a national nonprofit organization (501(c)(3)) devoted to education, advocacy, and research related to:

- the early recognition and treatment of trauma-related stress in children;
- the understanding and treatment of adults suffering from trauma-generated psychological disorder

To support people with traumatic stress conditions, and to educate mental health professionals and the public, Sidran has developed the following programs:

The Sidran Press publishes books and educational materials on traumatic stress and dissociative disorders. Recent titles include *Managing Traumatic Stress Through Art, Soldier's Heart: Survivors' Views of Combat Trauma, Trauma Research Methodology,* and *The Dissociative Child.*

The Sidran Bookshelf on Trauma and Dissociation is an annotated mail order catalog of the best in clinical, educational, and survivor-supportive literature on post-traumatic stress and dissociative disorders and related subjects.

The PsychTrauma Infobase is a comprehensive computerized information database of resources, including listings of therapists, organizations, conferences, trainings, and treatment facilities.

The PsychTrauma Resource and Information Service, drawing from the Infobase and Sidran's extensive library, provides resources and referrals at no cost to callers from around the English-speaking world.

The Dissociative Disorders Low-Cost Psychotherapy Clinic, a demonstration project, provides both supervision for therapists inexperienced in the treatment of dissociation and low-cost therapy for clients who otherwise could not afford treatment. This unique clinic was honored by the *Peter F. Drucker Foundation for Nonprofit Management* with an award of special recognition for nonprofit innovation.

PsychTrauma Education and Training, is currently developing an introductory trauma treatment curriculum for use in training mental health professionals and paraprofessionals who work in public mental health agencies. Sidran has also developed public education workshops on the psychological outcomes of severe childhood trauma for a variety of audiences: adult survivors, partners and supporters, caregivers of abused children, and non-clinical professionals (such as teachers, social services personnel, clergy, etc.).

For more information on any of these programs and projects, please contact us:

Sidran Foundation and Press
2328 West Joppa Road, Suite 15
Lutherville, MD 21093
Phone 410-825-8888 Fax 410-337-0747
E-mail sidran@access.digex.net
Website www.sidran.org